FIRING ON ALL CYLINDERS

The Service/Quality System for High-Powered Corporate Performance

Jim Clemmer

with Barry Sheehy and Achieve Associates

Macmillan of Canada

A Division of Canada Publishing Corporation

Toronto, Ontario, Canada

Canadian Cataloguing in Publication Data
Clemmer, Jim, date
   Firing on all cylinders : the service/quality system for high-powered corporate performance

1st paperback ed.
Includes bibliographical references and index.
ISBN 0-7715-9133-0

1. Customer service — Management.   2. Quality of products — Management.   3. Success in business.   I. Sheehy, Barry.
II. Achieve Group Inc.   III. Title.

HF5386.C54 1991   658.8'12   C91-093380-4

1 2 3 4 5 WC 95 94 93 92 91

Cover design by David Wyman
Cover photo by Jim Allen

Macmillan of Canada
A Division of Canada Publishing Corporation
Toronto, Ontario, Canada

Printed in Canada

To Heather, Christopher,
Jennifer, and Vanessa:

We can make a difference.

CONTENTS

ACKNOWLEDGEMENTS

This book brings together the experiences of Achievers in working with Clients using Achieve's Service/Quality System. The development and on-going refinement of this improvement process is the result of a number of Achievers, associates, and Clients giving freely of their successes, failures, insights, and observations.

The following Achievers deserve special recognition and thanks for their pioneering efforts:

Barry Sheehy — your experience, vision, determination, and belief in the critical importance of service/quality improvement, along with your guidance in taking Achieve down an unfamiliar path has been an example of outstanding leadership. The Service/Quality System would likely not exist today without your invaluable contributions.

Art McNeil — your founding vision of "changing the rules of the consulting game" through helping clients become self-sufficient in moving strategies beyond lofty plans to effective implementation provided a solid base. Your energy, conceptual creativity, and "big circle" possibility thinking continue to build an ever-stronger foundation and is a source of constant inspiration.

Rob Ell — your "twelve cylinder" model and "storyboarding" process provided the vital framework. Your experience, research, and observations of how top service providers move ahead of the pack continue to be invaluable insights.

Paul Levesque — your experience with the quality "guru" processes helped to fuse service and quality improvement in a new and unique way. Your contributions to "The Three Rings of Perceived Value" and the Team Tactics cylinder have been substantial.

Mark Henderson — your marketing research and support have contributed immensely to Achieve's success in understanding and reaching those organizations determined to improve their service/quality levels. You've continually kept everyone on track by putting those concepts and strategies into practical and useful action.

Peter Strickland — when it comes time to transfer personal or organizational development processes into useable implementation steps that clients can manage themselves, you're always there. Your ability to take complex processes, simplify them, and "instruct the instructors" is proving to be a key component in the long-term success of the improvement effort.

Achieve Associates Zenger-Miller, Inc. and Roland Dumas have also added significantly to our understanding of the many facets of service/quality improvement. Their research of the critical (but often overlooked) role Personal, Coaching, and Team leadership skills development plays in the success of improvement efforts has been groundbreaking. The resulting leadership skills development programs produced by Zenger-Miller are now at the heart of the Service/Quality System.

We have also benefitted enormously from the pioneering efforts of a number of key Clients. Together we have learned when service/quality theory is not enough or is off track. They have also helped us to understand the keys to successful improvement. Special thanks to Merv Stanley at the B.C. Telephone Company, Judi Blackwell, Frances Horibe, and Emmett Hossack of Transport Canada's Training Directorate, Bob Latham and Eileen Truckle at Bell Cellular Inc., Georgia Stevens and John Webster at POI, Ken Henry of North American Life Assurance Company, Sid Fattedad at Canadian Airlines International, David Curry of The City of Ottawa, and Ron Clark at The Regional Municipality of Ottawa-Carleton, and many others too numerous to mention.

Every emerging field has pathfinders and pioneers. Service/ Quality improvement is certainly no exception. Anyone writing or consulting in this field owes much to the work of Ron Zemke and Karl Albrecht, who gave us new insights into high service performers in their popular 1985 book *Service America!*

In 1989, Ron Zemke and Dick Schaaf published the results of an exhaustive eighteen-month study of top service providers. Their book, *The Service Edge: 101 Companies That Profit From Customer Care* was the source of numerous examples and insights found in this book.

Ron Zemke, Dick Schaaf, and Karl Albrecht continue to light the way to an ever clearer understanding of how the best service organizations do it. I am indebted to their research.

INTRODUCTION

"Quality is never an accident; it is always the result of intelligent effort."
                    —John Ruskin, English art critic and historian

Any attempt to improve, it's been said, can be compared to a parade. Essentially, three groups of people are involved: (1) the small number of people in the parade; (2) the larger group of people watching the parade; (3) and the mass of humanity left saying, "Huh? What parade?"

When it comes to attempts to improve service, any North American manager unaware of the parade either has been living in a cave for the last ten years or just doesn't care about his or her organization's future. For those leading the parade, improvements in service/quality have contributed to growth, cost containment, and profitability at almost obscene levels. And for the rapidly growing mob watching, learning, and waiting to join the parade, service/quality improvements are clearly the way to survive in a radically changing world.

Throughout this book the term *service/quality* is used. We coined the term at The Achieve Group to convey the dual focus — quality and service — of effective efforts to improve performance. Our focus on "quality" will be familiar to readers who have been part of, or who have been watching, the "quality improvement" parade of the past few years. The systems and technology to improve quality that are in popular use today can be traced

1

back to four "quality gurus": W. Edwards Deming, Joseph Juran, Philip Crosby, and Armaund Feigenbaum. All promoted an integrated approach, but stressed different focal points. Each drew on a different discipline for his core methods or technology. These technologies included variations of Statistical Process Control (SPC), Just-in-Time (JIT), Cost Of Quality (COQ), and employee participation (Quality Circles/Improvement Teams). However their methods may have differed, they all emphasized one common principle: *Control the quality of the process, not the product.* In other words, quality must be built in from the start; it can't be added or "inspected in" later.

As we'll see in Chapter One, service improvement has rapidly emerged as the strategic issue of the day. Numerous polls and surveys show that improving service is the top priority of a growing majority of North American executives. Typical is a Gallup poll of 615 executives taken in 1987 and quoted in a feature article in *Fortune* magazine on the service improvement explosion: "The winner by a mile: service quality, picked by 48 percent, well ahead of productivity and government regulation. Remarkably, even executives who turn out goods, not services, said that offering their customers better service will be nearly as important as making higher-quality products."

While this book covers both quality and service improvement, much of the focus will be on the latter. We'll go behind the scenes at a number of leading-edge corporations and government agencies that are making significant progress in their service/quality journey. We'll see how they are bringing together the best quality improvement processes with trail-blazing work in service enhancement. As we'll discover, these organizations are getting the best of two worlds: first, they are substantially reducing costs and increasing their productivity by getting their production and administrative processes under control; second, they are reaping higher revenues and growing market share.

Achieve's experience in service/quality improvement began with the outstanding leadership-training work done by our consulting associates of over a decade now, California-based Zenger-Miller Inc. Zenger-Miller has led the field in the research and development of employee, supervisor, manager, and executive non-technical performance-skills training. The effectiveness of their programs can be measured by the numerous professional awards they have received and, most convincingly, by the only true test of enduring quality — a highly competitive marketplace.

In 1982, Zenger-Miller developed a team leadership skills program called groupAction. This series of sessions helped Quality Circle (there's a throwback to another era) leaders develop the group process and problem-solving skills so vital to getting people to work together effectively. While the program has worked very well through the years (in fact, it is still being used), it gave us our first look at the formidable cultural obstacles that quality improvement faces.

In 1983, Zenger-Miller and Achieve worked with Tom Peters (author of *In Search of Excellence*, *A Passion for Excellence*, and *Thriving on Chaos*) to develop a process to bring an organization closer to "excellence." Called "Toward Excellence", this process added extensively to our understanding of the critical steps needed for long-term service/quality improvement. Over a six-year period, we learned much from the hundreds of North American organizations that used the process to reach for higher levels of performance. Many, such as Campbell Soup, B.C. Tel, Canron, and others, succeeded in dramatically improving their service/quality performance. In most of these cases, the "cultures" of the organizations were recharged and transformed.

Other organizations, however, failed in their use of the process. Service/quality not only didn't change, but the attempt became a source of cynical internal laughter and derision ("Well, we've all been 'excellenced'; what's next?").

Our experience with "Toward Excellence" taught us a great deal about the vital role that vision and values play in building a leadership base for cultural change. We also came to understand the effect that employee commitment has on service/quality improvement. (While quality *might* be driven higher solely by technomanagement — management systems and technology — service goes *nowhere* unless employees decide to improve it.)

Most importantly, we learned what is needed to improve an organization's environment and to foster a commitment to outstanding performance. As well, we discovered what conditions and steps are necessary for successful innovation.

In 1986, Zenger-Miller's extensive research and our own experiences showed us that the focus had shifted from improving "excellence" to improving service/quality. At that point, we recruited Barry Sheehy to join The Achieve Group to provide supplementary consulting services within service/quality improvement and related areas. Barry had been director of organization effectiveness for the telecommunications manufacturing giant, Northern Telecom, which used quality improvement systems and technologies from a number of the gurus. Of even greater interest, however, was Barry's involvement in a highly successful service improvement program for the City of Calgary. While in the Engineering Department there, Barry helped design and manage a groundbreaking program in North American public-sector management. During a period of severe cutbacks and reduced tax revenues, the city's Service Improvement Program (SIP) saved millions of dollars while improving service. SIP built on the best service/quality approaches in use by leading public organizations such as New York City's sanitation department, the City of Phoenix, and Florida Light and Power. SIP has become highly recognized throughout North America for its effectiveness. It was awarded the Canadian Society of Industrial Engineers' National Award of Excellence in 1986 and nominated for the society's prestigious International Award of Excellence — the first time in the award's 45-year history that a government agency was so honored. Barry has since been invited to chronicle his experiences for *National Productivity Review*, *Journal of Industrial Engineering*, *Public Works* magazine, and others.

In 1987, Achieve joined forces with 3M's new Quality Management Services division out of Minneapolis, which had developed a highly effective Total Quality Management system, which combined the best technology and approaches being used. For a time,

4

we teamed up to introduce organizations to the system and to help them implement it.

Total Quality Management is a powerful and effective process. Working with 3M, we added significantly to our understanding of what it takes to improve quality over the long term. We also saw how the manufacturing, product-driven view of quality improvement narrows the field of focus. *Harvard Business Review* editor Ted Levitt succinctly articulates our experience: "The organization must learn to think of itself not as producing goods and services but as buying customers, as doing those things that will make people want to do business with it."

The Service/Quality System outlined in this book is based on the process of the same name developed by The Achieve Group. It is built on our varied and broad experiences, as well as extensive research on the common elements shared by the highest service/quality providers. This approach is now being used by dozens of leading North American and Pacific Rim corporations and government organizations. This book pulls together the key concepts, examples, and actions outlined in Achieve's Service/ Quality executive retreats, management workshops, and academy.

I hope that you find this book chockful of action ideas you can use to map and take your service/quality journey. I have written *Firing on All Cylinders* with the belief that you want less a description of *what* high service/quality looks like and more on *how* to lead your organization there.

The English essayist and critic William Hazlitt once observed: "Great thoughts reduced to practice become great acts." I hope this book inspires great thoughts and ideas for you and that you come away from our time together a great deal richer than when you started. And for the sake of our North American economy, and the future of our kids, I hope you decide to improve your organization's performance on this critical do-or-die issue. But, most of all, I hope you *act.*

Jim Clemmer
October 1989

CHAPTER ONE
The Service/Quality Revolution

"Continuous improvement is vitally important in today's business environment. The world is full of savvy, agile competitors who know quality makes the difference. We are seeing a revolution in quality throughout the world."

—E.S. Woolard, Jr.
Chairman and CEO, Du Pont

A revolution that began in North American organizations in the early eighties has had sweeping effects. In less than a decade, management theories and practices have been fundamentally reconstructed. Complete (and for many organizations calamitous) changes of circumstance turned many industries and public institutions upside down and inside out. Gone forever are the days of stability, predictability, and continually growing revenues.

A myriad of changes occurred around 1980-81 to begin the revolution. Chief among them was the worst "correction" of runaway inflation the industrialized world has seen since the Great Depression. As North American managers fought back by "downsizing" and slashing overhead, Japan relentlessly assaulted our manufacturing sector. "Productivity" quickly became management's rallying cry. "Doing more with less" became an imperative. Those corporate dinosaurs whose productivity languished are long gone today. Many were acquired by or merged with more nimble corporations. Those that still exist have been so radically altered that they are mere shells of their former selves.

But the focus on manufacturing productivity was short-lived. It soon became apparent that getting those widgets out the shipping dock doors in high numbers was no longer enough. In too many cases, the quest for higher productivity caused quality to be sacrificed for quantity. Consumer preferences shifted dramatically as Japanese and other world-class companies provided high-quality alternatives at reasonable prices. Just ask our automobile industry. Back in the late seventies, Detroit's productivity was increasing — but it was turning out high quantities of junk. Reflecting on those bad old days, a car rental executive said, "It was embarrassing to get a shipment of new cars. We wanted to put them on our lots at night when no one was looking. Not only did the doors not fit, and the trim fell off, but we always seemed to be fixing something."

As it became clear that quality was to be the next competitive battleground, North American car manufacturers learned a major lesson about the relationship between productivity and quality. If there was one thing that pulled our automotive industry, and indeed many manufacturers, back from the brink, it was this critical shift in perspective — driving *up* quality while pushing *down* costs. As Philip Crosby pointed out in his popular book *Quality Is Free*, managers found that it really is possible to have the best of both worlds: higher quality as well as higher productivity.

Talk about revolutionary thinking. Since the dawn of our modern industrial age with its focus on mass production, manufacturing managers had accepted that increased quality cost more or took longer to produce. Then along came the Japanese with higher shipping costs and, in the late eighties, a rising yen, relentlessly producing cars, computers, and electronic products of ever-higher quality while maintaining or even reducing their costs.

We can be proud of how North America's manufacturing sector responded to the threat. Faced with the prospect of — and in too many cases actually losing markets to — superior competitors, our manufacturing managers pulled their act together. As the English author Samuel Johnson observed, "When a man knows he is to be hanged in a fortnight, it concentrates his mind wonderfully."

Not that we've won the battle yet. A number of industries still haven't made the shift or are moving far too slowly. There will be more victims. Even among the "early improvers," the pressure to continue improving is intense. For example, Ford dramatically improved the quality of its vehicles in the eighties with its "Quality is Job 1" program. The results were a dramatic rise in market share and an increase in productivity with a drop in costs. That led to a correspondingly sharp rise in profitability that propelled Ford's earnings beyond those of slower-moving General Motors for the first time in corporate history. Despite those impressive gains, Ford's quality has still not caught up with its Japanese rivals, who continue improving at a relentless pace. And at home, the gap between Ford's quality and that of its rivals is being vigorously pursued by Chrysler and GM, with signs that they are catching up. Of course, the European car manufacturers are not to be ignored on the quality issue either. Raymond Ablondi, Ford's director of market research, sums up the fiercely competitive world that all manufacturers live in today: "Quality is the price of admission to the marketplace these days. You must have it going in or no one pays attention to you."

THE NEW SERVICE BATTLEGROUND

So, just to play the game today, your company's products must be continually improving — unless you're prepared to let your competitors gain a strategic edge in a highly quality-conscious marketplace. But that will only keep you even. You'll remain one of the pack offering "me-too" products with similar features and quality. If your company is to grow and prosper, you need a strategy that will leap-frog you past your competitors. Unfortunately, high quality and competitive pricing through improved productivity by themselves won't do it.

In today's world economy, high quality and reliability are becoming the norm. Failure to meet high quality standards can be fatal. Any sluggishness in your ability to improve and stay abreast of your industry will quickly take you out of the race. However, unless your competitors are slouching badly in quality and productivity, you will likely have a difficult time pulling ahead on these alone.

In a world awash in good products, service is quickly becoming the competitive battleground. In studying this emerging trend, *Fortune* magazine concluded, "As global competition intensifies and companies around the world invade each other's markets, cost [from improved productivity] and quality differences among all sorts of goods and services are shrinking. The company that coddles customers best has a competitive edge."

The expectations of North American consumers are also changing. In a major cover story on this issue, *Time* magazine reported, "Disgruntlement with services runs almost counter to the prevailing attitude about products. Consumers show a reasonable level of satisfaction with the merchandise they buy, thanks largely to technological advances. But the harsh world of the service economy intrudes once again on their contentment when a modern product suffers a breakdown."

The automotive industry is well into the service battle now. We saw the sign of things to come (but didn't recognize it) back in 1982, when we were approached by a Japanese car company to help them improve service in their local dealerships. Executives at the company saw a problem that anyone who has ever owned a car has experienced. It may be the best car available, but when we take it in for service we're treated as though we had a communicable disease or were there to con the mechanics out of their precious time (which is, of course, much more valuable than ours). What these executives had come to realize is that car buyers are a funny bunch. When we are treated as subhumans by the backshop tyrants or as gullible "marks" by the showroom sharks, we tend to think less highly of the company whose name is so proudly hanging on the building — despite a car that may be an engineering, ergonomic, or quality masterpiece.

The perception that we tie service and product quality together is backed up by extensive research conducted within major industries throughout North America by the Strategic Planning Institute in Cambridge, Massachusetts. They found that "customers value good repairwork, delivery, and sales assistance almost as much as they value the quality of the product itself. Those who get top-notch service often think more highly of the product they have purchased." *Fortune* has been studying the sweeping changes hitting the automotive industry: "If Detroit manufacturers can keep improving public attitudes toward the dealer — long the most vilified figure in the car business — they will have taken a competitive step just as important and at least as difficult as improving the quality of their cars."

Although manufacturers are just now learning the rules of the service game they must master, you would think service-sector companies would be well along their way in the game. You would be wrong on two counts. First of all, our service sector is just starting to recognize that they can improve. In a provocative *Harvard Business Review* article entitled "Will Services Follow Manufacturing into Decline?" James Quinn and Christopher Gagnon observe, "Daily we encounter the same inattention to quality, emphasis on scale economies rather than customers' concerns, and short-term financial orientation that earlier injured manufacturing. The costs of losing this battle are unacceptably high."

Second, "service company" is usually an oxymoron, a contradiction in terms like "bittersweet," "jumbo shrimp," or "original copy." As you and I know only too well from painful personal experience, service is usually the first thing promised and the last thing delivered. The service of most service companies is appalling, frustrating, disgusting, horrendous . . . In other words it is virtually non-existent. Robert Kelley, writing in the *Wall Street Journal*, said, "Our service economy is in for a big shock. The quality of most services today is like the quality of many manufactured goods 15 years ago."

As if there wasn't enough reason for companies to take drastic action to improve their service/quality, consumers are being incited to revolution by North American media. Typical is a feature article in the *Toronto Star*. Headlined "Disappearance of Service with a Smile Leaves Consumers Nostalgic and Angry," the opening lines expressed the frustration we're all feeling: "Remember service with a smile? Today, about the only way to get it is at the point of a gun." *Time* ran a cover story entitled "Pul-eeze! Will Somebody Help Me?" A special supplement in *Fortune* was called "Rediscovering the Customer." A *Forbes* article wonders, "It's Supposed to Be a Service Economy . . . Where's the Service?" Ron Zemke, an editor, author, and emerging service guru, says that as far as the business media is concerned, "service has become *the* major story as companies struggle against each other, foreign challengers, and larger economic forces."

The combination of competitive forces and changing consumer expectations has made service *the* management issue of the nineties. A number of surveys now confirm that improving service is the highest priority of executives across North America. A Gallup poll commissioned by the American Society for Quality Control found service quality to be the single most important business issue faced by more than 615 CEOs in both the manufacturing and the service sectors. Yet the pressures to improve productivity and quality are as strong as they've ever been. Higher service levels have now been added to the business success mix. However, as you'll discover in this book, productivity, quality, and service are interconnected. And they are turbocharged by a key improvement force — innovation.

THE PAY-OFFS OF HIGH SERVICE/QUALITY

Companies with high levels of service/quality enjoy riches most lesser corporations only dream about. High service/quality companies are able to keep down their costs while driving up revenue by increasing their market share, by their ability to command premium prices, and by their growing sales figures. The net

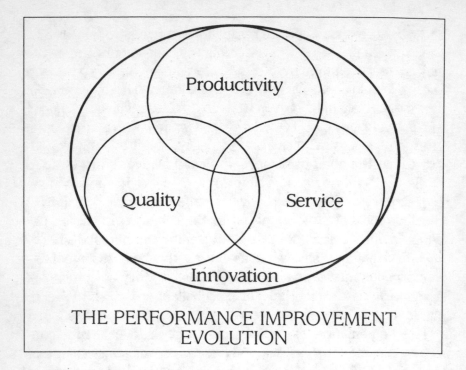

THE PERFORMANCE IMPROVEMENT
EVOLUTION

effect is a wonderful double whammy on the bottomline — profits soar.

Much of the "magic elixir" effect of service/quality on corporate performance would be just so much hot air were it not for the irrefutable, solid proof of the PIMS data base accumulated since 1972 by the Strategic Planning Institute. SPI is a non-profit organization dedicated to the advancement of management strategy with more than 200 member companies in the United States, Canada, Australia, Western Europe, and other countries. The authoritative PIMS (Profit Impact of Market Strategy) data base contains the good and bad experiences of more than 2,000 business units (division, product line, or profit center).

By examining the effects of the strategies that companies were deploying, SPI found that "service is becoming in many cases the *only* road to competitive excellence." According to SPI's research, the reason for this situation is that "we are entering an era of global product standardization."

Many financial types treat service as a nice-to-do add-on that is delivered by the sales, customer service, or field people. This attitude on the part of those who so proudly watch the bottomline and "manage by results" shows incredible naivete or just plain ignorance. If you find yourself having to broaden the view of such tunnel-vision managers in your organization, use the following sections to dazzle them with the brilliant light of a new management age that's dawning. (But make them buy their own book!)

SERVICE/QUALITY'S IMPACT ON PRICE

The Strategic Planning Institute concludes, "With the PIMS data base we can test and quantify [the] relationship between price and performance. The data clearly show that, on average, better products command higher prices." In fact, PIMS shows that price index relative to competition puts those companies with low perceived service/quality at 98 percent compared to high service companies who are at 107 percent. In other words, high service/quality companies can charge *almost 10 percent more* for their goods and services.

This jibes, no doubt, with your personal experience. After we have experienced the pain and frustration of shoddy merchandise or lousy service, we are willing to pay a little more for decent treatment or a product that lasts longer with fewer breakdowns. The rise of consumerism in our society is making it easier for buyers to make these judgments and is contributing to the service/quality revolution. Having bought our share of lemons, my wife, Heather, and I always consult *Consumer Reports* and other such publications before making a major purchase. Not that we take the offered analysis as gospel, but it is helpful to have some basis for evaluating value and comparing one product with another. Inevitably, we end up investing a little more money to buy long-term peace of mind and hassle-free use. Maytag has been riding this wave to outstanding market and financial performance for years now by attracting the growing crowd of consumers who agree with that time-worn adage, "The bitterness of poor quality (or service) remains long after the sweetness of low price is forgotten."

As businesses and consumers become better at discerning long-term value for their dollars, high service/quality providers will enjoy even greater opportunities to charge premium prices. Even those companies that thought that they were competing in a commodity marketplace are finding ways to add value through higher service/quality.

American Express provides an excellent example in the commodity travel and financial services markets they have come to dominate. Their basic card service is similar to that offered by many banks. Yet American Express charges a hefty premium and continues to attract cardholders and businesses. Spencer Nilson writes a credit card newsletter and is often very critical of American Express and its dominant industry position. Yet he clearly understands how AMEX has developed and maintained its commanding edge: "There is no getting around the fact that American Express's service is far and away the best in the industry." Now AMEX is poised to use its superior service reputation and financial strength to invade traditional bank markets for card and bank services.

A number of studies are coming to the same conclusions as the Strategic Planning Institute regarding the powerful effect of perceived service/quality on price:

- The Retail Council of Canada found that "shoppers are willing to pay a little more to get better service."
- The American Business Conference commissioned an exhaustive two-year study of high-performing "mid-sized" (revenues of $25 million to $1 billion) companies. As a group, the companies studied had more than doubled in size and profits from 1978 to 1983. They dramatically outperformed the economy and the *Fortune 500* in sales, jobs created, market value, and profits. Now here's the point — 43 of 45 winners highlighted in the study compete *by delivering higher value rather than lower price.*
- Management consultant Milind Lele, and Brooker Professor of Research at the School of Business of the University of Southern California Jagdish Sheth, spent two years studying customer satisfaction and service levels of 15 firms

14

in 13 diverse industries. They conclude, "In industry after industry, happy customers are willing to pay extra for the additional satisfaction they derive."

- In the property and casualty insurance business, the consulting firm of Temple, Borker & Sloan found that many companies try to make up for poor service/quality through low pricing. But when this strategy is contrasted with the financial results of service/quality leaders in the insurance field, the researchers concluded that low service/quality performers "will discover the importance of quality, not as a competitive weapon, but as an imperative for survival."

- The PIMS studies show that "beating competitors in a race for a relative quality advantage is a more certain route than trying to win a price war. To improve the customer-perceived quality of your products and services relative to those of your competitors — and thereby gain the ability to increase prices — is the less perilous route to renewed competitive advantage."

Low levels of service/quality often lead companies into a negative downward spiral. Unless they pull out of it, many end up crashing. The fatal spin is set in motion by three powerful and destructive forces. These are the dark side of the same forces that work so effectively to boost high service/quality performers out of sight financially. First, poor service/quality companies must spend ever greater amounts to replace the customers who are charging out the back door vowing never to return. These sales and marketing activities must also counter the negative word-of-mouth advertising that spreads the horror stories of just how bad (or mediocre) the experience of dealing with that company really is. Second, low service/quality providers have higher costs, because they are not doing it right the first time. Their production and delivery processes are out of control. This situation exists despite the illusion of tight management by bottomline slash-and-burn managers who have boldly "trimmed the fat," "tightened their belts," and otherwise brutalized the organization to cut operating costs.

Many downsizing efforts are not only necessary but long overdue. If they are handled properly, the organization emerges leaner, smarter, and faster. But all too often, downsizing is handled with all the finesse of a butcher wielding a chainsaw. When that happens, the effect can be devastating. Ill-conceived across-the-board cuts (such as reducing the workforce by 10 percent) can severely damage service/quality levels. They reduce service levels by crushing the spirit of the front-line employees whose voluntary efforts are the *only* means by which high service is delivered to customers. After all, management is not out there providing the lion's share of customer service.

Those who advocate traditional cost-containment efforts also rarely question the current methods used to produce and deliver products or services. Instead they whip employees to speed up the inefficient processes and then tie their hands by reducing the resources available to support their efforts. Of course, these managers are then very puzzled when employees not only don't appreciate the heroic efforts being made but are even bitter about them. This bitterness leads to a widening of the we/they gap between management and employees — and efficiency plummets further.

Third, low service/quality providers must lower their prices to attract business, especially if the company has failed to carve out a market niche and is competing in a commodity market with "me-too" look-alike products or services.

So as we can see, these companies suffer the worst of all worlds. Their sales and marketing costs are high; they are inefficient with low productivity levels; their prices are low and revenues are dropping. They're well on their way to decline and death. It's just a question of how long and how agonizing the process will be.

SERVICE/QUALITY'S IMPACT ON MARKET SHARE

Your company's market share is a direct reflection of the value that its customers place on it. Quite simply, when enough customers believe your products or services provide the highest value for their dollars, you will beat out your competitors and gain a higher share of available customers. It should come as no surprise that the PIMS data clearly shows that high service/quality providers are gaining the market share given up by low service/quality providers. In fact, the difference was a loss of 2 percent per year for low performers versus gains of 6 percent per year for the high performers. The rich truly are getting richer. Those companies perceived by their customers to produce and deliver high service/quality are moving ahead of their lesser competitors at a rate of *8 percent a year*! You don't have to be a marketing genius to realize that at that rate it doesn't take long for top companies to move into commanding positions in their markets. And the weak performers' position continues to weaken — victims of the service/quality revolution.

As low service/quality providers get pushed further into the background, they often take desperate measures to fight back. Rather than competing on service/quality, many lower prices to get noticed and chosen. This is a deadly game to play. As soon as competitors notice customers moving because of price, they respond with similar action. Companies that play this game are often signaling to their customers that a low price is all they have to offer that's different from the rest of the pack. In today's world, with increasingly sophisticated buyers who know that value is defined by much more than just low price, price cutting is often the last desperate gasp of a company on its deathbed.

Based on nearly twenty years of studying these kinds of strategies with more than 2,000 business units, the PIMS research again provides solid evidence: "Competitors that cannot keep up in the race for higher value will find their market share eroding. . . . The price cutter often finds itself in a weakened position, with the same share but less revenue. . . . In the long run, superior quality allows you to hold on to the high-value position and reap permanent gains in market share. . . . When we examine the options for maintaining the lead in value, we find that changes in relative quality have a far more potent effect on market share than do changes in price."

SERVICE/QUALITY'S IMPACT ON SALES GROWTH

Higher service/quality also means higher levels of sales growth. The PIMS data shows that high service/quality providers have average annual sales growth rates more than double that of the low service/quality providers. The research shows that the low performers have been increasing their sales at an average rate of 8 percent per year. Considering our inflation rates since the data was first collected in 1972, that's not very impressive. High performers, on the other hand, have been increasing their sales at a rate of *17 percent* a year.

Those figures should be especially troublesome for you if your company is one of the masses that spend heavily on sales and marketing to buy sales growth. A typical misguided organization invests only about one-tenth of 1 percent of that amount of money and effort in driving up its service/quality levels. That's not to imply that high service/quality companies don't invest in sales and marketing. IBM, Marriott Hotels, McDonald's, American Express, Disney, and other high performers are heavy investors in sales and marketing. The big difference is they also make substantial investments in continual service/quality improvements to keep their customers coming back year after year and bringing their friends or associates with them. They work just as hard to make these investments pay off as they do with those they make in business development.

James D. Robinson III of American Express sums up the philosophy of many top service/quality companies: "Customer service is American Express's patent protection. Our goal, simply stated, is to be the best in the service industry." An *American Banker* study showed that the second biggest reason people moved their principal financial business to another institution was problems related to service or errors. The biggest reason? A change of residence. So despite the offers of toasters or interest calculated hourly, customers move because they are fed up with daily indifference and constant little mistakes. While the hopeful new customers are lured in the front doors by promises of something better, disillusioned former customers are storming out the back with their closed-out account books in clenched fists.

SERVICE/QUALITY'S IMPACT ON PROFITABILITY

It doesn't take a financial genius to figure out that higher market share, higher prices, and strong sales growth all add up to higher profitability. What is astounding is just how much more profitable top service/quality providers are. On this key measure of performance, executives of lower service/quality firms might be tempted to dismiss the PIMS data out of hand because the profit levels seem like something out of fantasyland. But the research is too extensive, broad-based, and solid to do that. Low service/ quality companies have a return-on-sales averaging just 1 percent. High service/quality companies have a return-on-sales averaging *12 percent.* That is a difference of 11 percent. It means that high service/quality providers have a profitability more than *ten times higher* than their lesser counterparts!

Those numbers are astounding. Executive teams will sweat blood for days on end at budgeting and planning time figuring out how to squeeze 5, 10, 20, or maybe even 50 percent more profitability out of their financial statements. All the while the golden key to undreamed-of riches lies close by but doesn't get so much as a passing glance. Why? One of the reasons is plain: simple ignorance. The American teacher and philosopher Amos Bronson Alcott once said, "To be ignorant of one's ignorance is the malady of the ignorant." Most executives of low service/quality companies have never seen first hand the overwhelming power of an intense service/quality improvement strategy. So they dismiss the results highlighted here as an aberration or put them down to special circumstances the high service/quality companies "lucked into."

Many low service/quality executives are of the old management school. They think it costs more to deliver top service or high quality. They equate "service" with being servile or with literally serving customers, like waiters in a restaurant. They believe that high-service restaurants have more waiters running about answering their customers' every whim. So to increase service is to increase costs. It all sounds terrifyingly familiar to the arguments that manufacturing managers gave in the seventies to explain why they couldn't afford to build quality into their products.

As we'll examine in later chapters, one of the reasons high service/quality companies are so incredibly profitable is that they have lower costs than their competitors. Talk about having your cake and eating it too! The PIMS data shows that these companies enjoy the best of two worlds: their revenues grow while their costs proportionately shrink or remain tightly under control. They are able to do what many Japanese firms do so well: add perceived value while reducing their Cost of Quality. That essentially means they are driving down the astronomical costs of not doing things right the first time. They are more efficient and productive than their competition. They are able to do more with less. But the wonderful thing is, they can charge more than their competitors and still offer better value.

To corroborate the PIMS data, John Groocock, retired vice-president for quality at TRW, applied the same analysis to that $6-billion highly diversified conglomerate. Using the customers' evaluations of quality, he measured 148 product lines in 47 TRW business units and compared them with 560 competitors' product lines. He found that the top third of TRW's quality providers (as measured by their customers) had returns on assets three times higher than those of the bottom third of quality providers. Groocock made a penetrating comment based on this discovery: "The PIMS results are so impressive that it is surprising that they have had so little effect on management."

A final note from the PIMS data: "The impact of high quality goes beyond the bottomline. Businesses that improve quality also improve their economic market value."

THE PENALTIES OF LOW SERVICE/QUALITY

As we've just seen, the costs of not improving service/quality are the opportunities lost. But what are the costs of maintaining the status quo? It's been said that business is a lot like rowing upstream — the minute you stop, you automatically drop back. Let's look at what is lost when a business decides not to row strongly up the service/quality stream.

Losing Customers

Remember this old joke? "Doctor, when I hold my arm up like this I get an awful pain shooting through my shoulder." "Well, then, don't hold your arm up like that."

Most of us are averse to pain. Unless we have psychological problems, we generally stop doing those things that hurt. Customers are no different. If they are continually treated with thinly disguised contempt, or are met with hostility or indifference, they'll look for alternatives. *Canadian Grocer* magazine found that 60 percent of shoppers who felt they had been snubbed or hassled simply switched stores.

Several studies have looked at the reasons customers quit. Typically, the findings look something like this:

Customers who died	1%
Customers who moved	3%
Customers whose friends influenced them	5%
Those who changed for competitive reasons (often price)	9%
Those who were dissatisfied with the product	14%
Customers who perceived an attitude of indifference on the part of an employee	68%

Unfortunately, we're all familiar with that "attitude of indifference." Often it's the little things that get us. Seldom does one major problem send us across the street. It's usually a series of little nagging signals that all add up to one big "We don't care about you and your petty little problems. Can't you see we're busy doing more important stuff?" One car owner went back to the dealership (with the familiar inconveniences) three times to have a transmission repaired on a new car. On the fourth trip he demanded to talk to the factory rep. His complaints were summarily dismissed with a nonchalant "They all do that." Guess who he no longer buys his cars from?

It's clear that you can't maintain the status quo and expect to retain your current market share or customer base. North Americans may not be sticking their heads out their windows and declaring their anger to the world, but they are getting fed up with current service levels and they aren't going to take it any more. So unless you're pushing hard *now* to improve your service levels, you are about to — or already have started to — drift back in sales and operating costs.

Customer Complaints: How Big Is Your Iceberg?

Complaints from dissatisfied customers can be either a problem or an opportunity, depending on how you handle them. Clearly they are only a small tip of a large iceberg. Technical Assistance Research Program (TARP) is a Washington, D.C.–based non-profit organization that has made a specialty of researching consumer complaints. Like the Strategic Planning Institute, they have amassed a large, solid research base that can shed a lot of light on a key area of service/quality. For years they have studied when, why, and how many unhappy customers take action to let the offending organization know of their displeasure. They have also tracked the consequences of unhappy customers.

TARP has found that one customer complaint represents a very large group of equally unhappy customers who never bothered to complain. Depending on the size of the purchase and the industry, only about 4 to 30 percent of unhappy customers bother to register a complaint. But the iceberg is even larger than that below the surface. In studies of consumer complaints in the gas and telephone utility industries, TARP found that a huge number of customers didn't bother to complain any further if their complaint was rebuffed by their first level of contact. Since these complaints are not recorded, TARP found that as few as 1 in 2,000 customers registered a complaint beyond the first level of contact.

Why don't more customers complain when they don't get what they pay for? After all, how can you be expected to know there's a problem unless someone tells you, right? Wrong. As far as most customers are concerned, it's not up to them to manage your business for you. Think of how often you run into uncaring, indifferent, or even rude service at restaurants, hotels, car dealers, banks, home-repair services, and the like. How often do you bother to register a complaint beyond a snide passing remark to a cashier?

The reasons you don't bother to complain no doubt mesh with TARP's findings. First, you may not know whom to complain to. Do you demand to see the manager? Is there a "customer service" department (a real contradiction in terms for those very companies that need improvement the most)? Next, is it worth your time and trouble? In most cases, your dissatisfaction was not caused by anything major. It was more a sense of being treated as a nobody enough times to get the message. Besides, who needs the aggravation? It will probably result in a confrontation and conflict. Or you will sound like a sourpuss who has pickles and lemon juice for breakfast. So weighing all that out, along with the sad fact that such treatment has become rampant every place we go these days, you throw up your hands and storm out, vowing never to return.

If you do take the time to complain, you will no doubt run smack into another problem TARP found is all too common. Most complaints are so poorly handled that most customers never return again. I once had a day of frustrating delays due to equipment problems on an airline flight. The captain never told us what was happening or when we might reasonably expect to be under way. When we were finally airborne, four hours past our departure time, the captain made no apology, and the cabin crew came through charging for drinks and headsets. I wrote a scathing two-page letter to the airline president. I never received a reply. That was over five years ago. I still refuse to fly with that airline.

We've all experienced the futility of complaining. It is yet another reason that we don't bother. The sad irony is that those companies who deliver that uncaring "get lost, you're bothering me" service are the same ones that make it hard to complain and seldom take action when some "persistent cuss — er . . . customer" does get through to some manager. TARP's research shows that 81 percent of consumers with minor unresolved complaints ($5 or less) won't buy again. They also found that more than 54 percent of consumers with major (over $100) unresolved complaints won't buy again.

Complaints Can Be Great Opportunities

The good news is that handling complaints effectively can build customer loyalty. TARP says, "Complaining consumers give business a chance to rectify their problems. Responsive companies are rewarded by the greatest degree of continued brand loyalty." In fact, the research shows that when complaints are resolved quickly, *up to 95 percent* of customers will return and buy again. Clearly, then, recovery after your product or service fails is a critical factor in holding your customers. As much as companies are pushing themselves to deliver top service/quality the first time, customers will be very forgiving if they feel the organization wants to make things right after a service/quality breakdown. Had that airline captain been concerned about his passengers' inconvenience, or the cabin crew showed empathy for our frustration, there clearly would have been far fewer angry passengers like me who took their travel business elsewhere.

If your company uses complaints as a barometer of how well you're doing, then you need to get a sense of how many unhappy customers that one complaint represents. How many customers don't bother to complain beyond saying something to your frontline servers or deliverers? Could it be in the hundreds or even thousands? Of those who do lodge a complaint, how many dissatisfied customers does that one person represent? Is it five, ten, twenty, or as high as twenty-seven, as in TARP's findings of North American averages? And how effectively does your organization handle the complaints it does get? If you don't have the answers to these questions readily available based on solid research and feedback from your employees and customers, you're losing golden opportunities every day. Ignorance may be bliss — for a while.

The key question is, how much can your company afford? Even if you are prepared to pass up the potential pay-offs of service/quality improvement, can you afford the potential losses? Can you hold your ground against competitors who will grab your unhappy, or even just less-than-delighted, customers? *Customer loyalty is just lack of a better alternative.*

Our experience, and a growing mountain of evidence, clearly say you can count on these four facts: (1) your customers expect sharply higher levels of service/quality; (2) your competitors are already working flat out (or getting ready to) to entice your customers with higher perceived value than you've been offering; (3) to the victor will go the spoils; (4) if you're currently at or near the top of your industry and don't have an aggressive plan to dramatically improve your service/quality levels, you're already behind and in serious trouble.

The Gossip Can Kill You

While only a tiny fraction of your unhappy customers bother to tell you about their dissatisfaction, they are eager to tell lots of your potential customers about the crummy products or service you provide. TARP has studied the ripple effects of dissatisfied customers and word-of-mouth testimonials. The results will rock anyone concerned about sales and marketing. They found that each dissatisfied customer will tell *nine to ten* other people about his or her negative experience. For products and services in excess of $100, those disgruntled rumor-mongers will tell *sixteen* others about their unhappy experience. On the other hand, happy customers tell only half as many people about the delightful experience they may have had with you. That's a sad comment on human nature. We are far more willing to gripe and complain than to talk about the good things.

We all have our favorite "can you top this rotten, lousy service" story. And should the topic stray anywhere near the area of cars, financial services, stores, or wherever our latest sad service saga comes from, we're only too ready to lay out in detail just how agonizing it really was. Of course, the conclusion drawn for any of our audience who are considering a similar purchase is "stay away from Brand X or ABC Services."

How Much Do Your Unhappy Customers Cost You?

Based on TARP's findings, let's take a look at the cumulative effect of one unhappy customer who "lost" over $100 and didn't bother to complain:

The original customer who won't return	1
Potential customers not gained because the original customer didn't tell them how satisfied he was	8
Potential customers lost because the original customer told them how *dis*satisfied he was	16
Total customers lost from *one* unhappy customer	25

Now here's the $64,000 (for many companies, $64-million) question: What does it cost your company to get 25 new customers?

If those numbers make you sick, it gets worse. Writing in the authoritative *Harvard Business Review*, marketing guru Regis McKenna (author of *The Regis Touch*), said: "With so much choice backed by service, customers can afford to be fickle. As a result, references have become vital to product marketing. And the more complex the product, the more complex the supporting references." For marketers who ignore the impact of service/quality word-of-mouth, here's a marketing study to chew on: "General Electric found that it [word-of-mouth] can be an even more influential factor than mass media advertising. . . . Only 29 percent of those surveyed found manufacturer's advertising 'useful' during the prepurchase period. On the other hand, *61 percent* felt that the 'opinions of friends' were 'useful.' "

Top service/quality providers not only capitalize on the word-of-mouth effect for marketing, they also have very high customer retention and repeat business rates. For example, Walt Disney World facilities average between 65 to 70 percent return rates. Disney fanatic Paul Levesque of The Achieve Group is so captivated by the facilities and service atmosphere that he has been to Disney's parks nine times. In its study of the automotive industry, *Fortune* magazine found the same pattern: "The leverage in satisfying customers is enormous. Satisfied customers are twice as likely to stick with their old make and three times as likely to return to the dealer who sold them the car." In the construction business, it's common practice for real estate developers to maintain a blacklist of bad contractors who won't be used again at any price because dealing with them is too much hassle.

TARP found that the average North American company spends five times more to get new customers than to retain an old one. Take a long hard look at your company. How much does it cost for marketing, sales, and administration to attract and set up the relationship with a new customer? Every time you lose a customer, you can kiss that amount of money good-bye. Many companies are like a home owner who leaves all the doors and windows open in the midst of a cold snap and turns the furnace on full-blast to heat the house. Heavy investments are made to bring heat (customers) in, while little attention is given to retaining existing heat (customers).

Stew Leonard and his thriving dairy store in Norwalk, Connecticut, have become famous through videos such as *In Search of Excellence*. He operates his store with an unparalleled obsessive focus on customer service. His sales-per-square-foot set records unimagined in the U.S. grocery business. *The Service Edge* newsletter reports that Leonard likes to talk about a conversation with the chairman of one of America's largest supermarket chains. He asked this executive about the average wait his company's customers experience at the check-out counters. The chairman had no idea and basically didn't see the need for someone at his level to be concerned with such operating details.

Yet when you and I go into a grocery store, what's the major beef we all have? That's right: it's the wait at the counters. We couldn't care less about inventory turns, capitalization, or whatever else the chairman and his boardroom buddies are sweating over. The king of grocery sales, Stew Leonard, puts it in perspective: "What could be more important than customer satisfaction?" He goes on to outline a way of looking at his business that we find is common among that tiny group of top service providers: "Our average customer spends $100 a week; that's $5,200 per year or $52,000 every 10 years. When I see a dissatisfied customer, I see a potential loss of $52,000."

When you look at the effects that delighted customers have on a business, it's not hard to explain the findings contained in the PIMS data. Companies with top service/ quality increase their market share, their revenues, and their profits by building loyal, long-term customers. Not only that, they are broadcasting positive testimonials that have twice as much effect as mass media advertising. And as our information age leads to information overload, the word-of-mouth and customer-loyalty trends promise to grow even stronger.

CHAPTER TWO
Service/Quality in the Public Sector

"Public-service institutions such as government agencies, labor unions, churches, universities and schools, hospitals, community and charitable organizations, professional and trade associations and the like, need to be entrepreneurial and innovative fully as much as any business does. Indeed, they may need it more. The rapid changes in today's society, technology, and economy are simultaneously an even greater threat to them and an even greater opportunity."

—Peter Drucker, professor and author, considered the father of modern management

Our government agencies and public institutions are headed for a major crisis. Public-sector managers who cut their teeth during the go-go expansion years of the sixties and seventies became increasingly nervous during the restraint years of the eighties. They ain't seen nothin' yet.

This chapter will show public-sector managers how service/quality improvement can, and — in a small but fast-growing number of cases — is, making major contributions to conquering the enormous challenges that lie ahead. The same magnitude of improvement that we explored in the last chapter for the private sector is possible through service/quality improvement in the public sector. Many of the same cost reductions are applicable. A number of the same reasons for "customer" dissatisfaction also apply. However, the consequences of unhappy customers are different. The public can't easily go down the street and hire a different supplier of electricity, street cleaning, highway repair, or firefighting. That's not to say that competition doesn't exist. Many public-sector managers are waking up to find work they performed badly or services they provided poorly have been contracted out to the private sector. Others are finding their monopolies eroded or their industries privatized.

A WORLD OF CHANGE

To say we're living in changing times is a cliché. In the sixth century B.C., Heraclitus said, "Nothing endures but change." We've certainly been getting our share of "endurance" in the last few years! Every part of society has seen massive and far-reaching changes. But most public-sector institutions are about to be, or have been, swept away on a virtual flood of change caused by a number of small streams and tiny eddies that are converging to form a mighty river . . .

External Factors
Many societal trends have made today's world almost unrecognizable from our grandparents', or even our parents'. Foremost among those changes is the explosion in technology, which for public-sector managers can be either a threat or an opportunity. In almost all cases, technology poses difficult dilemmas and makes for agonizing choices.

Technology threatens poorly managed institutions the most. Poor managers are finding fewer places to hide. In our information age, it is easier for auditors, other managers, and the press to find out what is going on in many of the nooks and crannies of the bureaucratic maze.

Technology can, when it's well used, provide incredible management leverage. Information technology can pinpoint strengths and weaknesses and lead to improved performance. Technology related to the services the organization provides (policing, safety, regulatory controls, construction, park maintenance) can strengthen considerably the organization's ability to provide those services effectively.

But technology also forces difficult choices, especially around its costs and benefits. Today, as never before, public-sector managers have more tools at their disposal than they can likely use or afford. There's no better example than the health care field. Medical breakthroughs and technological advances are almost daily occurrences. And many of them are expensive. Which ones to choose? Because we can prolong a life or perform a procedure, should we automatically do so? But we can't do it all. Where do we draw the line?

Recent economic swings have also made things tough for public-sector managers. Rapid growth, inflation, and sudden economic downturns have made long-term planning extremely difficult and hazardous. Getting ten economists to agree on an economic forecast beyond next week is about as difficult as getting ten politicians to agree on the best public policy for the next few years. As George Bernard Shaw said, "If all economists were laid end to end, they would not reach a conclusion." Even less complimentary things have been said about politicians' ability to provide consistent, solid guidance to their organizations.

Marshall McLuhan's global village is here. Travel and communications technology have shrunk our world considerably. Because of, or as a result of that, interdependence and cooperation among nations have increased dramatically. And trade barriers are starting to fall. In North America, it's the Free Trade Agreement between Canada and the United States. In Europe, it's the Common Market agreement of 1992.

Changes in world trade patterns will have far-reaching effects on public institutions. One will be the unpredictability of economic directions as even more variables and unknowns are added. Will the economy flounder or flourish under Free Trade? Will there be large dislocations? How are they to be handled? Will there be pressures for growth and expansion, or reduction and downsizing?

Another effect will be the impact of political changes on public policies. As politicians wrangle with their new trading partners over subsidies and the "level playing field," there will likely be substantial changes to social or economic programs. How might that situation change the funds available and the public services expected?

But the biggest implication for public institutions of our global village could well be the shift in expectations of the customers they serve. As the old saying goes, "How you gonna keep 'em down on the farm after they've seen Paree?" As companies and individuals become "world class" in their experience and outlook, the kind of government they may once have accepted is radically altered.

Public Mood and Expectations

Nestor Yurchuk, executive director of the Courts Administration Division for the Ministry of Attorney General in Ontario, is a manager with a clear view of the need for improved service/quality in the public sector. He believes that all government agencies should feel the competitive heat on this issue: "Our competition is all those private-sector firms who are working so hard to raise their service/quality. As they succeed, it changes the expectations of our customers. They will increasingly want to see the same kind of effectiveness and treatment from us."

The service/quality revolution, fueled by free markets and highlighted by the media, is changing the way taxpayers look at the services they pay for. As companies, especially those in the service sectors, improve the quality of the work they produce and the customer coddling they provide, public-sector customers will become more sensitive to their governments' effectiveness in these areas. As the gap widens, discontent will grow and business-as-usual will become impossible.

In addition to better-quality public programs and services, John Q. Public continues to want — no, *demand* — more of those programs and services. We've raised a generation of citizens who are not only comfortable with but encourage massive government intervention at the municipal, provincial or state, and national levels. Many North Americans expect social safety nets, protection from or compensation for natural or man-made injuries or disasters, economic support or intervention, environmental clean-up . . . that's only the beginning of the long list of perceived needs.

At the same time the political pendulum has swung back toward conservative economic policies. The power of capitalism and free enterprise to improve a society's quality of life is being widely recognized. Even staunchly communist states are realizing that government intervention and control only strangles economic growth. An economy can't function efficiently without the discipline of price mechanisms. But we're not likely ever to return to the days when government spending accounted for a small amount of the Gross National Product.

While everyone is all for "getting governments off our backs," there's much screaming, wailing, and gnashing of teeth if "our" airport, rail service, firefighting, bridge building, economic development, or pet program should be the one to be cut. As our changing world violently shakes whole industries, regions, and countries, most people conclude that the government "ought to do something." The incomparable American wit, Will Rogers, put his finger on the problem when he said, "The business of government is to keep the government out of business — that is unless business needs government aid."

The Crunch

Rising public expectations are on a crash course with another powerful force sweeping North America: revenues are drying up as deficit reduction becomes a top priority. Taxpayers are turning their pockets inside out and telling their governments there's nothing left to give.

On one side is the rock — shrinking dollars to fund public expenditures. On the other side is the hard place — rising demand for more public programs and services. Few private-sector managers are in as tight a spot. And it's only just begun.

PUBLIC-SECTOR MYTHS AND REALITIES

In the heyday of government growth and expansion, a career in the public service was considered worthwhile and even prestigious. Many of the best and brightest gravitated toward government. Today that's changed. Most North Americans now stereotype public-sector managers and employees as ineffective, fat cat bureaucrats.

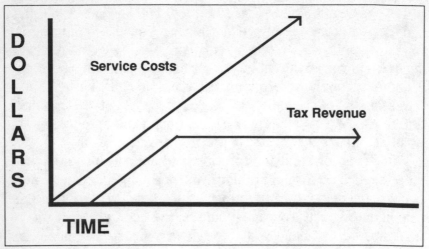

A number of common myths about the public sector should be exploded:

- "The public sector is not well managed." Many people feel that our governments have become overgrown, bloated organizations that cavalierly throw money away.
- "The public sector lacks coherent values or sense of purpose." Most people believe the only values government employees hold are to work less, earn more, control everything, and make a big deal out of small tasks. As one wag put it, "If you took every grain of sand and laid them end to end, you'd be working for the government."
- "Public-sector employees don't work hard." It's generally felt that public servants arrive at work around nine or ten, take two-to-three-hour lunches, and leave at four.
- "Public-sector employees don't care about customers." C. Northcote Parkinson (Parkinson's laws) sums up the feeling of many: "If there's anything a public servant hates to do, it's serve the public." A cynical old joke expresses the same

sentiments: "What are the two most common lies? — (1) The cheque is in the mail, (2) I'm from the government and I'm here to help you."

- "The public sector needs more private-sector practices." Most people, especially business people, feel that governments suffer because they don't have the discipline imposed by the bottomline. As one businessman put it, "Anything that the private sector can do, government can do worse."

So on top of higher demands and less money with which to fill them, public-sector managers also have a huge public-relations problem taking shape. In addition, everyone now expects high-quality services (from both private and public sectors) delivered by service-minded employees who stretch to satisfy them. That means that public tolerance and forgiveness for mistakes, bureaucratic run-around, or lackadaisical service will be close to nil. Unless dramatic improvements are made, complaints, bad press, and political intervention are destined to rise sharply, while public cooperation falls just as steeply.

Public-Sector Realities

Let's contrast the list of common public-sector myths with what we find are the realities of public-sector management:

- The public sector in North America is basically well managed and has coherent values. Government leaders from around the world regularly come to Canada and the United States to learn how we've developed and maintained some of the most effective governments and public institutions ever known. Many civil servants truly want to make a contribution to society. The basic value of service to their public, patients, or taxpayers is deep-rooted. For many, it's the reason they chose that career in the first place.

  Does that mean there's not a lot of room for improvement? Absolutely not! Just as in 90 percent of private-sector organizations, the public sector has poor productivity, lousy quality control, and all too often crummy, indifferent service. The difference is that it's more visible than in most companies. After all, how many company managers have politicians and the press watching their every move? If they did, the same kind of ineffectiveness and poor performance would be in the spotlight for all to shake their heads at in disgust. Those business managers who are so quick to criticize their governments would do well to take a long hard look in the mirror. Their costs are likely way out of line, their quality, though improving, is likely still mediocre, and the service their company provides is probably appalling.

- Employees in the public sector are no different from those in the private sector. Many do care, and most do work hard. Nurses, police officers, researchers, auditors, engineers, systems analysts, inspectors, and a long list of other civil servants want to protect, heal, improve, ensure fairness in, and serve society. Many, in fact, are quite idealistic about the contributions they want to make to the lives of others. The challenge for their managers is to harness the vast untapped energy that employees want to offer but aren't able to.

Many managers feel that "you can't get good help today" or "nobody wants to work anymore." Those popular views are cop-outs. The fact is we all want our work to be meaningful, and we all want to make a contribution. People *do* want to work today. They just may not want to work *for you*.

- Increasingly, public-sector organizations must compete with private-sector companies. There is not a single function of government, except maybe defense or tax collection, that has not felt substantial efforts to privatize. Fire, police, prisons, airports, road maintenance, social assistance — you name it, and someone somewhere is trying to privatize it. Before this shake-out is complete, public-sector organizations will find themselves out of many of the businesses traditionally regarded as the sole prerogative of government.

- A public-sector organization can't be run like a company.

The constituents that public agencies must serve are broad and diverse. These include politicians, taxpayers, unions, the government bureaucracy, employees, special-interest groups, and the media. Every decision must be measured against its effect on these powerful constituencies. It takes a skilled manager to chart a course through such treacherous waters.

- Our government deficits can't be sustained. For those institutions operating with balanced budgets (municipalities, hospitals, school boards, etc.), the problem may be an unrealistic feeling of security. As long as we keep our budgets balanced, we'll be fine, right? Dead wrong. Federal, provincial, or state deficits will increasingly choke off funds as these governments attempt to reduce their own expenditures. With the flick of a pen, a program is cut or funding is reduced, and a balanced budget quickly becomes a serious financial shortfall. Every indicator points to this trend picking up momentum in the coming years.

So no matter what the level of government or type of institution, future revenues look slim indeed. "Doing more with less" will continue to move from a catchy phrase mouthed by public-sector managers as they cut a little here and a little there, to an imperative calling for drastic changes in how public organizations are managed.

Changes on the Inside, Too

As if the challenges posed by external changes weren't enough, public-sector managers also must deal with a number of potentially damaging internal changes. If dealt with ineffectively, these changes could seriously hamper the organizations' ability even to maintain status quo, let alone improve performance.

Every manager in any organization today faces a radically different work ethic. It shows up in many ways and takes many forms. A bumper sticker I saw captured one of the key philosophies of today's worker. It said simply, "Question Authority." Raised in the liberated spirit of the 1960s, today's workers don't just expect involvement and participation in organizational decisions affecting them, they *demand* it. Richard Walton, professor of business administration at Harvard Business School, argues that managing today's workers requires a move from traditional command-and-control approaches to one that builds commitment in the workplace. He says, "This commitment cannot flourish in a workplace dominated by the familiar model of control."

The affluence, high employment levels, and social security programs of the last few years have also changed workers' attitudes toward their jobs. Where once they were grateful to get a steady paycheque, today's workers view a job as their right. And doing a job they hate just to collect a paycheque so they can get on with living the rest of the week is no longer enough. Today we want meaningful, fulfilling work that also pays well. Some experts studying these trends argue that the decline in church attendance and religious activities leaves many people searching for a type of spiritual fulfillment from their work. It's no surprise then that when workers are turned off by their jobs, their sense of frustration is more intense than their fathers' may have been. And they will vent that anger on the organization, its managers, and its customers.

The decline in the popularity and strength of unions in the eighties may lead public-sector managers to overlook the pressure unions can still exert on the organization. They still have lots of muscle-power left, and we can expect to see them flexing their muscles and spoiling for a fight as pressure is increased on the public sector. But managers can't afford a fight. Everyone's time and energy must be devoted to improving effectiveness — a fight for survival.

Management's challenge is to involve unions in the critical struggle for survival. It won't be easy. In the first place, managers are inclined to fight back with command-and-control authority when challenged. But that's like poking at the eyes of a wounded bear. As unions push to protect their power block, managers need to lead or pull together their teams rather than pushing them back into the arms of a hostile union. Second,

38

managers need to find the common ground between themselves, unions, and employees. In a relationship built on conflict and confrontation, that is a tall order. Players on both sides are used to finding and exploiting each other's differences. However, some leading public-sector managers are showing not only that it *can* be done but that it *must* be done if organizational performance is to improve.

Good Help Will Be Even Harder to Find
Given the changes and problems we've reviewed, it's not surprising that pride and morale in the public sector have slipped badly. This situation compounds another problem now showing up in many parts of North America: the growing shortage of skilled candidates for key positions. This problem plagues every organization, though it is particularly deadly for a mediocre or poorly run public-sector organization. Just as their budgets tighten and they can least afford it, mediocre public-sector organizations have to try to attract good people to a place with a poor public image, slipping morale, reduced budgets, and few, if any, promotion opportunities. As that proves harder and harder to do, the organization spirals into a vicious circle of hiring less-qualified people who are less effective — which helps lessen morale — making it harder to attract good people — which lessens . . .

Contrasting the Public and Private Sectors
In 1986, David Zussman and Jak Jabes from the University of Ottawa compared the managerial attitudes of 1,981 managers in the top five levels of the government of Canada with 1,289 managers in parallel positions within Canadian private-sector companies. They found that "the managerial cultures of the public and private sectors differ significantly." They especially noticed a big difference among various managerial levels of the government respondents. However, there was little difference between levels with the company managers. Here were their key findings:

- **Commitment and Pride** — Private-sector managers had

a somewhat higher level of commitment. Their pride in the industry and organization they work for was also higher.

- **Loyalty** — In the private sector, managers felt a high degree of loyalty to their company and CEO. In the public sector, managers' loyalty was *to the public*. In fact, five levels below the deputy minister, managers felt 20 percent lower levels of loyalty to their deputy minister than their private-sector counterparts felt to their CEO.
- **Organization Development** — "There were substantial differences between the two sectors in the degree to which they perceived their senior management to be committed to the future development of their organization." Again, those managers furthest down in the public sector held views sharply more negative than their most senior managers did.
- **Service** — There was a high degree of similarity between the two groups in this area. Both sectors agreed that service to their clients was their organization's most important orientation. Improving the quality of service was also seen by all managers to be a critical goal for both organizations.
- **Innovation and Creative Management** — While neither group rated themselves especially high, public-sector managers rated themselves at *half* the levels of their corporate counterparts on this critical organizational renewal issue.
- **Job Satisfaction** — Public-sector managers were less satisfied with their jobs. However, there was a marked difference in the intensity of those negative feelings further down the organization. This situation showed, once again, the gap between senior management and the rest of the organization. But, overall, "almost twice as many public-sector managers indicated agreement or strong agreement with the idea of quitting their job."
- **Morale** — Given many of the problems and negative differences found in the public sector, morale there was felt to be much lower than in the private sector. More than 40 percent of public-sector managers indicated morale to be a

serious issue, compared with just 13 percent in the private sector.

Zussman and Jabes concluded their report by highlighting the "striking" differences in opinion between those at the top of the managerial hierarchy and those closer to where the real work is done. They show that these two groups live in very different worlds: "In effect, the data suggest that they belong to a separate management culture." Zussman and Jabes found that particularly alarming, since the lower-level managers are the largest group and are the ones most visibly carrying management messages to employees and the public.

Our experience suggests that first-level supervisors and their work teams constitute yet another, much larger block of organizational members who feel even further removed and alienated from the organization than do middle managers. Here, commitment, pride, loyalty, job satisfaction, and morale are at all-time lows. The problem is exacerbated by senior management who don't recognize the extent of the problem because they live in their own separate, privileged world, hearing what those around them think they want to hear.

CAN PUBLIC-SECTOR CUSTOMERS QUIT?

Where's the motivation for public-sector organizations that aren't threatened by someone else taking over their work if they fail to perform? Karl Albrecht, coauthor of *Service America!*, is extremely critical of government service/quality in his follow-up book, *At America's Service.* He writes, "This lack of any force in the government organizations that might threaten their existence makes it plain why indifference is found in all of the nooks and crannies of their operations. It becomes an all-pervading cultural norm to which all but the most self-motivated and idealistic individuals eventually succumb."

The challenge for managers in the public sector is to help their staff understand just how critical service/quality is to survival or at least to improving the quality of work life for everyone. The training directorate of Transport Canada is a good example. This organization provides training for Canada's air traffic controllers, Coast Guard officers, and maritime pilots. In the late eighties, pressure was building to dramatically increase the number of controllers. Bottlenecks were building at Canada's major airports, especially in Toronto, because of an explosion in frequency of flights. At the same time, Canada's government, struggling to contain its burgeoning debts, imposed a series of tough spending restraints on all federal departments. The training directorate was ordered to slash 15 percent from its budgets at a time when demand for its services was increasing. Here's how Emmett Hossack, the executive director, assessed their situation: "We had two choices: carry on as best we could, let change occur, and hope to react well enough; or more directly influence our future by actively searching for and developing innovative ways to take charge of it." Emmett's challenge was to help his staff see the dangers of not taking charge of their own destiny while not allowing them to feel overwhelmed and helpless in the face of events beyond their control.

Public-sector managers need to help their organizations see that there are essentially two ways that their customers can "quit." One is fairly visible; the other is much more subtle. The visible way that public-sector customers quit include privatization, contracting out, forming pressure groups, and deregulation. The subtle forms of quitting include tax resistance, complaints, apathy, and conflict.

All too many public servants don't recognize many of these quitting problems as service/quality issues they can do something about. Because these problems are often wrapped up in political issues, they are seen as issues to be solved in that arena. But would a politician who is concerned about courting the popular vote even dream of dismantling an institution that is perceived to be delivering a vital public service efficiently and cost-effectively? Would widespread tax revolts or public outcries develop any momentum if the government concerned was perceived to be extremely customer-driven and responsive?

42

No, we don't live in a perfect world where doing the right thing is always recognized and rewarded. Popular opinion can indeed be fickle and unpredictable, and so can the politicians who try to catch those waves. But public-sector managers must help their staffs build a broad base of delighted customers. For that is the organization's only avenue to long-term security and quality of life for everyone. And it's the only way for the public sector to weather the powerful storm clouds building on the horizon.

What makes public-sector customers "quit" or punish the organization that's supposed to be serving them? Essentially, the same thing that we find in the private sector — an attitude of indifference. It's the public's sense that "I'm just a number, or a coronary case, or a voice associated with this paperwork to be dealt with and dismissed before break time." Even in those rare cases where a public-sector customer feels the organization has been efficient in the service or program provided, there needs to be a sense of humanity and caring for the experience to be rated as effective. Otherwise, it's just one more example of why the bureaucratic, wasteful machine needs to be torn apart, or at least rebuilt.

The health-care field provides an excellent example. Many doctors and medical professionals consider making patients physically better to be their only purpose. Unfortunately, that often means that Mr. Jones who's in for a hernia operation becomes "the hernia in room 302."

When indifferent, uncaring service is delivered by an institution that has grown fat and stupid in its cost-effectiveness, we have an organization ripe for political picking. Publicly flogging it or forcing it on a diet of bread and water while whipping it to run 10 miles a day is seen as a mere beginning that's long overdue. With the public in a black mood over rising taxes and falling service levels, public organizations must be seen as being well run and responsive. Otherwise some ambitious politician will offer up less fit public agencies for a few headlines.

43

WHAT'S THE BEST STRATEGY FOR THE PUBLIC SECTOR?

The pressures building on the public sector are enormous. The bloodletting, pain, and change about to be experienced by a majority of our governments and institutions will be intense. It will certainly rival the massive restructuring we've seen corporations go through in the last few years. Many public-sector organizations and their managers are about to be tested as they may never have dreamed they would be. Only the strong will survive.

To prepare for the storm, public-sector managers need an overarching strategy that:

- protects their market share by making the search for alternatives unnecessary;
- pleases the public and gives them a strong sense that they are getting good value for their money;
- ties into the existing values and strengths of the organization;
- improves service/quality while reducing operating costs;
- empowers employees without alienating unions;
- delights politicians with results they can take back to their constituents.

Service/Quality: A Key Strategic Issue for Improved Public-Sector Performance

To the uninitiated, claims that service/quality improvement can provide the unifying strategy that addresses the many challenges faced by the public sector may not be believable. How can one strategy be so powerful? It smacks of selling snake oil and swampland. Of course, any strategy is only as good as its execution. A brilliant plan poorly implemented is useless. But the evidence is there for sceptical public-sector managers to examine.

A well-executed service/quality improvement effort has turned a number of public-sector organizations from victims to masters of the changes blowing in on them. Service/quality improvement will:

- **Improve the level of service delivered to customers.**
  Service, like beauty, is in the eye of the beholder. When it
  comes to judging service, the perception of the customer is
  all there is to go on. Public-sector organizations that implement a service/quality improvement effort effectively report a dramatic improvement in how their customers rate
  their service delivery. When these real improvements are
  well communicated to the public being served, a strong
  sense of "getting our money's worth" develops.

  A municipal garbage truck fleet was able to improve average operational "up time" for their fleet from less than 50
  percent to more than 90 percent. A city department improved service levels with a drastically reduced budget. A
  federal agency was able to improve service levels and morale, handle a 15 percent budget cut, and identify over $1
  million in additional savings.

- **Reduce operating costs by doing more with less.** This
  "quality" side of the service/quality equation is the area that
  astounds public-sector managers. The amount of waste and
  inefficiency to be squeezed out of daily operations is
  unbelievable.

  Operating costs are reduced through a combination of
  doing it right the first time and changing the kind of activity,
  program, or service being delivered. Just asking employees
  "What's the dumbest system we have around here?" or
  "What hinders more than helps you deliver good service/
  quality?" can produce high-yielding changes. The same
  kinds of questions should be asked of customers. They too
  can identify which services or programs are the highest
  priority and which may be no longer needed.

  During Barry Sheehy's work with the City of Calgary, the
  engineering department measured how much they saved as
  a result of their service/quality improvement effort. In one
  year, they documented several million dollars saved from
  such things as improved billing processes, better inventory
  control, innovative approaches to pavement patching, and

more effective parts delivery to repair crews. All these improvement ideas came from front-line performers.

The City of Ottawa and the Regional Municipality of Ottawa-Carleton have experienced similar results from their focus on service/quality improvement. They have documented hundreds of successful service/quality improvements throughout their organizations.

From his research, Tom Peters asserts: "Among the best [organizations] in the public sector, the customer is identified and made central to all affairs. . . . A quality revolution will allow [the organization] to have its cake and eat it too: improve service delivery and cut its cost simultaneously."

- **Enhance public image and support.** As discussed earlier, public-sector organizations that have their act together are far less vulnerable to indiscriminate slashing and burning when tough budgets are imposed from on high. In *The Service Edge* newsletter, Milt Honea, of Arkansas Louisiana Gas Company, explains, "If we provide the best possible customer service, then the people [who] regulate our industry can justify allowing us better wages, benefits, and expenditure levels to help pay for that excellent service. If our customers are happy and our regulators are pleased, . . . our jobs are more secure."

- **Unify employees, politicians, and managers.** How can anyone associated with public service be against improving service/quality? Obviously, some groups, most notably employees and their unions, can feel threatened by any service/quality effort that is imposed from above. However, service/quality improvement can build on the common ground and can forge stronger relationships that move everyone toward the same goals. "We're all in this together" can take on a new, unifying meaning.

- **Create a context for enthusiasm and teamwork.** In my and Art McNeil's book, *The VIP Leadership Action Planner*, we introduce a concept we call "context and alignment." Basically, it summarizes an approach we see the best leaders unconsciously using to increase their employees' energy and commitment to the organization's goals. They provide a context or overarching purpose for the organization's existence around which they align everyone's (most especially management's) daily behavior. Tom Peters observed the same approach in the high-performing organizations he's been studying. He calls the context "superordinate goals."

We have all seen context and alignment in action at times of crisis or great calamity. The war effort during the Second World War was an example. So is the clean-up and relief work after a natural disaster such as after a tornado has hit. In those kinds of situations, people put aside their differences and personal goals for the attainment of a greater common good.

Service/quality improvement may not appear to have the same galvanizing potential. However, effective managers are able to maintain an intensity of purpose that can have a similar effect. When everyone involved understands the gravity of the situation, improvement can be a powerful rallying point. This is further reinforced by early feelings of success and "we're making a difference."

- **Improve morale, pride, and quality of work life**. One of the biggest killers of morale is a sense of powerlessness. If we feel that our work doesn't amount to much or make any difference, our pride and satisfaction will be low. In the public sector, the "useless bureaucrat" image is now so widely held that public servants begin to feel (and subsequently act as if) it's true.

IT IS BEING DONE NOW: A REVITALIZED PUBLIC AGENCY

A growing number of public-sector organizations are throwing off the shackles of their traditional way of management and are redesigning their organizations with a focus on service/quality improvement. Depending on the selected approach, these organizations are enjoying varying results.

One such organization is the Bureau of Labour Information, part of Labour Canada. The bureau collects, analyzes, and disseminates information on collective bargaining to the industrial relations community across Canada. Until April 1987, the services offered by the bureau were delivered by six sections. This situation resulted in customer confusion, lack of innovative new services, and retention of old services of questionable value. In 1985 and 1986, extensive downsizing was forced on Labour Canada as part of the federal government's expenditure reduction drive. At the same time, pressure was growing to improve service (sounding familiar?). Given the severity of the situation, senior management (from the deputy minister down) decided to refocus the organization through an intensive service/quality improvement effort.

They began by talking with their customers to identify their priorities and needs. The responses confirmed that a "single window" approach to serving clients seeking industrial relations information was the way to go. With this structure, customers would have to deal with only one group or entry point in the organization. This change led eventually to the practice of holding regular "meet the client" sessions. These approaches moved the organization from being product-driven to becoming much more client-oriented and market-driven. It also led to dropping some services, adding others, and streamlining many of the rest.

Early in the organizational redesign, employees were brought into the process. A "zero-based" approach was used, starting from a collective vision of what the organization should ideally look like. Teams were formed to redesign technology, equipment, and the processes for information collection and retrieval. A number of steps were ultimately eliminated or greatly reduced. These changes led to a dramatic reduction in error rates ("doing the right things right the first time"). Training and retraining were also heavily emphasized. In fact, more training was done in a two-year period than in the previous twenty years combined. Highly participative management approaches focused on people ("our only significant assets ride up and down in the elevators"), beyond the same tired old lines mouthed by every manager.

So what were the results of this radically new service/quality approach? Pessimists, naysayers, and we-tried-that-once-beforers, prepare to have your crutches kicked out from under you. By 1988, the bureau's service volumes were up by *400 percent*, but — get this — those sharply higher levels were handled by *39 percent less staff.* The bureau's files are now bulging with unsolicited letters from delighted customers who aren't used to such effectiveness from their governments. There is also a very low turnover rate and a lengthy list of applicants wanting to transfer to this revitalized organization (everybody wants to play for a winning team). The Auditor General of Canada cited the bureau as "one of eight well-performing organizations in the federal government."

CHAPTER THREE
What Does "Service/Quality" Mean?

"The organization must learn to think of itself not as producing goods and services but as buying customers, as doing those things that will make people want to do business with it."
— Ted Levitt, editor of *Harvard Business Review* and author of *The Marketing Imagination*

We complain that it is disappearing. We all want more of it. When asked to define "it," we say, "I'll know 'it' when I see 'it'."

Organizations want to be known for delivering high levels of "it." Many understand that "it" will increasingly determine their success. Employees would like to be known for delivering high levels of "it" to their internal and external customers. And they would like to be appreciated and rewarded for providing "it."

But when I talk about "it," and you agree your organization needs more of "it," are we talking about the same thing? Even more importantly, when you talk to your people about improving "it," are they seeing "it" the same way you are? Or is everyone signing up for "it," then heading off in opposite directions toward their own vision of "it"?

"It" — service/quality — is fast becoming the most talked about and least understood concept in organizations today. The problem is that it's intangible, qualitative, a term that's impossible to define once and for all. In seminars and executive retreats, I often ask participants to define what service/quality means to them. Here's a list of responses from a recent session:

- prompt attention to complaints or problems
- availability
- good customer communications
- showing respect and common courtesy
- keeping appointments and commitments
- educating maintenance people
- quality workmanship
- recommending future products
- appearance and neatness
- technical knowledge and ability
- a high-quality job

When you ask this question of employees on the front serving lines, another list usually develops. Some of the same definitions appear, depending on the mind-set of the employees and especially on the atmosphere of the organization. In some organizations, just showing up for work every day, in never mind how snarly a mood, is considered a heroic feat. A receptionist under siege on the switchboard might consider connecting the caller to the right department, regardless of how long they've been holding, as good service/quality.

So what's the point of all this? *Your organization needs a clear, well-understood, and consistent understanding of what service/quality means and how to deliver it.* Most organizations, and ultimately the managers and employees in them, know they want to improve service/quality, but they are not all reading the same road map. But then again, they're not even all heading to the same place.

Let's look at some of the above responses. Would a customer consider recommending future products good service/quality? Or would she see it as hard selling? How is an employee to understand what is meant by availability? Does that mean being on call 24 hours, being open Saturdays, or just checking into the office for messages once a day? Is an appointment or commitment kept if it's done within a half hour of the promised time? How about a day later? A week? That month? What is a quality job? According to whom? Using what measurements? And what are good customer communications? Does communication mean loading customers down with information? When are we telling them more than they care to know? Are we needlessly wasting their time with trivial details?

According to *The Service Edge* newsletter, Southern New England Telephone is a service/quality leader. CEO Walter Monteith declares, "We must redefine what service means within the context of a new and totally different business place." With the world moving at breakneck speed, what was considered good, or even innovative, yesterday could be substandard today. On top of that are a myriad of confusing and conflicting ideas of what service/quality means within just your management group, let alone the rest of your organization. Whether you use the model presented next or some other one, it's critical that you and your people develop a unified, consistent definition of service/quality. You've all got to be singing off the same sheet of music.

THE THREE RINGS OF PERCEIVED VALUE

Early in the evolution of Achieve's Service/Quality System, Ted Levitt's model of the Total Product provided an inspiration for a broader, clearer definition of what service/quality means. Widely renowned as the Harvard Business School's "guru of marketing", Levitt's classic book *The Marketing Imagination* outlined his four-ring model building on the organization's "Generic Product" to differentiate it in the marketplace.

Achieve's Three Rings of Perceived Value model was developed to help everyone throughout an organization better understand the relationship between the technology or expertise to produce an internal or external basic product or service, support for that product or service, and enhanced service that tops things off with a memorable experience.

The concentric rings show that as additional support and service is added to a high-quality product or service, the customer's perception of value increases. In high service/quality organizations, all three rings are strong and growing. Perceived value is high.

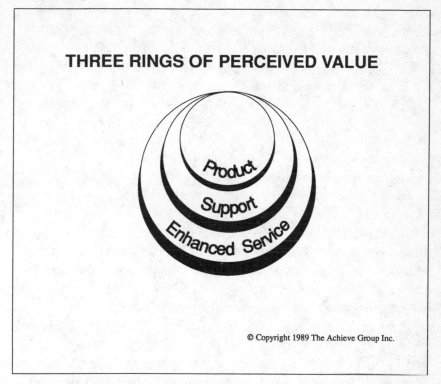

THREE RINGS OF PERCEIVED VALUE

© Copyright 1989 The Achieve Group Inc.

The inner product ring is the basic, bare product on its own. This could be a widget, a financial service, government program, hotel room, or complex technical system. Internally, it can also be a report for the boss, information for the manager in plant no. 3, training and development, or technical support. The size of this ring depends on the level of quality the customer feels he is getting. The customer appeal of that product or service depends on the extent to which it meets minimum requirements.

Today, the minimum standard that's considered acceptable in product manufacturing is much higher than it was 10 years ago. Similarly the standards of basic service requirements such as ease of access, flexibility, and the suitability of the service for the need are also rising. Just to get into the game today, you must

53

have a good, functional basic product — there is simply no market for products and services that don't work. However, in a world with an unprecedented supply of good products and services, minimum standards of acceptable quality are increasing exponentially. Just keeping your customers' perception of your product or service up to that of others is a tough job.

Those whose basic products or services are primarily for internal consumption also feel this pressure to improve. Changing requirements of external customers, coupled with growing pressures on every organization to do more with less, are radically shifting internal customers' bare requirements. Internal support groups need to keep their basic product strong and evolving to keep up with the fast-moving needs of their organization.

The Basic Product Is Not Enough

Just meeting product or service requirements has never been enough. Customers expect additional support services to back up the products or services we use. And their satisfaction will be in direct proportion to how closely they feel their expectations are, or are not, met. Those expectations are also elastic. They will change according to the price of the product or service, what the competition offers, the customers' prior experience with this kind of product or service, the promises being made by the delivering organization, personal values, and a host of other factors.

Let's take a hotel, for example. One of its basic products is a bedroom. Now, depending on the price you pay, you know your minimum requirements for the type of room you would call acceptable quality. (By acceptable quality, I mean a room you wouldn't immediately turn right around and check out of, or one that would make you fire off a scathing letter to your travel agent before you've even unpacked.) These First Ring requirements might include an attached bathroom with hot and cold running water, absence of bugs and rodents, privacy, a bearable room temperature, a bed with clean sheets, and a lock on the door, among other basics.

54

If you included a telephone and a color TV among your minimum requirements, you'd be illustrating how minimum acceptable standards change over time. It wasn't all that long ago when hotels advertised color TVs to entice people to stay there. Now we expect to find one in even the lowest-priced North American facility.

Though the absence of those minimum requirements in your room leaves you dissatisfied, those alone, no matter how high their quality, would not even begin to give you an overall satisfying experience. In addition to a room of decent quality, you expect to find a number of services and facilities. Again, your list of expectations is influenced by a host of factors, one of which is price. Your list of expectations is no doubt long, and largely unconscious. You don't enter a hotel with this checklist in hand, or even in head. But should some of your expectations not be met, you suddenly, and maybe painfully, notice the void. Here's a partial list of common support services we expect to find in a moderate-to-high-priced hotel: room service, easy check-in/out, a restaurant, meeting rooms, convenient location, a pool, exercise room, elevators, tasteful decor, responsive and friendly service, help with baggage, comfortable beds, wake-up calls . . . and on the list goes.

Now take a look at your own organization. It offers a multitude of basic products or services to external customers. Even more products, services, and departmental outputs are being delivered internally. Pick a few examples. What is the basic product being produced? What are the minimum quality requirements? What additional expectations do users of the basic product have concerning its support? What would it take to satisfy these customers?

In the early eighties, companies concentrated on expanding their small, inner "product quality" ring. By the late eighties that was no longer enough. Attention began to shift to the second "support service" ring. This change came in response to shifts in customer expectations. Regis McKenna draws on his extensive experience in the field of marketing to explain the trend: "The product is no longer just the thing itself; it includes service, word-of-mouth references, company financial reports, the technology and even the personal image of the CEO. As a result, product marketing and service marketing, formerly two distinct fields, have become a single hybrid. Now more than ever, marketers must sell every aspect of their business as important elements of the products themselves." Even the highly product-focused health care field is broadening its view of what makes for high perceived value. Treating patients as human beings is now being recognized as a Second Ring expectation. A Welland, Ontario, woman won a $450,000 lawsuit against a doctor. "All he had to do was say he was sorry," said Hendrika Jinks.

As you look at your organization's basic products and supporting services, you'll probably have some difficulty deciding what the minimum requirements are and what expectations would most likely lead to satisfied customers. If you took that discussion to your management team, a conflicting array of opinions would further confuse things. One way of clarifying what belongs where would be to ask those employees on the serving lines who hear what customers are asking for and commenting on. Their opinions have constantly been shown to be much more valid than those of management.

But the obvious people to ask are your customers. And there's the power and simplicity of the "Three Rings" model. Ask your customers what their minimum standards are and have them rate how you've been doing. Then do the same to find out what support services they expect and how you've been doing at satisfying those expectations. Get each employee team to do the same for the external or internal customers they serve and to communicate the results to everyone. Do that, and you've just taken a giant step toward developing a consistent definition of what service/quality means in your organization. You'll be starting to build a base. But it's just the beginning.

IS THE SECOND RING ENOUGH?

Most definitions of service/quality stop at the Second Ring. They are essentially variations on the theme of "find out what your customers want and give it to them." Customer satisfaction and meeting customer needs are important goals. Certainly there's nothing wrong with that as far as it goes. But it doesn't go far enough any more. Yes, we want satisfied customers. But that won't set us apart in today's world of skyrocketing expectations and dizzying arrays of options and alternatives. The crusty old man of quality improvement, W. Edwards Deming, said: "It will not suffice to have customers that are merely satisfied. Satisfied customers switch for no good reason, just to try something else. Why not? Profit and growth come from customers that can boast about your product or service — the loyal customer. He requires no advertising or other persuasion, and he brings a friend with him." Remember — *customer loyalty is a lack of a better alternative.*

Let's go back to our hotel example. If you came away merely satisfied with the basic product, would you be sure to go back to that hotel the next time? Not likely. If some other hotel was closer, booked by someone else for you, offered more airline bonus points, or just looked like an interesting one to try, you'd likely switch. One's as good as another, right? Take away the nameplates and fancy stationery, and you would have a tough time distinguishing just which hotel you were in this time. In fact, most hotels pretty much follow each other in meeting changing customer expectations. Remember when getting a little basket of shampoo, conditioner, and fancy soap was an unexpected extra. Now if it's missing we feel cheated. Our expectations have changed again.

The hard reality of the world we live in is that just to be considered a serious player in the market you must have strong First and Second Rings. But that won't get you noticed in the fight for your customers' hearts and dollars. As someone said, it's like housework: just keeping things clean doesn't stand out. That's expected. But let it slip for just one week and everyone notices immediately.

A Gallup survey conducted for the American Society for Quality Control found that Americans were more concerned in 1988 with attitude and courtesy, promptness, and feeling their needs were satisfied than they were just three years before.

These priorities eclipsed price, accuracy, or convenience (mostly Second Ring expectations) as areas customers felt needed the most attention.

THE THIRD RING:
THE NEW SERVICE/QUALITY BATTLEGROUND

Tom Peters once again hits the nail on the head: "Unfortunately, we can no longer afford to merely satisfy the customer. To win today, you have to *delight and astound* your customers — with products and services that *far* exceed their expectations." As North American organizations turn their attention to the Second Ring, taking similar "me-too" action won't put you ahead. At best, you'll just hold your own.

The Third Ring is where you can pull ahead. It's where those organizations that have been stealing market share and increasing their revenues at phenomenal rates have been operating for years. And they've had the territory all to themselves. With solid First and Second Rings, an expanding Third Ring gives your customers a strong sense of perceived value. It's one of the reasons strong Third Ring companies can charge more. Their customers feel they get their money's worth.

The Third Ring moves beyond customer satisfaction to *customer delight*. It exceeds expectations. At Stew Leonard's incredibly successful dairy, it's the "wow" factor. As Stew constantly drills into his people, "We want our customers saying 'wow' at every corner." And those "wowed" customers keep coming back for more — and tell their friends to do the same. That comes from *enhanced service* — which is the Third Ring.

The Third Ring is where the large investments you've made in basic products (First Ring) and supporting services (Second Ring) can multiply your pay-off. Third Ring enhancements are usually small investments with huge pay-offs. The Third Ring is where the human touch is added. It's those intangible signs of personal care and commitment that say, "We're pleased to serve you. We want to do whatever we can to make your relationship with us as delightful as possible." In the first two rings you can objectively point to specifications, selection criteria, equipment, facilities, support systems, and the like to give clear, rational reasons why that hotel did or didn't live up to your requirements and expectations. The Third Ring is much more intuitive and irrational. It's a series of tiny gestures and insignificant signals that make dealing with an organization a rare delight. It's a sense of warmth and attention that makes for true user-friendliness.

In the hotel business, getting a potential guest's consideration is an expensive series of First and Second Ring investments. What keeps guests coming back, and recommending the place, are all the delightful Third Ring enhancements. An *Advertising Age* hotel/motel poll showed Hyatt Hotels that guests rarely mention their expensive facilities. What gives them top marks is the quality and *consistency* (anybody can do it once in a while) of service. A study by Strategic Information Research Corp. for a resort developer found that 73 percent of travel agents, editors, travel bureau representatives, and meeting planners said "service was the most important element in rating a hotel". They were primarily concerned with the way a hotel's staff anticipated guests' needs and provided for them. Zemke and Schaaf report that a Gallup poll asked what makes people decide not to return to a given restaurant. The answer was typically Third Ring: 83 percent listed service ahead of food quality, ambience, and price.

Don't Confuse the Second and Third Rings

We often define the rare times we experience the Third Ring as outstanding personal service. These moments shouldn't be confused with the services found in the Second Ring. Services (Second Ring) are usually systematized and not personal at all, although many misguided organizations try to make them that way. A good example is the form letter you get when you raise a problem with a large organization: "Dear Valued Customer: Our computer cares about you. But, unfortunately, our policy is . . ."

The financial services industry is rife with examples of companies that can't tell the difference between Second Ring services and Third Ring enhanced service. Typical of most technomanagers (those who think productivity, quality, and service improvement are to be found in technology and management systems), many bankers expected automated teller machines to take care of those pesky customers who wanted more convenient access to their accounts, shorter lines, and an escape from rude tellers. Yet after 15 years, only 48 percent of U.S. bank customers ever use them. Research shows that customers don't trust the machines and miss the human contact (high tech, high touch). John M. Kolesar, president and CEO of American Trust Development Bank in Cleveland, explains, "Bankers can't understand why consumers don't appreciate all the investments we've made in new technologies. . . . It's because they don't define 'service' as convenience. The new consumers' concept of service is far more qualitative. We need to bring our concept of service into line with theirs." Alexander Berry III, senior vice-president of Signet Bank/Virginia, summarizes beautifully what most managers in all organizations need to understand about the Third Ring: "Bankers who equate better service with more people, more space, and more machines do not understand that service quality is 'heart,' not 'things.'"

THE THIRD RING:
LITTLE THINGS THAT MAKE A BIG DIFFERENCE

In the early days of the computer, IBM took a broader view than did its competitors. They provided what was at that time Third Ring, delightful service. The Strategic Planning Institute's research led them to conclude, "While competitors focused on hardware — what the machines could do, IBM focused on software and service — what the user could get from the machine. . . . It was this perspective on the 'soft' dimension of customer needs, so logical in hindsight, that was the trigger to IBM's rise to dominance."

Today, we expect more, and our higher expectations are pressuring leaders like IBM to improve their service/quality levels just to hang on to their current position. Providing Third Ring enhanced service in an environment where basic products and support services expectations are changing at a blistering pace is an enormous challenge. When you add to that the inflexibility that can come with an organization as large as IBM, you've got a major problem to deliver even a few Third Ring personalized enhancements. Can IBM keep its leadership position in the face of aggressive, ever-improving competition?

During an executive retreat I ran with the management group of an internal store systems group for a major retailer, the discussion turned to whether they were ready to focus on Third Ring service. The problem was that their basic product (computer systems, training, and support) was outdated and badly flawed. An all-out effort was under way to fix that. But, argued one group of executives, how can we provide enhanced service when the inner rings are weak? Smiling and politeness go only so far.

From the raging debate, a consensus formed. It's the same conclusion that top performing organizations often arrive at when they are overtaken by similar changes in their products and customer expectations. The group agreed that work on inner rings did not preclude getting the organization to provide personalized enhanced service of the Third Ring. In fact, they concluded, taking steps to ensure their customers were treated with care and consideration would go a long way toward increasing the overall impression of perceived value even though the inner rings were currently small. Once these rings were enlarged, the organization would have developed Third Ring habits that would lead to a combined perception of high overall value. In other words, they were committed to improving all three rings.

The Third Ring is made up of thousands of little things that either add up to a high "wow index" or that bit by bit drive customers nuts — a death of a thousand cuts. Buck Rodgers, one of the key executives who helped IBM become so dominant through a service/quality focus, says, "There's no way of quantifying how many customers are lost because of little human errors — not returning a phone call, being late for an appointment, failing to say thank you, taking an account for granted. As far as I'm concerned, these things can be the difference between a very successful company and a failure."

Performance consultant Joel Weldon sums it up nicely: "Elephants don't bite. It's the little things like mosquitos or blackflies that get you." Earl Fletcher, sales and management trainer for Volkswagen Canada, makes a similar point: "It's not the $1,000 things that upset the customer, but the $5 things that bug them."

Learning by Example
The Roman writer Seneca once said, "Rules make the learners' path long, examples make it short and successful." There's no better way to understand what Third Ring enhanced service looks like than to see it in action:

- The Canadian-owned and operated Four Seasons Hotel chain has become legendary for their exceptional service/ quality in the upscale and highly competitive international luxury-hotel market. Knowing founder Issy Sharp's passion for making sure everything is just right (and the rewards to staff for being equally particular), a housekeeper at the Boston hotel took him aside to point out what she thought was a misprint in the guest Bibles.

  A seminar participant told me that he and a party of four once dropped into the Edmonton, Alberta, hotel hoping that there would be rooms available for everyone. Luckily there were. "By the time we got checked in and up to our rooms, not only were the sheets turned down and the chocolates on our pillows, but we each found a hand-written note welcoming us by name!"

  Carol Resnick, the concierge at their Inn on the Park in Toronto, realized the pressure that a guest from Brazil was under. So she spent more than an hour helping him type his report and organize his presentation.
- It was a hot, steamy July morning in Toronto when the air conditioning failed in a major office tower run by North American real estate developer Bramalea Limited. As repairs proceeded, building management sprang into action. They began a series of communications through office-to-office visits and notices in hallways and elevators throughout the day updating tenants on the progress of repairs. The manager then took some of his promotional

dollars and hired an ice cream company to set up shop in the lobby with free ice cream, juices, and soft drinks. A carnival atmosphere prevailed as shirt-sleeved executives and office staff joked about the situation while licking ice cream.

The whole thing cost Bramalea a grand total of $1,815. The pay-off was incredible amounts of goodwill (higher perceived value), and not one single complaint was received.

- Hilltop Auto Service is right around the corner from Achieve's Mississauga offices. We all take our cars there because of the high service/quality. Their inner rings are strong — modern bays, licensed and competent mechanics, convenient location, the latest diagnostic and repair technology, and so on. But that's not really what sets them apart from many other similar shops.

  What makes Hilltop's perceived value higher are the little Third Ring acts of care and concern — returning phone calls, smiling and calling their customers by name, keeping promises. Once when I had my car in, they diagnosed the problem, then called me at the office to recommend I return to my dealer to see if I could get it fixed under warranty.

- New to town, a man went into a bank to cash a cheque. After looking over his identification, the teller disappeared leaving him wondering what the problem was. She promptly reappeared with other bank staff who sang him "Happy Birthday" (the teller had noticed his birthdate).

- The phenomenally successful and service-oriented Walmart Stores has a designated greeter at the front doors whose only job is to make customers feel welcome as they enter the store. He also thanks them as they leave.

- At Achieve, we try hard to practice what we preach. Here's a sample of some of the little unexpected Third Ring enhancements we've found delight our customers:

  - a welcome sign with the names of all Achieve visitors that day
  - fresh home-baked muffins, pastries, etc., for workshop participants

- • a peppermint candy in each order of materials or books sent to clients
- • a bowl of quarters for participants to make phone calls during public seminars we hold at hotels
- • when we do make a mistake or shipping error, we send our client a "Mugs and Kisses" apology (an Achieve coffee mug filled with chocolate candy kisses) along with an explanation of what actions we have taken to correct the situation

- • Rob Ell grew up focusing on service/quality in the family's Flintstones Bedrock City theme park in Chilliwack, British Columbia. One of their unexpected Third Ring enhancements involves patrolling the parking lot looking for cars with their headlights left on. A card left on the windshield of these cars invites the customer to turn it in at the main gate for a free boost.

- • Bryan Sue, promotions director at the Hockey Hall of Fame in Toronto, not only helped a visiting couple select a restaurant for lunch but he also drew a map for them showing how to get there.

- • A loyal customer raved about a hardware store he frequents: "It's just a little hole in the wall. It has only one of some things, and they're usually a bit more expensive. But the service is superb. There is always some knowledgeable, eager staff person just dying to help you find what you want. To get there, I pass a much bigger, more modern store loaded with heavily advertised specials and lower-priced merchandise. But if you do finally find somebody to ask for assistance, they stumble around with you searching for whatever it is you're after."

EXAMINING THE THREE RINGS
OF PERCEIVED VALUE

Your customers, employees, and management team all play parts in the Three Rings. Yet their roles are all different and sometimes conflicting. And while your employees control your Third Ring, management holds the keys to their performance.

Your Customers' Role

To be even considered by potential customers, your organization needs a strong basic product. Customers also expect support services with your basic products. The type and quality they expect will often be influenced by price. Most of us know that we get pretty much what we pay for. Some customers will bag their own groceries or freeze their hands pumping their own gas to save money. However, if price is not your leading draw point (and it's a dangerous, usually losing long-term game to play), then your customers have some higher expectations of the minimum support services you provide.

Your customers often experience the Three Rings exactly opposite to the way those inside your organization look at them. Customers start on the outside and move into your basic product from the Third Ring. If your Third Ring is weak or non-existent, they'll never notice. But if your Third Ring is large, their first impressions will be very positive. That gives you great momentum as customers move into your inner rings. Even the odd failure in one of the inner rings will be forgiven if everyone is delighting your customers in the outer ring of enhanced service.

However, managers and employees often see the three rings from the inside out. Most of the focus is put on the basic reason the organization exists — the products/services it provides. Administrative, support, and delivery services come next. And, if there's time, somebody throws a training program or catchy slogan at those front-line servers so they'll do more of that "people stuff."

How likely, or typical, is this scenario in your organization? A customer calls with a question, and the harried receptionist (generally overworked, undertrained, and underpaid) tries to get Joe. His phone rings and rings but no one answers. The call comes back to the switchboard (or the customer calls back), and the receptionist tries Sue. Sue reluctantly listens to the customer and passes the call to Brenda, because that's her area of expertise. Brenda is in a meeting. The customer leaves a message. When Brenda finally does call back (she's extremely busy be

65

cause so many people rely on her strong abilities), she tells the customer that the organization can't do anything to help him.

Sound familiar? Everyone did his or her job. But the customer was made to dance to that old familiar tune, "The Bureaucratic Shuffle." That's because the organization was organized for its own convenience rather than for the customer's. Looking from the inside out, everyone did his or her job. Looking from the outside in, the customer was greeted with a confusing mish-mash of departments and busy people.

So what about your organization? Do you have a one-call/stop entry point that brings your customers effortlessly into the organization? GE, for example, has brought all its service lines into one 800 number staffed by well-trained and supported people who will provide the answers or connect customers quickly with the right people. How easy are you to deal with? How do you know?

One of the causes, or certainly a big contributor, to the problem is that most organizations are product- rather than customer-driven. Campbell Soup was in that position before Dave Clark took over as CEO in 1983 and began a major organization renewal process. Over the next few years the company took steps to increase its customer focus. Those efforts (focus groups, surveys, having executives do their family's grocery shopping, and the like) brought to light the "wall of soup" problem. You've no doubt experienced it. There you were, in front of that wall of red-and-white soup cans looking for one little can of Cream of Whatever soup. The reason you couldn't find it was that Campbell's had laid out the display according to how they looked at the soup business. So they had consumer focus groups rearrange all Campbell's soup displays to follow soup buyers' rather than soup makers' logic. The results? Soup sales increased and store managers were passing along the thanks that they were getting from grateful shoppers.

A good indicator of whether your organization is set up for customer delight is the language that's used with the average, not terribly knowledgeable, customer. If it's a special brand of technobabble full of acronyms and jargon, then it's a safe bet that your people are trying to make your customers fit your organization rather than the other way around.

Your Employees' Role

Jan Carlzon, president of Scandinavian Airline Systems, popularized a simple, powerful concept in his miraculous turnaround of that company in the early eighties. His key concept, which he calls the Moment of Truth, is that any time a customer makes contact with the organization, whether by phone, fax, letter, or in person, some kind of impression is formed. In the course of a day in an organization of a few hundred employees or more, there are thousands of moments of truth. Each one is so minor it's almost insignificant. So what if the phone rings a few extra times? And does one little typo really make that much difference?

On its own, each moment of truth is pretty small stuff. The organization is certainly not going to sink or soar on the basis of that one tiny event. But each moment of truth is like a grain of sand placed on the scales of justice. Either that minute, almost weightless grain of sand goes on the side of mediocrity ("So what else is new? You just can't get decent service these days") or it is placed on the side of outstanding performance ("Incredible! What unbelievable service. They are a delight to deal with!"). Over time, the scale will start to tip in one direction or the other. Thus are apathetic, antagonistic, or enthusiastic customers created. And from such tiny beginnings are reputations made.

Service guru Ron Zemke sees the organization as a collection of many daily moments of truth. As he outlines in *The Service Edge*, impressions formed from moments of truth are often intangible feelings that cause customers to leap to their own conclusions: "The clerk who rings up an order with a telephone cradled in the crook of his neck, a personal conversation in progress, no eye contact, and a wad of gum in his mouth, is sending a clear message: 'You are not important enough for me to treat you with even a modicum of respect. You're a duty, not a person.'"

Who makes your organization's First and Second Ring decisions? Who decides what products/services and their supporting

services your organization will offer? In virtually every organization, large or small, the answer is management. Those are big-
buck, major investment decisions. The bigger they are, the
higher up they're made.

What about your moments of truth? Who decides whether to
bend a rule to help out a customer? Who decides whether to
answer that phone on the second ring? Who spots the error in the
invoice and pulls it out for correction? The answer, nine out of ten
times, is that employees make those Third Ring decisions. If you
studied a thousand moments of truth in a given day, no doubt you
would find that 900 of them were managed by an employee with
no supervisor or manager in sight. Employees live in, control, and
get their job satisfaction (or hatred) from the Third Ring. This is
their territory. They own it.

You've gone to that upscale restaurant where the linen was
made of a finer material than your suit, only to be snarled at by
your waiter. You've admired the polished brass and marble of a
spanking new financial institution's building, only to be treated as
a non-person who's interrupting the more important administrative work that's going on there. And you've had one of the
clerks in that government's new $10-million program berate you
because you didn't fill out their 200-line form completely and
accurately.

The net effect was a poor overall impression of the organization. Your perception of value received was much lower than it
could have been. Many of the dollars they invested in the inner
rings were wasted because of poor Third Ring performance. And
how much would better Third Ring performance have cost them?
Very little. Look back at our Third Ring examples on pages 62 to
64. The dollars involved are puny compared to the capital and
operating costs of the inner rings. But the pay-offs are enormous.
The return on investment can be in the thousands of percent.

Not only do committed front-line performers control the Third
Ring, but they also have the closest contact with customers and
are in an ideal position to identify ways to improve the inner
rings. How many millions of dollars could your organization save
by forming a partnership with your front-line people?

Management's Role

Many of management's concerns surrounding the Three Rings are based on the customers' needs and the employees' role. It's around these two groups that most of management's time and energy should be focused. If you believe that improving the Third Ring is an important element of your future success, then making sure that customers' needs and employees' requirements are met is a big part of how management should be defining its job.

It's in the outer ring that your inner-ring investments pay off. And when the management-employee partnership is working well, problems or opportunities flagged by employees in the outer ring direct the most strategic use of resources in the inner rings.

Some of the most effective consultants your organization could ever hire are already working for you. I love to be part of presentations that service/quality teams make to their own senior management on improvements needed to manage the business more effectively. Inevitably, once the presentation is over and the employees have left, members of the management group look at each other in wonder. "Where have we been hiding these people?" they ask. "Such insight and clarity. Why haven't we heard these ideas before?" Well, the reason is simple: nobody was listening. Most employees have good ideas they would love to see implemented. Maybe they even tried once or twice to pass them along. But the system, their supervisor, or simple lack of interest killed the suggestion. So why keep beating their heads against the wall? One employee expressed the frustration many feel by sticking this sign on a suggestion box: "Please don't put any more ideas in here. The handle is broken and it won't flush."

How do you develop effective Third Ring behavior? That is the key question. It is *the* critical issue for moving your service/quality improvements into the Third Ring. Unfortunately, the answer to the question is easy to give, but building consistent and constant Third Ring improvements throughout your organization is exceedingly difficult (if it was easy, we wouldn't all be experiencing such crummy service everywhere we went). Writing in *Fortune* magazine about the best service providers, Bro

Uttal observes, "Unlike products, services can't be made in a factory and stored in inventory; they are consumed at the moment of production, and whoever delivers the service, from telephone operators to washing machine repairmen, will do more than any management system can to determine quality."

The quick answer to how you develop effective Third Ring behavior is *build an environment that encourages, nurtures, and rewards "volunteerism."* It's about now that most executives roll their eyes, check their watches, and hunker down for another boring bit about "that people stuff." At least the technomanagers do. They don't believe, don't appreciate, or — this is closest to the truth — *don't know how* to motivate their people to voluntarily perform daily acts of mini-heroism in the Third Ring. Because it can't come any other way. As much as technomanagers continue to try, you can't command and control your people into the Third Ring. What are you going to do, take the firings-will-continue-until-morale-improves approach? If you beat your people hard enough, make the rules tough enough, ensure your "snoopervision" is overbearing enough, and make all the follow-throughs relentless enough, you'll get them to follow their job descriptions and, maybe, just maybe, do an adequate job of meeting Second Ring expectations. But you'll never get those moments of truth weighing on the side of outstanding Third Ring performance.

Many Technomanagers have tried to mechanize or capitalize their way into the Third Ring. It can't be done. Computers and other systems can support the delivery of Third Ring service, but they can't *do* it. Only people can. Futurist John Naisbett outlines the dilemma management faces: "The more that computers come into play in handling consumers, the more customers crave reassurance that humans will intervene when help is needed."

In the service/quality improvement process, you can make a fair number of gains on the inner rings with better management (systems, controls, planning, structure). But to move into the service/quality major leagues, you *must* have your coworkers enthusiastically pulling together to get there with you. *The Service Edge* newsletter quotes Lewis Lehr, retired chairman of

3M, as saying "We learned we could hire people, pay them well to do a job, but we couldn't force them to bring a quality attitude to their jobs. That's something they have to volunteer."

Nurturing and maintaining high levels of volunteerism across a large organization over a long period is extremely difficult. In most cases, it requires everyone — especially management —to change, and that demands a substantial cultural change.

Although employees directly control those critical moments of truth, final control and responsibility for the quality of their delivery rests with management. Management holds the keys. For it's management that ultimately sets the focus and atmosphere of the organization. And it's this atmosphere and direction that determines who gets hired, how they're trained, what values they see demonstrated every day, what behavior is rewarded, who's promoted and why, what gets measured, what support systems and controls are available, and what messages customers and employees are given.

Expectations Gravitate Inward

The Three Rings are dynamic. They ripple inwardly quite rapidly. In other words, what was once an unexpected delight eventually becomes a Second Ring expectation. What was once an expectation to satisfy additional needs becomes a minimum requirement. And minimum requirements keep rising. But each time an expectation moves from the extraordinary to the norm, it enriches the perceived quality of your basic product or supporting Second Ring service.

Service/quality improvement is a journey, not a destination. It never ends. You are always in the process of becoming. Or as the Japanese and our best high-quality producers teach us, it's a process of continual improvement. And that improvement starts with the culture and leadership skills provided by management, because it's the environment created and signaled by management that ultimately determines the intensity of the service/quality improvement efforts. Management gets exactly the service/quality it deserves.

CHAPTER FOUR
Deadly Assumptions

"Reading about the principles of quality and hiring an expert to explain them is easy. The hard part is making them work."

— "Victories in the Quality Crusade,"
Fortune magazine

Every executive wants better service/quality. "Yes, sir! Sign us up for ten tons of that service/quality stuff!" The need for improved service/quality is obvious to many. The pay-offs are just common sense. The need to meet customers' minimum product/services standards is obvious. The need to find out what customers' expectations are and to satisfy them is common sense. And the need to delight customers with enhanced service is also obvious.

If all this is so obvious and just common sense, why is service/quality so bad? Because common sense is rarely common *practice*. We all *know* much more than we *do*. Many executives can preach a pretty sermon, but only a few can practice what they so eloquently preach. Whether it's personal or organizational performance improvement, obviously the obvious isn't so obvious or many more executives would be doing it.

VALUES AND BELIEFS

The biggest influence on our actions is our values and beliefs. A leading Japanese academic put his finger on the North American value system that undermines many service/quality improvement efforts: "You will lose and we will win because your failing is within yourselves. In your hearts you really believe in Taylor's model of scientific management. You believe that managers do the thinking and employees wield the screwdrivers."

Before any service/quality improvement effort can begin, senior management must clarify its underlying values and beliefs. For many managers, declaring their intentions is fairly easy; the tough part is "walking the talk." All too often, executives talk quality while rewarding volume; talk service while personally avoiding customer contact; talk teamwork while behaving like Lone Rangers; talk about "people, our most important asset" and then kick them around or kick them out; talk about the importance of improved communications and then retreat to their offices and boardrooms, or talk about the need for training and development and then cut the training budget.

As you read through the seven deadly assumptions outlined in this chapter, check your knee-jerk response. Whenever you find yourself thinking "I knew that," or "Of course, that's just common sense," be tough on yourself. Examine your *actions*. Are you *proclaiming* one thing but *doing* the opposite? Better yet, solicit feedback on your behavior. How are your actions being interpreted by your customers? Employees? Your management team? What do your actions say about your underlying values and beliefs?

Don't guess. Ask them. Even as you read through these deadly assumptions, complete each one by asking yourself: "Would my management team, employees, or customers, say I acted as if I held this erroneous assumption?" Then muster up your leadership courage, swallow your managerial pride, and *go ask them*.

"OF COURSE WE BELIEVE IN SERVICE/QUALITY"

To many executives, service/quality is a motherhood issue. There is a sense of impatience, indignation, or even resentment at any suggestion that the organization needs to make a special effort to improve service/quality. "We've been a quality (or

service) organization for more years than you've been alive."
"Why, service is practically our middle name." "Hey, we're in
the service industry (or public sector), so we've always had to
emphasize service."

This deadly assumption is the most common and unrecognized
one that snares many an unwary executive. It's also the one that
managers or fellow executives identify as the biggest problem
they face in getting their organization on the high road to outstanding service/quality. It's a perfect example of confusing
knowing with doing — or in many cases, confusing intending with
doing. We also refer to it as the implementation trap. And it's
been plaguing organizational improvement for years. Although
those executives who fall into this trap would declare otherwise,
it comes from the command-and-control era that assumed "so it
was written, so it was done." These (fortunately dying) breeds of
executive see their role as strategists, planners, policy makers,
financial gatekeepers, and senior decision makers. Once the
decision, plan, or direction is set, they've done their job.

Actions Not Words Signal Beliefs
There is no stronger message senior managers can send about
their true priorities than their daily actions. When executives
play the service/quality tune but dance to something else, their
behavior drowns out the music. Service guru Ron Zemke paints
an all-too-familiar scene: "American boardrooms are full of senior managers who are all for signing service proclamations and
making bold speeches reminding 'those people down in the
trenches' how important customers are, but can't seem to find
the time to actually 'work' the problem of improving service."

Where is senior executives' time being spent? Are they busy
putting out fires because things weren't done right the first time?
Are they cost cutting the organization's pathway to long-term
profitability? Are they manipulating assets to increase book
value? Are they restructuring the organization? Are they looking
for ways to increase market share and grow revenues?

If you're a senior executive spending most of your time in
those areas, then you do not believe in service/quality, despite

Look Jones, the executive committee can't give this any more time...make us a service driven company.

what you may say to the contrary. As we showed in Chapters 1 and 2, there is no better way to cut costs and increase revenues than through service/quality improvement. If you truly believe in service/quality improvement, it would be your top priority. Period. And you would then make it the top priority of your management team. *Fortune* magazine says: "The most important factor in outstanding customer service sits in the corner office. When the CEO eats, sleeps, and breathes service, the rest of the troops catch the spirit pretty quick." What would your "troops" say you eat, sleep, and breathe? Would your actions leave no room for doubt that you truly do believe in service/quality?

Is Service/Quality Woven into the Fabric of Your Organization?

The president of a rapidly growing high tech company asked Achieve to help fine tune their service delivery. He was quite convincing when he explained that his was a service-driven company. "After all," he said, "we're in the service industry." He felt service was well ingrained throughout his operation. But he agreed to "indulge" us as we studied the organization to see if that was truly the case.

What we found was unfortunately typical of those executives who have fallen into the "of-course-we-believe-in-service/quality" trap. The company featured service in their marketing with convincing, clever ads; they had set up a customer service department, and they provided extensive technical and "customer handling" training. When we checked their operational systems and practices, we found that service was certainly conspicuous in their planning and budgeting, hiring, promoting, compensation, and performance evaluation. But it was conspicuous by its absence. It was nowhere to be found.

One litmus test of senior executives' true service/quality values and beliefs is the user-friendliness of the organization's technology and administrative systems. In far too many cases, systems and technology hinder more than help the delivery of high service/quality. It's often a wonder that performance isn't worse when you consider the defective tools and the interference many employees have to work with. The president of a major aircraft manufacturer puts the problem into perspective: "In a lot of ways, management has handcuffed and shackled our people, then told them to hop out there and build better products or deliver improved service. And then we beat them up when they fail to overcome the restraints we've put on them."

Far too often, the technology and especially the administrative systems are built for management's convenience. If employees think the systems or technology are hindering service/quality improvement, well, then, they obviously have an attitude or motivational problem or they don't know how to use the stuff properly. So let's give them a good stiff dose of training!

Even as you read this, someone in your organization is apologizing to a customer for your systems or technology. "I am sorry. I would like to be able to help you. But:

- it says right here I can't."

- the computer isn't set up to do that."
- I can't get authorization for that at the moment."
- the person who makes that decision isn't around."
- our process doesn't work that way."
- my hands are tied."
- I only enforce the rules, I don't make them."

How many times were lines like these given to your customers today? This week? This month? What impression did those moments of truth leave your customers with? What are they saying behind your back about your organization? What kind of reputation about the hassle/ease/delight of doing business with your organization is building out there? *How do you know?*

"WE KNOW WHAT OUR CUSTOMERS NEED"

"We did not always listen to what the customer had to say before telling him what he wanted."
—John F. McDonnell, chairman and CEO,
McDonnell Douglas

No executive would ever stand up and say "we know what our customers need." Instead, executives confidently mouth variations of "find out what your customers want and give it to them." But behavior often conveys an underlying contempt for customers. The *words* say, "We believe in uncovering our customers' requirements/expectations and meeting or exceeding those." The *actions* say, "I've been in this business for 35 years, I know our customers' requirements/expectations better than they do." Ron Zemke's extensive service consulting experience has put him face to face with the continual evidence of this deadly assumption. He says, "One of the greatest temptations is to believe that, because of years of experience in 'the business' . . . we know what the customer wants and needs even better than the customer does. Time and again, we find this is just not the case. Our logic is not necessarily the customers' logic, nor our perceptions of quality and value the same as theirs."

Despite what you're saying, what are you *doing*? Karl Albrecht's study of service improvement led him to conclude, "Many firms that have been in the service business for years have lost touch with customers' expectations and perceptions and don't even realize it."

One of the consequences of not truly listening to customers' needs is inconsistent levels of service/quality across the organization. Each employee, service/quality team, and manager provides the kind of performance they think their internal or external customer needs (assuming the care and commitment to do so is there — another dangerous assumption). So when customer concerns or problems arise, the response depends upon how seriously that individual or team views the problem, *from their own perspective.* Since the customer's true needs are not understood or appreciated, they are often minimized. But as one manager put it, "It's the customer's, not management's, opinion that counts."

Many executives sagely nod their heads at the need for getting broad amounts of customer input. But many of those same executives fool themselves into believing they are customer-oriented just because they're measuring service/quality levels and "looking at things from the customers' point of view." But the question is, who's measurement yardstick is being used? Jack MacAllister, chairman and CEO of "Baby Bell," US West Inc., says, "Ask anyone who worked in the old Bell system and they'll tell you an index was something posted in every office that purported to tell how well we were serving customers. It measured whether we met installation schedules, answered the phone in a proper amount of time, whether we repaired the phones within a certain time. But we didn't have a fix on what the customer thought was quality service — *these were internal indices.*"

So the challenge is to develop a consistent, across-the-organization understanding of customers' needs through the customers' eyes. That's where the Three Rings of Perceived Value can help. As everyone understands and uses this simple model, it forces the uncovering of customer expectations and provides a common language and viewpoint for delighting customers.

Examine your *actions*. How well do you listen to your internal and external customers?

"OUR EMPLOYEES KNOW WHERE THEIR BREAD IS BUTTERED"

Ask the average executive what's in it for their people and you'll hear a variation of "they get to keep their job." Well, doesn't that turn me on! You mean if I stay late, calmly soothe a customer who's berating me for your inflexible bureaucratic system, go out of my way to help a customer who's confused, or contribute improvement ideas I am rarely thanked for, I get to keep this great job? Wow!

If you're thinking is along those lines, you are living in a managerial fantasyland. It defies logic to expect exceptional Third Ring behavior from people who aren't treated exceptionally. If your employees don't get anything in return when they take those *voluntary* steps to providing outstanding service/quality, then why should they continue to supply that extra touch?

Again, the movement from the traditional management approach of command and control to building commitment becomes vital. You can't force anyone to move into the Third Ring. In *Total Customer Service: The Ultimate Weapon*, William Davidow and Bro Uttal write, "Most companies invest far too little money and effort in hiring, training, and motivating their employees. Companies known for great customer service outspend their competitors to ensure that customer-contact workers do a superior job."

One way to increase employees' commitment to higher service/quality is to involve them in uncovering customers' expectations and planning how to exceed those expectations. Remember, if they help plan the battle, they won't battle the plan. If one of my jobs is answering the phone, imagine my degree of commitment to response times imposed from on high. "Hey, I have a lot of work to do here. I'll get to the phone as soon as I can." But if my service team and I connect with our customers and develop a compelling sense of how answering the phone quickly can help build positive first impressions, then my commitment to the service standards we collectively set will be much stronger. And the peer pressure to meet those standards will be higher than any of my boss's "snoopervision." That's assuming rewards, measurements, and a number of other influencing factors are also in place.

Another, often overlooked factor in building strong commitment to a service/quality improvement effort is the quality of coaching provided for front-line contributors. Far too many managers and supervisors maim and wound their employees, scold them for leaving pools of blood on the floor, then send them out to perform exceptional acts of Third Ring service. It's yet another example of a naive view of human nature. If a manager dresses down an employee, is it any wonder that the employee will pass along that feeling of disrespect? And if management truly acts as if customers were their most valuable asset, what better way to get back at "management" (read "the boss") than by hurting that which they seem to value so highly? Now, most unhappy employees are not dumb enough to take overt action, especially if they want to keep this source of income. Rather, they will find ways to reduce service/quality while appearing to be committed to improvement.

But before you go blaming your supervisors and managers for killing the improvement energy available to be harnessed, take another look in the mirror. They are imitating *your behavior*. Over time, an organization's levels of service/quality mirror the organization's management practices. People will manage customer relationships in the same way they are managed.

"FIX OUR CUSTOMER-CONTACT PEOPLE"

How reasonable would it be to hold a shipping dock worker responsible for the quality of the goods in the boxes she is shipping? Not only would that be unfair, it would be illogical. Any good manager would argue, quite rightly, that the manufacturing process should be traced back to find the ultimate source of the defects.

All right, then, how reasonable is it to hold the final deliverer responsible for the quality of the service he is delivering? True, the analogy doesn't hold up completely because the service deliverer has more control over his actions than the shipper has over product quality. But to a large extent, the person on the front serving line is a symptom carrier, not the source of the problem. While he or she may be contributing to low service delivery, blaming him or her is also not only unfair but unproductive. Besides, who hires, trains, rewards, coaches, and measures that person? Davidow and Uttal report that a Pan Am executive blamed their stewardesses' upbringing when asked why Pan Am's service was lower than Singapore Airlines. They conclude, "By pinning the blame on his workers, of course, he simply revealed his own incompetence."

The quality of external customer relationships is a direct reflection of the quality of internal customer-supplier relationships. Just as a chain is no stronger than its weakest link, an organization's service/quality is usually no stronger than its weakest internal customer-supplier relationship. The service deliverer is but the last link in the chain. Granted, he or she may well be the weak link, but usually he or she is no worse than the many who provide the myriad of production and support services backing up that person. In fact, many front-line servers provide delightful Third Ring service *in spite of*, not because of, the organizational support and systems. Given the many obstacles, it's a minor miracle that service is being provided at all by some exceptionally caring employees!

A glaring action symptomatic of a management group that believes in "fix the customer-contact people" is the delegation of service/quality to a customer service department. This approach is not unlike the outdated practice of leaving quality improvement to a quality control department. As manufacturers have learned, a customer service department, like a quality control department, may serve a useful purpose. But it is *not responsible* for the organization's service/quality levels. In *Service America!*, Albrecht and Zemke pose a critical question: "If you have a customer service department, what's the rest of the organization doing?"

Everyone in the organization must be responsible for service/quality. At *all* levels, in *all* jobs, in *all* parts of the organization. Karl Albrecht puts it into proper perspective: "If you're not serving the customer, your job is to serve somebody who is."

Turn Your Organization Upside Down

A useful concept that will help everyone focus on customers and those serving them is the upside-down organization chart. However, like many useful organizational development ideas, this one has become overused and trivialized by many executives. The question becomes, once again, not whether you believe in this approach, but what are you *doing* about it?

A key principle of viewing the organization this way is that service/quality is produced by the organization and delivered by the front line. *Everyone* beneath the front-line servers needs to understand and, even more importantly, *act* to serve and support those further up the line.

Most managers and executives will agree with this principle — so long as it applies to the rest of the organization. But few truly see this approach affecting their jobs. At least they don't behave as if it did. Managers at all levels need to understand the dual nature of their role in building a high service/quality culture. On the one hand, they must manage and lead the organization from the top down. One the other hand, to be effective service/quality managers they must also *serve those who serve the customers.*

You've heard it said that no one can serve two masters. In a traditional organization with its top-down hierarchy, that means that employees focus on serving the boss as their master. In high-performing service/quality organizations, the upside-down organization chart keeps everyone focused on the only master who counts — the customer who's paying the bills. James E. Burke,

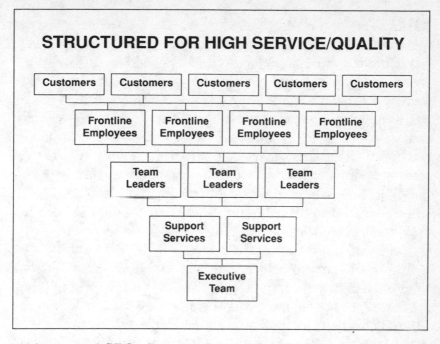

STRUCTURED FOR HIGH SERVICE/QUALITY

chairman and CEO of top-performing Johnson and Johnson, said, "The energy in this business comes from the bottom up. Not the top down. They [the employees] run us [the management], not we them."

Until front-line contributors feel served and supported, they can't serve customers consistently well. In every study of retail service/quality, Nordstrom Department Stores always gets top marks. In *The Service Edge* newsletter, management consultant Ken Blanchard relates a conversation he had with an employee there who thought her boss was "a little weird": "Three or four times a day, he asks if there is anything he can do to help me. He acts like he works for me." Exactly.

Who's serving whom in your organization? If you're not happy with your organization's level of service/quality, get out that mirror again. The performance level that people on the front line deliver is less their fault than yours. Their performance is a reflection of the organization's environment — an environment set and controlled by management.

"TRAIN THE TROOPS"

"Customer service training can be a potent corporate weapon, but without proper workforce training, well-intended service strategies quickly run aground. Unfortunately, many companies confuse customer service improvements with quick tune-ups of front-line employee attitudes. But front-line workers don't create service quality, they deliver it. A key to effective training is a holistic approach spearheaded by management to create a company-wide spirit committed to outservicing the competition." So Bob Grimm, director of training and development at Hecht's retail stores is quoted in *the Service Edge* newsletter. He came to those conclusions after an extensive study of customer service training practices.

The "train the troops" deadly assumption flows naturally from "fix our customer-contact people." Training is critical, but there is a difference between a series of training events and long-term cultural change. The first sews on a few pieces and produces a patchwork quilt of effective, less effective, and ineffective service/quality improvements. The second changes the pattern and color of the organization. As Bob Grimm found, "The big question is not are we doing enough customer service training? It's are we doing the right kind of training with the right people?"

Because service/quality improvement has become such a critical issue, many trainers have dusted off their old customer relations programs, stuck in some "moments of truth" stuff and a few Tom Peters or Ron Zemke quotes, and called it their "new" program. Employee training is vital to service/quality improvement, but it is only one piece of the puzzle. Training contact people how to provide better service is, in fact, the easy part. The really tough part is reorienting the organization to produce and support outstanding service/quality *consistently*.

Danger: Half-Baked Training Ahead

Let's look at the most common kinds of incomplete or ineffective service/quality training:

- **Cross-selling**: This training teaches front-line employees how to move customers into other products or services. When done effectively, it can provide excellent value-added service. However, it is sales training, not necessarily service/quality improvement. Cross-selling does not generally lead to long-term perceptions of increased value.

- **Smile Training**: These are the Courtesy 101 courses. Front-line servers are taught how to handle phone calls politely, to say please and thank you, and to mind their P's and Q's. There's no question these important service delivery skills are sadly lacking in all too many organizations. Rude, gruff, or indifferent treatment can quickly make those moments of truth negative experiences.

  But the painted-on smiles will be quickly wiped off trainees' faces by poor organizational support, lack of teamwork, or an abrasive supervisor. This kind of training can also send the wrong signals to participants about how bright management thinks it is. Many smile training packages or one-day-wonder seminars are insulting to employees with their simple-minded approach and "you're the problem" messages.

- **Inspiration Training**: This approach is often used when managers think that poor service/quality stems from a lack of employee motivation. "If we could just get them turned on to the need for improvement, we'd be all set." Toward that end, audio tapes, videos, motivational speakers, workshops, and seminars are used.

  There's no question that the more excited and energized employees are about improvement, the higher service/quality levels will go. But the real question is, why aren't they motivated? The answer is to be found in the day-to-day environment, not in short-term bursts of hype. While inspirational sessions can help kick off or revive a service/quality improvement drive, this approach has little lasting power on its own. All the best intentions and resolutions to

OK, OK, so we all feel unsupported, now, get out there and satisfy those customers!!!

©THE ACHIEVE GROUP INC. 1988

do better will have little lasting effect if skills, strategies, and systems are weak.

- **Customer Complaint Training**: Again, these are valuable skills that can help provide better Third Ring service. But if this and smile training are the bulk of your organization's service improvement program, it is seriously deficient. Why wait until customers complain? How about anticipating and exceeding their expectations? And what about that enormous body of unhappy customers who never bother to complain?

  Another problem with this training is the mind-set it too often conveys. That is, it teaches employees how to deal with "problem customers." It may seem to be just a silly word game, but there is a major difference between "problem customers" and "customers with problems." And that body of "problem customers" has a mysterious way of growing ever larger. You can tell when employees feel that unreasonable "problem customers" with their unrealistic expectations have become a raging epidemic. It's when those posters begin appearing that show a big gun and say, "Make my day. Tell me it's a rush." Or the one with the little guys rolling around in laughter saying, "You want it when?"

"IT'S ALL A MARKETING GAME"

We've all been sucked in by it: convincing advertising or sales come-ons promising high levels of service/quality, which are dashed by the reality of mediocre or rotten service/quality. Companies spending big bucks enticing customers with promises of high service/quality clearly have their priorities mixed up. If they spent a fraction of their advertising dollars on a well-planned cultural change effort, they would be miles ahead. But that takes much longer and demands dramatic changes in executive behavior. It's far easier to approve a marketing budget and keep running the business as before.

Who Are You Trying to Kid?

A great many organizations have also fallen into internal marketing traps. They've developed slick internal campaigns with snappy slogans on buttons, posters, hats, T-shirts, coffee mugs, and so on. These have often been combined with convincing executive speeches, videos, kick-off rallies, newsletters, and the like, all aimed at urging, prodding, or inspiring front-line performers to improve.

There is nothing wrong with solid internal marketing. In fact, the best service/quality providers are masters at it. There's a big problem, however, when marketing is too far ahead of real change in the culture or it constitutes the majority of the improvement effort. Richard Davis, senior vice-president for Security Pacific National Bank: "Don't play games with service quality. Don't create a program out of it, because that in itself is implicitly short-term. Create a focus, but don't even talk about it until you're ready to do something. The worst thing that can happen is to let it fall on deaf ears or to announce you're going to have a focus on the customer. 'The Year of the Customer!' That's ludicrous! What's next year going to be?"

The problem is, you've boldly declared "the dawn of a new age" before. The "flavor of the month" syndrome is probably well entrenched as a sacred management rite. "So what's the flavor this month? Service/quality, you say? Well, just sit it out and they'll be on to productivity, cost cutting, innovation, or God knows what soon." Lynn Shostack, chairman and president of Joyce International, says, "I don't think anyone is resistant to the *idea* that service/quality is important. But many are legitimately cynical about all the talk, 'touchy-feely' programs, and motivational claptrap they've been forced to participate in that has had no demonstrable results."

To what extent are you falling into the it's-all-a-marketing-game trap? Would your customers or employees say that your service/quality program is no more than smoke and mirrors? Would the words of Notre Dame coach Lou Holtz apply to your management team's efforts: "When all is said and done, a lot more is said than done"?

"WE CAN'T AFFORD THE EXTRA COSTS OF SERVICE/QUALITY IMPROVEMENT"

"[It is the function of the executive] to reflect sadly that one could have done it right in twenty minutes, and now one has to spend two days to find out why it has taken three weeks for someone else to do it wrong."
— R. Alec Mackenzie, *The Time Trap*

No executive would ever stand up and say "we can't afford to improve service/quality." In fact, most boldly talk of investing for the long term, of how service/quality doesn't cost — it pays, blah, blah, blah. But, once again, *actions* tell of a different set of beliefs. Maybe you have even put a little of your money where your mouth is, but what about time? Service/quality improvement takes a little money and *a lot of time* — yours, your managers', employees', and that of staff support resources assigned to act as trail guides on the journey. When it comes to putting in the time, do you suddenly realize what bad timing it is to go for that all-out effort right now? Maybe after the reorganization, or vacation periods, or year-end, or the new products are launched, or the next election, or you get profits up, or . . . . In the meantime, you think, let's get some people trained, the internal slogan ringing through the organization, or service/quality into our marketing.

The hoard of executives who are stuck on this treadmill just don't believe that service/quality improvement is worth the price — despite what they say. We encounter this reality when it comes time to move from concepts, ideas, and plans into allocating resources and getting on with the job. The talkers are separated from the doers pretty fast.

What Does It Cost You Not to Improve?

What percentage of your revenues are wasted as a result of less than perfect service/quality? Five, 10, 15, maybe 20 percent? In a Gallup poll commissioned by the American Society for Quality Control (ASQC), more than 70 percent of executives responding felt that their cost of poor quality was less than 10 percent. Twenty-seven percent admitted that they had no idea what those costs were.

With such misguided notions circulating, it's no wonder that service/quality is so bad in so many organizations. From the viewpoint of a company that has a good handle on its costs of low service/quality, David Kearns, chairman of Xerox Corporation, comments, "The [ASQC] survey shows that many people still do not understand the connection between cost and quality. You will not change the culture with that kind of data or those kind of perceptions."

What's misguided about an estimate of low service/quality costing organizations 10 percent of their revenues? It's far too low! The American Society for Quality Control has been studying these costs for years. They consistently find that the cost of quality (COQ) for North American organizations can run as high as *40 percent* of revenues. Those costs include the cost of prevention (training and planning), appraisal (inspection and checking), external failure (lost business, complaint handling, liability claims), and internal failure (correcting errors or redoing work). "By far the largest portion of those quality costs dollars is failure costs."

The "failure costs" come from not doing things right the first time. These are sometimes referred to as the price of non-conformance. And it can be mind-boggling to add up the direct costs and strangled productivity associated with this widespread epidemic. Not to mention the intangible wear and tear this enormous problem causes you, your management team, your employees, and, of course, your customers. The Strategic Planning Institute's extensive research on the pay-offs of service/quality improvement sheds further light: "Many companies still . . . underinvest in quality improvement because they have not learned to calibrate its strategic or financial payoff. . . . Our analysis indicates that a customer-oriented, quality-differenti-ated strategy can often lead not only to customer preference and loyalty but also to increased market share and lower costs."

Leading organizations are discovering the very profitable relationships between quality, productivity, and costs:

"Quality management is the route to being the low-cost producer and achieving a competitive advantage. We believe improving quality is the key to improving performance."
—Kay Whitmore, president, Eastman Kodak

"Every time we examined a quality issue we found a way to reduce costs. A lot of people think quality costs money. The exact opposite is true; poor quality costs a lot."
—G. Christian Lantzch, vice-chairman and treasurer, Mellon Bank Corporation

"We learned that a focus on quality is actually one of the best ways to control costs."
—John Young, CEO, Hewlett-Packard

"Quality improvement leads directly to bottomline improvement."

—Donald R. Frahm, president and CEO,
Hartford Insurance Group

Do These Costs Look Familiar?

There are essentially three costs of low service/quality. Because they've been with us for years, we tend to accept them as "the costs of doing business," but unless you act *now* to drive these costs down, your organization may not be doing business in a few more years. The three costs are (1) the price of not doing things right the first time, (2) lost revenues or "goodwill currency," and (3) intangible performance reducers.

1. The Price of Not Doing Things Right the First Time

Stanley J. Calderon, president and CEO of Bank One in Lafayette, Indiana, says: "We believe nearly one-third of a financial institution's non-interest expenses are attributable to the absence of quality or the correction of errors and/or exceptions. By paying more attention to doing things right the first time and thereby making even modest improvements in error rates, significant cost reductions will result." American Express is a financial institution that has been taking great strides in reducing the costs of poor quality. Over a ten-year period, they have saved more than $70 million by reducing cardmember application-processing time. Raymond Larkin, executive vice-president of operations, explains that hidden costs mount up in their business "if remittances are not processed, if billings are incorrect, if establishments are not paid on time, if cardmember benefits are not properly communicated. All this generates inquiries and additional processing — or what we call 'avoidable input.' Reducing avoidable input is the service equivalent to reducing rejects in manufacturing. . . . I can't emphasize enough that quality is as bottomline as a company can get."

The Technical Assistance Research Program (TARP) worked with a number of American gas utilities to determine the actual dollar costs of low service/quality. In 1981 dollars, TARP found it cost utilities from $20 to $300 *each time* a customer complained to an officer, asked for an investigation of a high bill, requested a meter check or a reread of meter, or delayed payment because of a complaint. TARP concluded, "Poor service results in substantial extra explicit costs. . . . These result in extra head count. . . . Many service calls are preventable." They found that one utility handled 2,000 calls a month from customers trying to read their confusing bill format. These calls alone cost $72,000 per year. In another gas company, 50 percent of all supervisors' time was spent talking to customers whom the representative couldn't satisfy.

A good indicator of service/quality problems is accounts receivable. In analyzing their issuance of customer credits, 3M found that only 15 percent of the time was credit given because of defective products. The balance of problems were pricing errors, billing errors, shipping errors, and order entry errors. Hewlett-Packard saved $150 million by improving the quality of their accounts receivable processes. They traced most slow or delinquent accounts back to problems with processing, shipping, or credit information. Ford Motor Company cut the number of problem bills from 34 percent to 1 percent while reducing average invoice-processing time from fifteen days to six.

Take a hard look at your organization. How many of the following costs are you nonchalantly accepting as a "cost of doing business"? How much are these all-too-common problems costing you?

- High accounts receivables
- Resolving customer complaints and problems
- Callbacks to correct problems from faulty installations
- Warranty claims
- Backorders
- High inventory because of long delivery lead times
- Additional systems and controls to solve service/quality problems

- Extra staff, overtime, or management costs to deal with the above and repair customer relationships
- Credits or giveaways to dissatisfied customers

These are just some of the costs of not doing things right the first time. Identifying and reducing these hidden costs can significantly boost your organization's financial health. The B.C. Telephone Company found that around 25 percent of their budget was consumed by the price of non-conformance (PONC). Their executive responsible for service/quality improvement, Merv Stanley, said, "We found whole groups who were diligently devoted to fixing up PONC problems. Now that we've identified our cost of not doing things right the first time, all our executives are feeling the pressure to bring it down." That same pressure is being brought to bear on itself by computer giant IBM. Says president John Akers, "We believe quality improvement will reduce quality costs 50 percent over the coming years. For us, that translates into billions of dollars of added potential profit and quality leadership in our industry."

2. Lost Revenues or "Goodwill"

In Chapter One we explored in detail the horrendous costs of dissatisfied customers. In Chapter Two we looked at the costs of unhappy customers to those public-sector institutions or governments with "captive" customers. You may want to review those sections in light of this discussion on the affordability of service/quality improvement. What hidden price are you now paying for poor service/quality in the eyes of your customers? How many of your advertising, marketing, sales, or public relations dollars are wasted? (Remember, it takes five times more money to get a new customer than to keep an existing one.)

3. Intangible Performance Reducers

How do you measure the impact of low morale, absenteeism, or turnover? How much do conflict, poor communications, low innovation, or overbearing bureaucracy cost your organization? These are just some of the costs of low service/quality. But since they're hidden or difficult to measure, they're often overlooked. Worse yet, these soaring costs are accepted by many organizations as normal.

Unfortunately, they are all too normal — to the average organization. But you don't want to be average. You want to be exceptional. A high performer. Then these costs are completely unacceptable.

Let's take turnover as an example. It carries enormous hidden costs: hiring, retraining, mentoring, extra burdens on management and team members (covering vacant positions, working with a rookie who's learning the ropes), lost experience, lowered morale, as well as providing a model of how to deal with the organization's overwhelming problems. And in the coming years, the pool of professional and skilled people will continue to shrink. That will make it ever harder to find and keep top performers.

WHAT ARE YOUR DEADLY ASSUMPTIONS?

Which of the seven assumptions do your actions show that you believe? Do you proclaim the virtues of service/quality without using it to drive your operations? How well and how often do you ask your customers to define service/quality for you? Are you actively looking for creative ways to nurture the employee volunteerism that is the *only* way Third Ring service can possibly be delivered? Do you act as if service/quality problems were the fault of your customer-contact people? Is your service/quality improvement program essentially a training effort? Are you overpromising service/quality to your customers?

And do you behave as if improving service/quality were too costly, especially in time and human resources? Are you trying to implement champagne plans on a beer budget? What is it costing you to live with your current service/quality levels? Can you afford not to improve?

These are all tough questions. George Bernard Shaw said, "No question is so difficult to answer as that to which the answer is obvious."

CHAPTER FIVE

At the Service/Quality
Crossroads

"Two roads diverged in a wood, and I —
I took the one less traveled by,
And that has made all the difference."
— Robert Frost, "The Road Not Taken"

If you have decided that you want to take your organization to higher levels of service/quality, you are now standing at a critical crossroad. You must decide which road will take you to that higher ground. You have two choices: training, and cultural change. Be careful as you look down the two roads. First appearances are deceiving.

The service/quality training road looks smooth and inviting. It's broad and well maintained. There's plenty of company, and the road appears to be going uphill in the direction you're heading. But around the first bend, conditions start to change. The road starts to get bumpier. As you continue, it gradually becomes apparent that this road will not take you where you want to go. The road winds its way downhill. Pavement gives way to a dirt track. This starts to get soft and muddy. Before you know it, the road has emptied into a bog. With a sinking feeling, you watch a few organizations struggling up the cultural change road far above. You realize that your organization is now firmly stuck and will have a difficult time getting back on track.

On the other hand, the cultural change road is not nearly as appealing at first glance. The grade is steeper; it will clearly require more effort. For the first while, this road runs parallel to the training route. In a number of places, they almost merge. You notice that some organizations appear confused and begin following the training route without even realizing it. But as the journey continues, the terrain gets tougher. Many traveling companions fall behind, drop out, or cut across to the training route. As you stay on this course, it gets very bumpy and narrow. In places it's all you can do to stay on the ledge high above the canyon floor. You notice you're almost alone. And the journey seems to be endless. But when you stop to look around, you find yourself in the company of high performers. You've never felt so strong. And then you begin to enjoy the fruits of your efforts . . .

WHICH ROAD WILL YOU CHOOSE?

Training, if it's well done, will give you some pay-offs. Chances are, if you're careful, you won't get stuck in the bog. But training will not give you the substantial revenue growth and cost reductions that top performers enjoy. At best, you'll see a few improvements here and there.

Top service/quality providers are distinguished by a markedly different set of values and actions than those of most other organizations. *Fortune*'s study of top performers pinpointed some of those differences: "They make outlandish efforts to hire only the right people, to train and motivate them, and to give them the authority necessary to serve customers well. They invest earlier and much more heavily than their competitors in technology to support customer service. They keep an especially sharp eye on the competition. And they constantly ask customers to rate the quality of service they have received." Though cultural change involves a heavy amount of training, it goes much, much further than that.

BUT ARE YOU READY TO PAY THE PRICE?

"It is a rough road that leads to the heights of greatness."

—Seneca, Roman statesman and philosopher

Quality is not free. Venture capitalist Arthur Rock said, "You can walk up to people on the street and ask them if they want to be rich, and 99 percent will tell you, 'Sure I want to be rich.' But are they willing to do what's necessary to be successful? Not many are." The same is true of executives who want to improve service/quality. Many declare this to be their strategy, but few are willing to pay the price to make the long and difficult journey toward higher service/quality. A huge majority of organizations are interested in improving their service/quality. A number have even put those good intentions into mission statements, strategic plans, and advertising. But only a tiny minority of organizations are truly committed to taking the necessary steps toward improving service/quality. And an almost minuscule number of organizations are prepared to stay on the course for the time needed to make permanent changes in their culture.

Cultural change happens only when service/quality improvement becomes *the* strategic issue for the organization:

> *"Quality is a long-term commitment. It means rethinking the way you do business; it may also mean restructuring your operations."*
> —The American Society for Quality Control

> *"You can change your advertising as easily as you change your underwear. You can update your look, your logo type, and your literature with equal dispatch. But changing your core corporate culture takes time, strategic and tactical thought, and considerable energy."*
> —Ron Zemke, *The Service Edge* newsletter

> *"In the service age, service is not just something managers should think about now and then. It **is** management."*
> —Karl Albrecht, author of *Service America!*

> *"Changing corporate culture is a necessary, essential, quintessential part of improving quality in our corporations."*
> —Michael Beer, professor, Harvard Business School

"One area in which a consensus seems to be forming among business leaders is a need for a change in the fundamental culture of the organization to enable quality improvement to take place."
— Gallup survey commissioned by
the American Society for Quality Control

"The biggest problem that most any company in the Western world faces today is not its competitors, nor the Japanese. The biggest problems are self-inflicted, created right at home by management that are off-course in the competitive world of today. Systems of management are in place in the Western world that for survival must be blasted; new construction commenced. Patchwork will not suffice."
— W. Edwards Deming

"This approach [becoming market-driven] demands a revolution in how businesspeople act — and even more important, in how they think."
— Regis McKenna, author of *The Regis Touch*

"Improving service is about as difficult a job as a company can undertake, because it means reforming attitudes and practices in nearly every department."
— "Companies That Serve You Best,"
Fortune, December 7, 1987

"Service quality improvement does not happen by accident. It requires and demands professional management and measurement systems. It requires that business decisions be continuously assessed in terms of their impact on quality. It requires a special and deeply ingrained commitment, sustainable over the years."
— "The Strategic Management of Service Quality,"
produced by the Strategic Planning Institute

MAPPING OUT THE TERRAIN

If cultural change truly is the road you want to follow, it is important that you have a clear idea of how this route differs from the training one:

Significant Components	The Training Road	Cultural Change
Process delivery	Training is driven by internal/external experts	Cultural change is driven by line managers
Building employee commitment	Using inspirational messages	An environment of "volunteerism" is encouraged
Technology and systems	Making better use of what exists	What exists is redesigned
Managing people	Training "fixes" front-line employees and supervisors	All hiring, orienting, promoting, performance management, and rewards are realigned
Senior management involvement	Management gives its "blessings" and makes guest appearances	All activities are focused on service/quality improvement
Roles and responsibilities	Improvement responsibilities are given to a few selected people	Cultural change determines all strategies, structures, skills, and accountabilities
Customer expectations	Management tells employees what customers expect	Employees uncover their customers' expectations and work to exceed them

DOES YOUR CULTURE EMPOWER OR ENRAGE YOUR EMPLOYEES?

During a session with Canada Safeway executives, discussion turned to indicators of a grocery store's performance. In a business with paper-thin margins, knowing the key variables to profitability is vital. One veteran executive said, "I can tell within a few minutes of entering a competitor's store what the profit margin of that store is just by looking at a few key indicators."

When looking at levels of Third Ring service delivery, one key indicator never fails to reflect the level of "wow factor" customers experience from an organization. We can run customer audits and surveys, but getting a handle on this indicator unfailingly shows what the customers' responses will be.

What's the key indicator? It's how abused or enthusiastic front-line performers feel in their jobs. The title of an article on customer service in the *Wall Street Journal* said it all: "Poorly Served Employees Serve Customers Just as Poorly." It explains the phenomenon this way: "Service providers treat customers similar to the way they as employees are treated by management. In many organizations, management treats employees as unvalued and unintelligent. The employees in turn convey the identical message to the customer." Tom Peters agrees wholeheartedly: "I can think of no company that has found a way to look after external customers while abusing internal customers [remember the upside-down organization chart]. The process of meeting customer needs begins internally."

It's really just common sense. Beat up your people and they'll beat up your customers. Research is now providing documented evidence of this phenomenon. Zemke and Schaaf report in *The Service Edge* that management professor Benjamin Schneider from the University of Maryland compared the levels of satisfaction employees felt in the levels of service they received from the organization with levels of customer satisfaction. He found that when employees feel well treated, when they have the right tools available to do the job, and when they have management's strong support for delivering high service, customers see higher levels of service being delivered. Professor David Bowen of the University of Southern California found the same thing in his study of 51 branch banks. He concluded that (1) there was a strong correlation between customers' and employees' views of service/quality and the internal service climate, (2) favorable views by employees of human-resource policies are reflected in favorable views by customers of service/quality, and (3) a positive work climate directly improved service/quality levels.

Executives of organizations working hard to improve their level of service/quality have come to the same conclusions regarding the cause-and-effect relationship of internal and external service/quality. Herbert Kelleher, chairman of Southwest Airlines, says, "The way you treat people inside manifests itself in the way you treat people outside. And if you treat them lousy inside, they're going to respond the same way in handling passengers."

The next stage is empowerment. That means giving employees the ability, tools, and latitude to exercise power and control in making those critical moment of truth decisions. Since they control the Third Ring, help them to do so effectively. A few years ago when Jessie McClure was trapped in an old well, a Federal Express employee authorized the airlift of special equipment in the middle of the night to help free her. When senior executive James Barkdale was asked how an *employee* could approve such a major operation, his answer spoke volumes about the unique culture that has carried FedEx to the top of the service/quality heap in a fiercely competitive industry: "My job is to see to it that we hire, train, and pay people to make that kind of decision right there on the front line. If that person calls me at home in the middle of the night to okay doing something important, I've failed as a manager." Roland Dumas has thoroughly researched service/quality improvement throughout North America and Japan. He succinctly sums up much of his experience this way: "Service/Quality is a leadership issue. How management thinks, behaves, and structures systems is *the* pivotal issue."

BUILDING A HIGH SERVICE/QUALITY CULTURE

How do you build an environment that consistently encourages, nurtures, supports, and rewards strong service/quality across all

101

Three Rings of Perceived Value? The answer is really quite obvious: focus the entire organization on its customers, find out what customers' expectations are, and get all employees and management to work together continually to delight customers by exceeding those expectations.

But getting everyone in an organization to serve their customers better while improving the quality of internal production and delivery processes is no small task. It requires strengthening a number of skills, strategies, processes, systems, procedures, techniques, and approaches. Where to start and what to do can get very confusing.

The Service/Quality System provides both a framework to identify the areas that have the greatest impact on improvement, and a process for an orderly, long-term implementation. For organizations just beginning the service/quality journey, the system can be used in its entirety with modifications to meet special needs. For those further along, the Service/Quality System provides a map that allows for choices on which road to take.

At the heart of the system is the twelve-cylinder framework. (This approach was first brought to Achieve by Rob Ell, who used it in his consulting work. We took his novel concept and modified it to incorporate our ten years' experience with hundreds of North American organizations, and with 3M's Quality Management Services, Tom Peters and the Toward Excellence process, and Zenger-Miller's award-winning leadership-skill development systems.)

The cylinders isolate the twelve areas in which long-term cultural change must be made before service/quality levels can improve. Rob Ell used the analogy of a twelve-cylinder engine to illustrate the need for organizations to try to "fire on all cylinders." The beginning point is to determine the "compression ratings," or scores for each area. Then the real work starts: improving selected cylinders. Of course, to make the most effective use of the twelve-cylinder framework, a broad base of input and planning from customers, employees, as well as managers is essential.

Ahead of implementing any of the twelve cylinder improve-

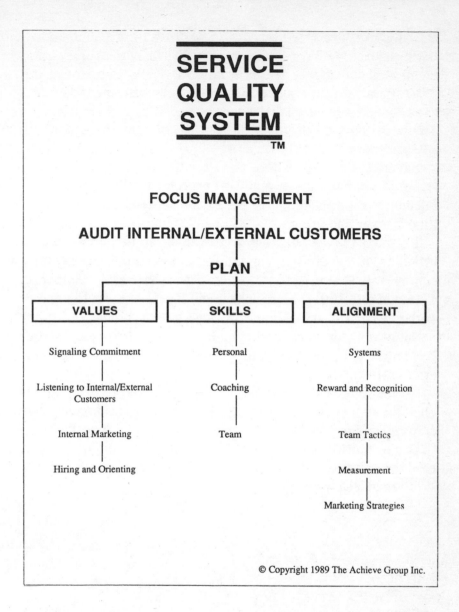

SERVICE
QUALITY
SYSTEM
™

FOCUS MANAGEMENT
|
AUDIT INTERNAL/EXTERNAL CUSTOMERS
|
PLAN

VALUES	SKILLS	ALIGNMENT
Signaling Commitment	Personal	Systems
Listening to Internal/External Customers	Coaching	Reward and Recognition
Internal Marketing	Team	Team Tactics
Hiring and Orienting		Measurement
		Marketing Strategies

ments are three critical steps. (These will be discussed in detail in Chapter 19.) The first, absolutely vital step is focusing management. It starts by bringing together the senior management team to define what service/quality means within the organization's reason for being, to clarify core values, to determine strategic issues, and to develop an energizing vision of the preferred future. The second step, audits, provides vital input at this point. These audits are generally surveys of customers and employees to find where the organization now stands. Getting "real" data on how employees and especially customers perceive the levels of service/quality being provided by the organization can sometimes be useful in shocking management out of its complacency.

Having determined where the executive team wants to take the organization, you're ready to proceed to the final step — implementation planning. It's here that the structure, resources, time frames, and firing order of cylinder improvements are set.

The next twelve chapters will examine in detail the twelve cylinders. If you are determined to build a high service/quality culture, rate your organization's compression in each cylinder on a scale of 0 to 100. (The Pitfalls and Traps section at the end of each chapter can act as your checklist.) Zero means you've got nothing going for you in that cylinder, and 100 is a perfect score. Better yet, get your management team, employees, and customers to rate you.

As you look at the amount of effort required to bring about enough improvements in enough cylinders to change your culture, you may find yourself asking, is this what it really takes to be a top performer? You bet! All that and then some. The high road to improved service/quality is not an easy one. That's why it is the road less traveled.

CHAPTER SIX
Cylinder One: Signaling Commitment

"Examples lead us, and we will likely see
Such as the prince is, will his people be."
> —Robert Herrick, English poet

Service/quality improvement starts at the top. And the length and intensity of the effort is a direct reflection of senior management's resolve to improve. Senior engineer and project manager in quality assurance for IBM, H. James Harrington, hits the nail bang on the head with these words in his book *The Improvement Process*: "A corporation takes on the personality of its top management. . . . The process starts with top management, will progress at a rate reflecting management's demonstrated commitment, and will stop soon after managers lose interest in the process." Adds Ray Boedecker, IBM's director of quality: "When the CEO says 'Let's go. Let's learn. Let's do it' — that's when quality begins. It's the single most compelling, motivating factor."

As service/quality improvement experts and executives of organizations striving to improve reflect on the steps involved, a key word keeps coming up:

*"A **commitment** to service excellence must be*
unequivocal. It radiates from senior managers, who
must eat, breathe and sleep customer service as the
nucleus of their corporate culture."
> —Karl Albrecht, *At America's Service*

"We must engage all our people to take ownership of, and pride in, the entire chain of events that delivers effective products or services to a customer. That requires management **commitment,** *starting at the top."*

—James E. Olsen, president, AT&T

"Commitment *to quality as a way of business life must come from the top. If senior management thinks they can delegate this problem as they have tried to do so many times in the past, they are mistaken."*

—E. Frank Mead, president, Tech Medical

"If there is **commitment** *at the top, the people at the bottom quickly become committed themselves. They're saying, 'Where have you guys been all my life? We know how to do the job. Give us the tools and let us get on with it.' "*

—James R. Houghton,
chairman and CEO, Corning Glass Works

There are two steps to developing a high-compression rating in the Commitment cylinder. The first critical one is getting the management team to agree wholeheartedly that service/quality improvement is *the* strategic issue for the organization. They must also be prepared to devote substantial resources and personal time for at least *three years* of intensive effort to launch the process. But that's not the focus of this cylinder.

In the Service/Quality System, the very first step, focusing management, is where commitment is developed and tested. If it is weak, there's no point in advancing any further. More than once we've stepped out of, or scaled down, a service/quality improvement plan because the senior group was clearly preparing to talk a lot and act a little.

Once it is clear that senior management is prepared to stay the course for the long, tough journey, the next step is to build this commitment within the rest of the organization. This cylinder deals with the visible *actions* senior management takes to signal their strong commitment to service/quality improvement.

HOW STRONG ARE YOUR SIGNALING SKILLS?

Art McNeil coined the term "signaling skills" and wrote extensively about these vital executive actions in his book *The "I" of the Hurricane*: "Every action you take sends a signal about your beliefs, whatever they happen to be. . . . Few executives realize the power that their personal day-to-day behaviors [signals] have on others. . . . Signals from senior officers move quickly. The signals you send today will probably spread through your organization before you get back to the office and empty your mail basket. . . . The essential ingredient to success is to be so visibly committed to the organization's vision and values that you send clear, consistent signals instinctively, regardless of the velocity of day-to-day turbulence." Dave Clark, chairman and CEO of the Canadian division of the revitalized Campbell Soup company, says: "We have a statement that we developed to remind ourselves, particularly in senior management, about [signaling skills]. It is, 'You are what you do, not what you say you are.' Our people know enough to ignore our words and instead observe our behavior."

If you are telling your people to prepare for the long and dusty journey toward higher service/quality, you and your management team must be *visibly* in front of the procession, actively leading the way. If there is some doubt about whether you're in it for the long term, people will start dropping out when you hit those first ruts in the road.

Are You Giving the Message You Want Them to Get?

Assuming that you are serious about, and highly committed to, driving up levels of service/quality, how do you communicate that to the multitudes who will make or break the effort? Consultant Ron Goodman and Rider College (New Jersey) Business School dean Richard Ruch spent years studying organizational communications. They concluded that "much of the responsibility for the low quality of corporate communications today and the widening gap in the corporate suites lies on the mahogany desk of CEOs. . . . Yet it is impossible to pick up a business journal or a serious publication commenting on corporate life without finding an article quoting some CEO on the importance of good communication." Your people are getting your message, all right. They are *seeing* it loud and clear.

Effective CEOs Are Chief Evangelical Officers

Executives in highly effective service/quality organizations spend much more time "managing by wandering around" with employees and customers than traditional technomanagers do. This marked difference inspired Donald Clifford and Richard Cavanagh to identify the CEOs in the high-growth companies they studied as the "Chief Evangelical Officers." That label is both accurate and misleading. It's accurate in that it captures the emotional, even spiritual, dimension that a powerful vision and set of core values taps to release energy for organizational renewal. Corning chairman James R. Houghton has it right when he says, "The real job in front of you is convincing people about your cause, not your tools." However, it can be misleading in that it implies a kind of fire-and-brimstone charisma that galvanizes people into action. While some executives do epitomize that approach, many highly effective ones are very low key and soft-spoken.

But the typical technomanager deals in a world of paper, not people. In one of his scathing *Fortune* columns on this widespread problem, Walter Kiechl III asks a good question: "If the top dogs are going to be paid so much, why can't the rest of the kennel reasonably expect a little more of them by way of guts? Guts enough, for starters, to go out and talk to their people face to face, if that's what it takes to make the company work." Thomas Melohn is no gutless technomanager. He and his company, North American Tool and Die, have been featured in videos and articles as an example of a renewed, now dynamic, quality provider. How does he do it? It's starting to sound familiar: "First, you have to live it — 24 hours a day. Second, you have to practice it — every day, every night. You can't ever deviate, or the whole thing crumbles. Third, you must preach it, over and over. Notice I emphasize action first — live it, practice it — and preaching second. Make your actions count and reinforce them by preaching quality again and again."

STRONG COMMITMENT IN ACTION

There are hundreds of ways you can signal your unshakable commitment to service/quality. Here are just a few:

- Hold regular meetings with employees in groups and individually to discuss your progress toward higher service/quality. Provide plenty of "cheerleading" for achievements.
- Make sure service/quality issues have the most prominent place in your meeting agendas and are never bumped for more "pressing" matters.
- Bring customers, customer advocates (salespeople are excellent ones), and front-line service deliverers to key planning and operational sessions.
- Be sure that you and your management team spend the bulk of your time out of your comfortable offices. Keep your paper-management and people-leadership activities in the right proportion. And be sure to spend that time with customers or those people who are actually producing or delivering your products or services.
- Put on an apron, or pick up the phone, and serve customers without being introduced as the brass. You'll be sending important signals. And you might even learn something.
- Get in the habit of reading, circulating, and responding to feedback solicited from customers. You'll be amazed at how quickly your people will show a new concern for what your customers are saying. This paperwork will do more for your organization's long-term health than "bean counting." Haven't you hired good people to do that for you?
- Take a hard look at how innovators are treated. Are they

quietly knee-capped, or are they hailed as heroes? Don't let your bureaucrats grind them down. How many little wastebaskets are there between you and the front-line performers who are full of outstanding service/quality improvement ideas? Give them a process to take what action they can on their own or to get the support they need from the organization. *Move your "status quo managers" out of positions of power. They are getting in the way.*

- Serve your producers and servers. Continually ask them what management can do to help them provide higher levels of service/quality. Hold your managers accountable for serving the organization.

- Set and live by this ironclad rule. *All promises to customers are kept.* Period. Overtime and other expenses are secondary once your organization has given its word. This rule also puts pressure on everyone to be careful about the promises he or she makes.

- Celebrate, honor, cheer, applaud, laud, praise, extol, and otherwise reinforce all service/quality achievements. Do this often and consistently enough and your people will start to think you just might consider "this service/quality stuff" important.

SIGNALING COMMITMENT

Following are only a few examples of how some executives and managers signal their strong commitment to service/quality. Some of the organizations and managers mentioned here have been top performers for years and are working hard to stay there. Others are striving to improve.

- Members of the senior management team in the Training Directorate of Transport Canada identified their core values as quality, service, and respect for the individual. They also decided that their Reason For Being was best captured in the statement "In Training for Your Safety." This vision and these values were used to guide a very successful effort to deal with a severe budget cut. In addition to absorbing the budget cut, the organization significantly improved service while enhancing organizational cohesion. The directorate has emerged stronger and healthier. Millions of dollars in savings have been identified.

- At Ben's Deli Restaurant, a thriving Montreal delicatessen, 85-year-old Ben still sits at the door greeting customers as they come in. He stops at each table to ensure that customers are delighted and thanks them as they leave.

- At Northern Telecom, Bill Delroy is an executive who, throughout his long career, has become a champion for quality improvement. Early in the improvement effort, he looks for opportunities to shut the line down when quality slips. Knowing the costs of that move, everyone in the plant quickly gets the message that defective products are unacceptable.

- Since 1984, B.C. Tel has taken a number of steps to transform its culture. The strong vision and commitment of senior executives continues to be signaled in dozens of ways. Here are a few:

  Early in the process, executives met quarterly to review progress on the multitude of "mundane action plans" they or their managers had initiated. These sessions were video-taped, and the highlights were used to kick off similar meetings that ultimately included all 2,500 managers and supervisors. This approach not only signaled the degree of commitment but it also put pressure on the executives and managers to keep the momentum going and excitement high.

  Vice-presidents and area general managers now travel throughout their entire region (it's a big, far-flung province) meeting with supervisory and front-line performers to discuss direction and celebrate contributions. These "Infonet" sessions have become an important forum for discussions. In one year, one executive talked to more than 4,000 people in his region in groups of 50 or fewer.

  When a new training program was introduced, most executives elected to attend the sessions rather than just give the same message by videotape. For some executives, that meant showing up in front of more than a hundred groups each year.

At least one group of front-line performers is invited in to every executive review session to report on the success of its improvement efforts.

- Toronto-based Four Seasons Hotels has occupancy and repeat rates that constantly beat the industry. Chairman Issy Sharp says that, since he started the business in 1960, "A single purpose dictates our priorities — to operate the finest hotels in every city in which we're located." To keep his executives in touch with the real world, each of his seven regional vice-presidents who oversee three hotels must also serve as general manager for one of them.

- A fine-paper manufacturer, a large hospital, a producer of medical devices, and a federal government department demonstrated their clear commitment to service/quality by making the budgets for these efforts "sacred and off-limits" during painful budget cuts.

- David Andrews, president of Alberta Blue Cross, signalled his commitment to management and employee teamwork by personally meeting employees through becoming "office mail boy" and pushing the mail cart through every department.

- The senior executives of Mac's Convenience Stores and the Canadian Imperial Bank of Commerce (CIBC) Information Services Division, are the instructors for a major coaching and team leadership skills development effort that will equip every manager and supervisor to live the new culture.

- Corning Glass Works' State College plant was running at capacity making television bulbs. Some bulbs went slightly off spec, yet the desperate customer said he would take them anyway. But the plant manager refused to ship a product that wasn't up to standard. Comments chairman James R. Houghton, "It took about five seconds for the people in the plant to understand that he was serious about quality. Those are the things that have to happen because people are always asking, 'What do you want? Quality or profit?' The answer is 'Both'."

- As part of Walt Disney World's cross-utilization program, management staff go out during peak periods and work as hosts, cooking or serving hamburgers, fries, and popcorn, sweeping the streets, or working the attractions. In this way management keeps in touch, brings teams closer together, and signals how valuable they consider these front-line functions.

- Executives at Paul Revere Insurance Group developed their own unique approach to "management by wandering around" and signaling called PEET — Program to Ensure that Everybody's Thanked. Each of the fifteen executives receives a monthly PEET sheet, which lists the names and leader of three Quality Teams they are to visit to discuss service/quality. After the visit, the executive notes the visit's highlights and sends the PEET sheet to Quality Team Central. A monthly summary of highlights and trends is compiled and circulated to the executive team.

- Campbell Soup executives held meetings in the backs of grocery stores to keep everyone focused on their customers. All executives also agreed to become the weekly grocery shopper in their household.

- Levi Strauss executives spend one Saturday a month on the sales floor of a major retail outlet selling jeans. "It's quite an eye-opener to sell our own [brand] and watch people decide to buy other people's jeans," says one senior manager.

- Bell Cellular put together a video for internal distribution that begins with a journalist reporting on the telecommunications industry four years into the future. The video portrays the outstanding service/quality success of the company as if it were history. The journalist goes on to describe the increased market share and unparalleled standards Bell Cellular has established. The video then cuts back to the present with an interview featuring the president, Bob Latham. He describes the extensive plans, changes, and training under way to make that vision of the future a

113

reality. This video is shown at employee orientation sessions, training kick-offs and graduations, planning sessions, operations reviews, and so on.

COMMON PITFALLS AND TRAPS TO SIGNALLING COMMITMENT

Big Talk, Little Action

There are three keys to long-term service/quality improvement: (1) follow through, (2) follow through, (3) follow through. You and your managers cannot set bold new directions and then delegate their implementation. Your time and attention needs to stay focused on service/quality improvement. Obviously you can't get wrapped up in all the details. But you must stay the course.

Managing by Muddling Around

If you're out to "snoopervise" or do bed checks, you'd do better to stay in your office. Many executives with weak coaching or team leadership skills inadvertently reduce openness and trust by their ineffective interpersonal skills. Of course, they are usually the same ones who are too busy to build their own skills but send their overworked supervisors to be "fixed."

Ivory Tower Visions

There is a delicate balance between senior management getting their vision, values, and plans together and building consensus and commitment through broad input. Visions and plans should not be developed in backrooms without the involvement of those people who will make it all work. An even greater danger is low customer input. Many an organization has squandered precious resources providing top-notch products or services nobody wanted.

Month-End Myopia

If you have developed a Reason For Being statement that boldly proclaims "zero defects," "delighted customers," or "only the

114

highest quality," watch yourself when the heat is on. This is one of your managerial moments of truth. What standards will you *really* accept? If you knowingly ship marginal-quality products or deliver poor service, your service/quality improvement process is finished.

Catch as Catch Can
A disciplined, regular process for communicating senior management commitment is essential. Someone must be assigned the role of orchestrating executive appearances and activities.

On a Wing and a Prayer
American writer and publisher Elbert Hubbard once said, "People who want milk should not seat themselves on a stool in the middle of a field in hope that a cow will back up to them." You've got to be aggressive when you go after service/quality improvement. All your best intentions to signal vision and commitment will have little impact if you don't have plans, structures, and processes in place to take you through the long haul. People just won't get on board if you announce a million-dollar destination and then pull up in a patched-up old bus with two kilometres of life left.

CHAPTER SEVEN
Cylinder Two: Listening to Internal/External Customers

"Listening, really listening, is tough and grinding work, often humbling, sometimes distasteful. It's a fairly sure bet that you won't like the lion's share of what you hear."

—Bob Waterman, *The Renewal Factor*

How can it get any simpler? What could be more obvious? Find out what your customer wants, and then exceed those expectations. Robert Desatnick, former vice-president, human resources, for McDonald's, says, "We would ask customers in our restaurants, 'How can we improve our services?' We then incorporated their suggestions into our service policies and practices. They started coming back more frequently — and bringing their friends with them." Or ponder the profound advice of *Fortune* magazine following their study of "companies that service you best": "The best way to develop a service strategy is to listen to customers." Really complex stuff, right?

But talk about common sense rarely being put into common practice! Like good nutrition and exercise, we know what needs to be done. It's actually making a disciplined habit of *doing* it that's so tough. You know you *should* be regularly listening to your customers, but are you?

116

LISTENING SHARPENS YOUR EDGE

Why do so many managers do so much talking about the importance of good customer listening, then do so little of it? Mainly because they believe "we know what our customers need." The Strategic Planning Institute's research shows just how deadly that management assumption can be:

- Managers don't always know customers' purchasing criteria. "Even when the criteria are correctly identified, management may misjudge the relative importance of individual criteria . . . *sometimes by a factor of 3:1."*
- Managers often misjudge how their customers perceive the organization's service/quality. "Those differences in perceptions of performance may exist for the most basic of criteria."
- Managers can fail to see how their customers' needs have changed and evolved because of "competitive product developments, technological advances, market or environmental influences."
- "Rather than focusing on customer preferences, management tends to evaluate the quality of products from an *internal* perspective."

If you're scrambling to make your company more competitive through higher service/quality, you have no choice but to get very close to your customers. You no longer have the luxury of waiting to see which way the wind is blowing before setting your strategic sails. As Tom Peters warns, "Listening to customers must become everyone's business. With most competitors moving ever faster, the race will go to those who listen (and respond) most intently." And, points out Richard E. Heckert, a Du Pont chairman, you need to pick up the pace: "As the world becomes more and more competitive, you have to sharpen all your tools. Knowing what's on the customer's mind is the most important."

Top service/quality providers make every attempt to understand their customers' world and speak their language. Intensive listening keeps them in touch and in tune with their customers.

117

And that pushes them to become more user-friendly. We all know organizations that aren't. Their customers are expected to speak the organization's language. They have their own secret code of acronyms and buzzwords that sounds like some foreign tongue. That's because it is.

Effective customer listening helps you to use your resources better. You can probably think of two or three organizations you've done business with that expend enormous time, energy, and money to provide you with services you don't want. That's one of the key reasons that high service/quality providers have lower costs. Leonard Berry, David Bennet, and Carter Brown provide a good insight to this in their book, *Service Quality*: "When management fails to understand customer desires for the service, a chain reaction of mistakes is likely to follow. The wrong service standards. The wrong training. The wrong types of performance measurements. The wrong advertising. And so forth. It is tough enough to satisfy customer desires without the added burden of not really knowing what desires to satisfy."

An increasingly important strategic issue today is innovation. And customer listening is at the heart of highly innovative organizations. Brian Quinn, a management professor and author, has found that the innovative practices of large and small organizations are remarkably similar: "Many experienced big companies are relying less on early research and more on interactions with lead customers. Hewlett-Packard, 3M, Sony, and Raychem frequently introduce radically new products through small teams that work closely with lead customers. These teams learn from their customers' needs and innovations, and rapidly modify designs and entry strategies based on this information."

HOW'S YOUR NAIVE LISTENING?

Tom Peters finds that top service/quality providers do an incredible amount of what he calls naive listening. He exhorts any manager interested in improving performance to listen "naively, continually, systematically, and from as many angles as possible." Too many times, when managers do bother to listen to their customers, they do the "yeah, but" kind of listening. They aren't really listening at all, they are rationalizing, explaining, excusing, or defending. "But our customers don't understand our business," or "If only it were that simple. You see, we have some unique problems . . ."

One way to check the type of listening done in your organization is to look at how customer perceptions are treated. Are they seen as facts or as misguided, uninformed opinions? Your customers' perceptions *are* facts — whether or not they agree with your own view. When dealing with the highly subjective areas of quality and service, the *only* perceptions that matter are your customers'. According to Jack Welch, chairman and CEO of General Electric and chief architect of the company's revitalization, "The customer either rates us better or worse than somebody else. It's not very scientific, but it's disastrous if you score low."

There are a multitude of ways to listen naively, continually, and systematically to your customers. Top service/quality performers use most of the following methods in dozens of variations. *How many are you using?*

- **Customer Surveys** — These can be complex and incredibly detailed or as simple as the check-off-five-questions type you've seen in hotels and restaurants. They can also be conducted by your staff or by a third party. They can be done on the phone or in person. When these questionnaires are used as measurement or a performance feedback, they are fairly tightly structured around specific service/quality indicators. To encourage "naive" input, they need to be very broad and open-ended. And that means asking more than just those questions you feel comfortable dealing with.
- **Market Research** — This tends to be a fairly rigorous and in-depth method. It can help you get a handle on emerging markets you may want to identify and serve, or stay abreast of the markets you're currently serving. Focus groups, surveys, and studies of demographic and psychographic trends are the techniques most commonly used. Your indus-

try probably has data available to help you identify patterns and changes in your markets.

- **Close-Up and Personal** — The simplest way to listen to your customers is to meet them face to face and ask them what they look for in your type of product or service. There really is nothing like getting out on the front serving lines and hearing the candid comments first hand from the bosses at the top of your organization chart. (Of course, if you would rather just *talk* about how "our customers sign our paycheques" instead of *acting* as though you truly believed it, why bother to listen to "ungrateful customers who just bellyache and complain"?).

  Done frequently and broadly enough, face-to-face discussions can help clarify inner-ring standards and expectations you've gathered from other listening sources. In *The Service Edge*, Ron Zemke explains, "The customer who says your company is 'lousy at communication' may have in mind one unpleasant phone call, periodic frustration with a poorly written manual, years of puzzling over incomprehensible bills, or any combination of a dozen other things. You only know what they mean when you ask the right questions."

- **Customer Hot Lines** — *The Service Edge* newsletter calls the toll-free 800 number "one of the most frequently used and most effective methods for staying in touch with customers." Getting managers to listen in regularly on calls is also an excellent way to help them keep both feet on the ground. Numerous companies study their calls for trends and ideas for new products and services.

- **Customer Complaints** — Keeping files on complaints and tracking their resolution helps top performers analyze how well they're doing. However, considering that one complaint represents a major block of equally unhappy customers, these companies shoot for "zero complaint" levels. As long as complaints are not used to criticize people, circulate them and ask, "What can we do to respond?" Even more importantly, ask, "What can we do to prevent these?"

- **Service Team Visits** — Increasingly, groups of employees are visiting their customers and seeing their products or services being used or passed on. This approach is especially effective for production employees in manufacturing or data processing. It's easy for these people to lose sight of who will ultimately use whatever it is they are producing. Support staff such as accounting, administration, or human resources benefit from this same focus on "why we all come to work every day." During those visits, service teams get a better understanding of their customers' standards and expectations.

But, you may be thinking, it costs a lot of money and "down time" to send these people out there. You're right. And what's the cost of not sharpening your axes? But, you may be tempted to respond, we're no different from anybody else. Exactly.

- **Focus Groups and Advisory Panels** — These come in all sizes and varieties. They may be combined with market research, service team visits, surveys, and face-to-face listening. Retailers, electronic manufacturers, and consumer product companies are among a growing list of organizations using this very effective listening approach. Customer focus groups can provide invaluable feedback and guidance on designs, standards, typical expectations, pricing, styles, trends, and more.

  Tom Peters urges that "informal 'focus groups' of a few customers ought to be called in every operation — manufacturing, distribution, accounting, not just marketing — on a bi-weekly or monthly basis. Debriefings with key accounts (annually or semi-annually) must include formal survey questions and open-ended discussions with all levels and functions in key account operations."

- **User Groups and Conferences** — This method of staying close to customers is used extensively in the computer business. Groups of customers meet to share ideas and experiences about the use of particular systems. Meetings may be initiated by the company for its customers, or by the users themselves.

Customer conferences and educational events can be a way not only to provide Enhanced Service but also to listen to customers.

CUSTOMER LISTENING BEGINS AT HOME

If you're competing in the marketplace for customers, there is one group of front-line performers who are an especially rich source of customer information. And their contributions are usually overlooked. These are your salespeople.

Sales strength is one of the key factors that pulled IBM far ahead of the pack in the last couple of decades. One of the key builders of that strength was the now retired VP of marketing, Buck Rodgers. He explains the critical role salespeople play in staying close to the customer: "The real heroes in every truly market-driven company are the sales reps. It is they who find out what the customers want and need, and where it all begins. Thanks to the marketing reps, IBM's engineering and manufacturing departments build what the customer needs." But even mighty IBM found out just how tough staying in touch can be. According to CEO John Akers, the company lost touch with its rapidly changing customer needs during the eighties. As a result, it lost ground in a number of key markets. IBM is now rededicating itself to customer listening and keeping its salespeople closer to its customers.

How does that compare to your company? Are your salespeople key strategists in plotting how you can move ahead through higher service/quality? Or are your salespeople treated as "necessary evils who would give away the store if we let them"? Buck Rodgers: "It bewilders me that some companies consider their sales force to be a necessary evil, something they wish they could eliminate — an expense they are forever whittling away at. These companies have little or no respect for their salespeople and more often than not treat them as though they were adversaries. They cut territories unnecessarily, raise quotas unrealistically, reduce commission rates whenever they can, and try to bully their salespeople into performing. The company usually gets what it deserves — a sales force that's angry, unhappy, unresponsive and nonproductive."

At Chaparral Steel, not only is the sales force treated as key players in improving performance but everyone is directed to behave more like salespeople. President Gordon Forward says, "We made everyone in the company a member of the sales department. That means people in security, secretaries, everyone. If we have bent bars coming off our production line that are causing a problem for our customers, we might send a superintendent over with the salesperson or the person who did the bundling or somebody from production or metallurgy. It's everyone's job. We mix crews. . . . We want them [employees] to see Chaparral the way our customers do, we also want them to talk to each other."

LOOKING IN ON GOOD CUSTOMER LISTENING

There are hundreds, if not thousands, of ways to listen to your customers. No one or two ways are best. The key is to use as many as you can to get the broadest view possible of your customers' needs and expectations. Good listening is also combined with strong feedback and measurement systems (the topic of Chapter 17).

The following examples will give you and your management team ideas on just some of the ways others have found to listen to their customers.

- Real estate developer Bramalea Ltd. found that around 80 percent of their new-home buyers lived within a 2.5- to 3-kilometre radius of the subdivision. To build homes that appeal most to those local tastes, Bramalea uses extensive marketing surveys supplemented by personal interviews. As house models and styles begin to take shape, focus groups are used. Former president and instigator of the customer focus at Bramalea, Ken Field, explains what happens next: "We get them talking in a very free-spirited way about the things that they would really like. About something that they may have seen in another city, or that a friend might have. We ask them if they were starting from scratch to work with an architect to build a home for themselves, what is it that they would really like to see?"

- Plant managers at Campbell Soup take employees out to tour the grocery stores they supply. The problem of dented cans was repeatedly identified as a way Campbell's could improve their service/quality. Employee teams threw themselves into reducing the problem because of the new perspective the visits gave them on this age-old issue.

- A growing number of companies in retailing, financial services, and the hospitality industry are hiring "Mystery Shoppers". Posing as regular customers, these trained professionals provide detailed reports on the service/quality levels encountered.

- General Electric provides the GE Answer Center as a 24-hour toll-free service for their customers. Staffed by more than 250 front-line agents and technical specialists, the center handles millions of calls each year. One of their innovative approaches is a What's Fair Policy for dealing with complaints. This involves asking unhappy customers what would be the fairest way to deal with their problem. GE finds "consumers are reasonable."

- All employees at Church's Fried Chicken spend at least two weeks working in one of the fast-food outlets.

- Everyone at Tony Lama, the Texas bootmaker, is expected to spend some time in the complaint department tuning into customers' concerns.

- IBM executives from manufacturing, development labs, administration, as well as marketing not only spend time traveling with salespeople but have key accounts assigned to them. They ask customers for suggestions, make recommendations, present updated information, and express thanks for the business. As Buck Rodgers explains, this is done in cooperation with the local IBM rep: "In addition to a first-hand view of some of the day-to-day problems of the customer, the executive gets a real education about the problems of selling in the field."

- An architect built a cluster of office buildings in a large green area. He waited to construct the sidewalks until people started wearing traffic patterns in the grass between the buildings. The sidewalks were then laid to follow the efficient, smoothly curved pathways established by the buildings' customers.

- When Ron Contino became commissioner of New York City's Sanitation Department he discovered that over 50% of their fleet was off the road because of breakdowns. In order to get the operators and mechanics committed to service/quality improvement, Ron solicited suggestions. He quickly provided lunchroom facilities and other changes in working conditions that were requested and went on to act on the suggestions for improving vehicle maintenance, such as a robotic paint system. The number of vehicles on the road jumped to 97% and the department began contracting in maintenance work from other fleets.

- At Stew Leonard's grocery, service teams scout out their competitors, looking for better ways to "wow" customers back in their own store. Focus groups are also used every week to give management feedback on the store's pricing, displays, selection, specials, and so on.

- Canadian Airlines hired researchers to fly along with customers, who were paid an honorarium for participating. The researcher met the customer before departure and they traveled together to the airport. Customer and researcher went through check-in procedures, flight, and arrival procedures together, and the researcher asked for the customer's perceptions of the service provided.

- Rolland Inc.'s fine-paper distribution division found that customer surveys produced dozens of opportunities for new products and enhanced services. At first, salespeople had resisted the surveys because they felt they already knew what their customers needed. However, as new perspectives and improvement opportunities emerged, salespeople clamored to get involved and extend customer listening.

- To turn around plunging Cadillac sales, GM planners met with a total of 2,500 Cadillac owners over three years to discuss design ideas and suggestions. The engineers sat in the back seats of prototypes, noting how customers responded to the instrument panel, switches and knobs, seatbelts, door handles, and the like during test drives. Based on the input, the newly customer-designed Cadillac took off when it hit the showrooms in the fourth quarter of 1988. The experience taught the division "a very tough lesson," says John Fleming, general director of marketing and product planning. "We learned to pay great attention to the customer."

- Techsonic Industries had brought out nine new depth-finder products for fishermen to track their prey. All had failed to compete successfully in a sophisticated, crowded marketplace prior to 1985. Chairman James Balkan then interviewed 25 groups of fishermen and found that what they wanted most was a gauge that could be read in bright sunlight. The year after this customer-designed product hit the market, sales tripled and propelled Techsonic to over 40 percent of the U.S. market. The company's motto is The Quality of Any Product or Service Is What the Customer Says It Is.

- Each month, managers at the turbo-fired mail-order house Lands End get an eight-centimetre-thick computer printout of customers' comments. These are studied religiously and used to fine-tune the merchandise offered in the next catalogue. In 1987, customers asked for a line of children's clothing. A year later, $15-million worth of the new product was sold.

- Every March since 1907, five carefully selected policyholders descend on company headquarters at Northwestern Mutual Life Insurance in Milwaukee. They spend five days interviewing officers and employees, as well as combing through documents, files, and statements looking for problems. The company prints their final, unedited report in its annual statement. Northwestern enjoys the industry's *highest* customer retention rate. Over 95 percent of policyholders renew their coverage.

- British Airways installed video complaint/comment booths at their main terminal at London's Heathrow Airport. The company replies to passenger comments within a week. The booths provide higher levels of feedback than if customers had to write or phone the company. The comments are also studied for product or service ideas.

- Radio consultant Lee Abrams is able to increase ratings for clients 92 percent of the times he's hired. Among his unorthodox methods are hitchhiking surveys; when he sees drivers punching radio stations on their car radio, he asks why they are changing. Abrams advises, "Don't worry about being scientific. Just be creative. If you're dealing with computers, go hang around a Computerland."

- One step in an intense new focus on customers (which led to a 50 percent increase in profits over two years) had Avco Financial Services executives contact ten customers by phone every time they visited a branch. They asked about the service and quality, requested suggestions for improvement, and thanked customers for their business. "They were quite surprised by the little things that could turn a customer off," reflected president Will Barrett. "And they became extremely concerned about the customers' perception of the relationship."

- B.C. Tel holds regular "defective tool days" to improve internal service/quality. Teams of telephone installers and repairers are invited to bring in the cables, switches, testing equipment, or procedures they are having the most trouble using. Internal and external suppliers sit and listen as a senior executive chairs the meeting. Suppliers are told to "shut up and listen. No excuses. No rationalization. Just take notes and ask questions only for clarity." At the end of the session, the chairperson records the dates by which the supplier will have the problem fixed or will report on progress.

- Three disgruntled customers were brought in to talk to a large group of mechanical contractors at their association conference. The customers outlined in detail the frustrations they felt with the group and the consequences resulting from shoddy service/quality. The consequences include secret blacklists, legal entanglements, financial holdbacks, or refusal to settle accounts. Many contractors were shocked to discover that dissatisfaction stemmed more from a series of little things (lateness, not returning phone calls, untidy work sites, not providing good information/updates, disorganization) than from technical incompetence or equipment failure.

- The Operations Branch of the Department of Engineering and Works at the City of Ottawa struggled to define who their customers were and how best to listen to them. They attended community association meetings and randomly sampled 10 calls per day of the 50,000 received at city hall each year. Acting on the information gathered, the department changed a section's name from Complaints Section to Information and Customer Service Section, established a five-day turnaround on requests (and significantly reduced repeat customer calls and those from politicians), revised "legalistic" bylaw notices to make them more user-friendly, and improved internal and customer communications.

- London (Ontario) Public Library hands out bookmarks with customer surveys on them for its customers to complete and hand in when they return the books.

COMMON LISTENING PITFALLS AND TRAPS

Among Friends

Don't just listen to your satisfied or old friendly customers. Be sure you're getting a balance of unhappy and dissatisfied ones as well. No reports or memos can capture the impact of being taken to task by a customer who's just had a run-in with your system.

You expect your people to take the flak. Quit hiding in your office and experience it yourself. It will bring service/quality into perspective.

"Yeah, But" Listening

If one of your colleagues didn't stop defending, rationalizing, or explaining long enough for you to give him feedback on a problem he's creating, would you consider him a good listener? Would you feel he heard you? Do you think the problem would be corrected? And how likely would you be to believe his sincerity if he told you he values your feedback? So how are you coming across to your customers?

Few and Far Between

Don't become overly reliant on just a few listening channels. You may be getting an incomplete picture. Many organizations rely primarily on complaints and maybe a few simple surveys. "The problem with such methods is they measure only the extremes," says Christopher Hart, an assistant professor at Harvard Business School who studies service industries. According to Hart, "You hear from Mr. Grumpy and Mr. Smiley, but not from Mr. Average."

Introverted Innovation

While there are examples of organizations successfully "springing" new products and services on their customers, the deck is severely stacked against winning this game. The evidence clearly shows that successful innovations happen "out there" in the real world with real customers. Paper studies and intuitive hunches that result in products or services being developed in backrooms rarely work. Your customers may have no idea of what product or service you could create, but they do know the problem they need solved or the opportunity they want to seize. Remember what has now become a marketing truism: we don't really buy the drill, we buy the hole that it will give us. Get close to your customers and work together to find solutions to their problems.

Hard of Doing

It should go without saying, but it has to be said: *act* on what your customers tell you. If you don't, you'll miss golden opportunities, and your customers and your people will stop talking to you. Ron Zemke says, "Listening is half a loaf. Doing something with what you hear feeds the multitude. Unfortunately, the corporate library chock full of customer research no one has ever tried to find a use for is far too common."

CHAPTER EIGHT
Cylinder Three: Internal Marketing

"Leaders who take culture seriously are bears for internal marketing, selling their points of view to the organization much as they would sell a product or service to the public, with slogans, advertisement, promotions, and public relations campaigns."
— William Davidow and Bro Uttal,
Total Customer Service: The Ultimate Weapon

Let's say that after listening to and working with your external customers, you've developed an exciting product or service that promises to take your customers by storm. Now you want to get the word out to your customers, and possibly attract new ones.

So you photocopy some leaflets, throw together a press release, ask a couple of overworked executives to give interviews, and just as you get the campaign under way, your executive team gets bored and wants to move on to something new and different.

How successful would your campaign be? What impressions would your customers be left with? What kind of return on investment do you think this approach would give you?

Ridiculous? Absolutely. But take a look at your *internal* marketing. Internal marketing — selling — of service/quality improvement, if it's done at all, is generally done poorly. It's amazing how many organizations will spend megabucks and megahours planning and executing powerful, slick campaigns aimed at their external customers. Many will then turn around and spend ten bucks and two hours bringing the people on board who ultimately decide whether those external advertising messages are fact or fiction. A few thousand blown moments of truth (and that's likely just a couple of days' worth in your organization) can quickly scuttle hundreds of thousands of dollars' worth of external marketing and public relations.

Some organizations rely too heavily on internal marketing to drive up their service/quality levels. Their sloganeering and slick internal newsletters, posters, mugs, hats, T-shirts, rallying speeches, and videos cover up the fact that that's all there is. The service/quality improvement effort is nothing more than window dressing. Inside, the room is empty. And some organizations make the opposite mistake. They build an improvement effort of substance and fail to keep the momentum and excitement strong with solid internal marketing.

INTERNAL MARKETING TOOLS

There are a multitude of ways to keep the process fresh and alive. No one method should be used exclusively. Just like an external marketing campaign, an internal marketing strategy begins with a clarification of the central message to be communicated, and the people to whom it is being directed. Next comes a marketing plan that combines as many media as possible to make the key message "top of mind" with the target audience. Repetition, impact, and consistency are keys to successful persuasion.

Here are a number of the most common internal marketing methods used by the top service/quality providers and those striving to shift their cultures:

- **Senior Management Signaling** — In their book, *The Winning Performance: How America's High-Growth Midsize Companies Succeed*, Donald Clifford and Richard Cavanaugh write: "The winning performers understand that their actions speak louder than words — but they also understand that the words may have to be repeated endlessly . . . so they never stop communicating. The leaders spend prodigious hours writing, speaking, visiting the troops in outposts, doing whatever's necessary to get the essential messages across." It just can't be said too often:

the message repeatedly given by senior management is the single most powerful channel for communicating the values, priorities, and strategies of the organization. But rather than leaving those opportunities to chance, careful planning should go into where and how members of the senior management team should invest their time in communicating and reinforcing service/quality improvement.

- **Orientation Sessions** — If employees are to improve the moments of truth they control, they *must* become partners in the improvement process. That means that a great deal of planning needs to go into the process of getting employees committed to, and involved in, the improvement effort. One of the best ways is to bring them together to meet with senior managers. These sessions may be as long as a day or as short as a few hours. Here's a typical agenda:
  1. Why Service/Quality Improvement Is a Critical Issue for the Organization
  2. The Three Rings of Perceived Value and the Role Employees Play in Improving Value
  3. Evaluating Our Service/Quality Strengths and Weaknesses
  4. Strategies for Improvement
  5. Our Plan for the Improvement Effort
  6. A Vision of Our Preferred Future

- **Updating and Recharging Sessions** — These can be planned and structured, or impromptu and informal. There is a direct relationship between the frequency of these meetings and the amount of sustained energy and commitment available for continuous improvement in your organization. These sessions are also great opportunities for celebration, recognition, and "hoopla."

- **Internal Newsletters** — There are some outstanding newsletters, and there are many poor ones. When used effectively, newsletters can be an excellent way to inform, inspire, recognize, reinforce, and market the improvement effort. Here are a few newsletter do's and don'ts:
  1. Do keep the style lively and readable.

2. Don't trivialize the issues or talk down to readers.
3. Do provide a balance. Combine recognition, people-oriented stories, and meaty strategic updates with hard business information and "how to" tips.
4. Don't let it go out looking like a third-rate production.
5. Do give it as much thought, planning, and resources as you would to a customer newsletter.
6. Don't let it become a social register or gossip rag.
7. Do have it produced by representatives of its readers.

- **Videos** — Like newsletters, the quality of your videos will signal how important senior management believes the whole effort to be. An effective video can highlight your organization's commitment, values, Reason For Being, as well as plans and processes for achieving higher service/quality. It can be used as an internal awareness tool and as an external sales, marketing, and public-relations vehicle.

   However, video can also backfire. Some organizations suffer from the it's-all-a-marketing-game syndrome. This deadly assumption leads them to produce slick, expensive videos that employees know are a whitewash or just pipe dreams. Like many other internal marketing tools, video can breed better cynics in your organization if it isn't supporting a much larger, fully integrated improvement effort with real substance and planning. If employees are left wondering, "Is that all there is?", videos may do more harm than good.

EXAMPLES OF INTERNAL MARKETING

- The turnaround of automotive manufacturer Tridon Canada Limited began with an all-employees meeting that laid out the financial position as well as the vision, values, and strategic plan. Internal communications have continued through Friday meetings in the cafeteria.
- D.H. Howden (Pro Hardware) sends out a quarterly video-tape "service newsletter" to all its retail stores across Canada. The tape features key messages from executives,

examples of outstanding service, tips for service improvement, and reports on its service improvement program.

- Bramalea Ltd., a major real estate developer, devised a service improvement slogan ("Proud. Me and Bramalea") and program to get its employees, contract tradespeople, and salespeople on board. They mail a trilingual newsletter to tradespeople at their homes. They put the slogan on peaked hats, coolers, decks of cards, T-shirts, and coffee cups for trucks. Each home under construction has a picture of the family who has bought it hung just inside the main door. When construction is completed, each tradesperson signs his name to the bottom of the picture for presentation to that customer.
- American Express's Optima Card was unveiled to employees through a nationwide teleconference before it was announced to the public.
- Regular CEO breakfasts, luncheons, and "tea breaks" have been used by Campbell Canada, Mark's Work Wearhouse, Transport Canada, POI Office Interiors, Bramalea Ltd., and others to get service messages to front-line employees. These also provide an excellent source of "non-filtered" ideas, suggestions, and feedback from employees directly to senior management. Pictures and anecdotes are put in newsletters and reports to add momentum to the organization's "service improvement bandwagon."
- Volkswagen Canada put all 5,200 of its dealership employees through a two-day customer service awareness program. Participants were identified by first names only, and dealer-owners learned alongside those who wash and prep cars.
- Many top service/quality providers post all customer letters — good and bad — in employee areas.
- Campbell Soup and others publish acts of "employee heroism," awards, and other recognitions in their annual reports.
- McDonald's, Disney, and many others use "Employee of the

Month" (week, or even day) to reinforce service improvement messages. Doing this forces management to get out and "catch people doing things right."

COMMON PITFALLS AND TRAPS TO INTERNAL MARKETING

Mixed Messages
Internal and external marketing must be tied together. Your staff need to hear the same message your customers are hearing. Too often employees are the last to hear about the wonderful service/quality they're being committed to provide.

Not Walking Your Talk
You and your management team must *behave* in a manner consistent with the messages being broadcast to your people. You do the strongest internal marketing (or blocking) of the true value and priority of service/quality with your tiny, seemingly insignificant *daily actions*. Nothing else will convince (or turn off) employees as effectively as senior management behavior.

Stale and Stalling
Executives involved in building a high service/quality culture are always shocked by how long it takes to get the message through to those who will make it happen in their organization. Often, just as executives are getting tired of repeating the same old vision, values, strategies, or rationale, people on the front line are just beginning to think, "Just maybe, quite possibly, they might be serious this time." If at about that time senior management gets bored and moves on to greener pastures, momentum is lost, and employees add yet another protective layer against your future "flavor of the month" campaigns. The watchwords are consistency and repetition, repetition, repetition . . .

Bits and Pieces
Internal marketing must be given the same planning and follow-through as external marketing. The stakes are just as high. If you don't believe that, you're on the wrong journey. If you do believe that, then carefully think through your internal marketing cam-

paign as any good marketer would. What's the position you are trying to achieve? To whom are you targeting what messages? How can you ensure continuity and repetition of key themes? What are the best methods to use?

CHAPTER NINE
Cylinder Four: Hiring and Orienting

"Get the brightest people and train them well."
— Charles Merrill,
Founder, Merrill Lynch

This cylinder most clearly separates the high service/quality providers from the talkers and dreamers. In our consulting, workshops, audits, and executive retreats, we find that most organizations consistently score lowest on this critical cylinder. Yet this area has been identified in almost every study as a key factor that sets apart high service/quality organizations from the rest of the pack. Ron Zemke's exhaustive study of 101 top service providers is a good example. He identifies hiring and orienting, particularly training, as among the most significant reasons these companies are on top: "As we have explored company after company, we constantly have been struck by the slow, careful, calculated way they approach the hiring process for even the lowest-paying positions. The 'get somebody, anybody, on those phones' mentality was nowhere in evidence."

Stack the deck by hiring the best people, those most likely to uphold your service/quality values, and get them off to a strong start with solid training and orientation. Add to that careful attention to the signals you send by your decisions to promote or dismiss certain people. Use these practices to focus and direct full attention to service/quality improvement, and you're well on your way to transforming your organization's culture.

ONLY THE FINEST INGREDIENTS

In far too many organizations, the hiring and selection process is done half-well, at best. Only sometimes are the candidate's knowledge, relevant experience, job skills, career aspirations, stability, motivation, and work ethic screened, tested, and checked. But rarely is the candidate's fit with the organization's values thoroughly scrutinized.

Slipshod hiring practices send clear messages about your values: "Ignore whatever we tell you about service/quality, it's not a top priority." Weak hiring and selection processes also sharply downgrade the new recruit's perception of the job's value and importance: "Looks to me like they will hire anybody for this job," or "If the job were worth anything, it wouldn't be so easy to get." We place the highest value on those things that are hardest to get. Whether it is a house, a relationship, or a job, when we've really had to work to get it, we cherish it. How do your new people feel? Are they just doing a job or do they consider themselves important links in your organization's service/quality chain?

One easy explanation for why so many organizations do such an abysmal job of hiring and orienting around their service/ quality vision and values is that they don't have any. Most organizations have a sort of warmed-over pablum culture that doesn't smell, feel, or taste like anything. It just is.

Highly effective organizations have a *strong* and *visible* culture. Potential candidates are either excited by and drawn to that organization's way of life, vision, and priorities, or repelled and turned away by them. Even if the candidate is perfect in every other way, top performing organizations want those who are turned off by their culture to look elsewhere. Although Walt Disney World recruits employees in Orlando, Florida, where there is a labour shortage, the organization refuses to lower the standards which eliminate 30% of applicants before the inter view stage. Top organizations know that every recruit will eventually integrate with and reinforce the organization's vision and values — or will detract from them. When it comes to service/

quality improvement, it's critical that everyone is heading in the same direction.

All the signs point to a tightening of many job markets in the coming years. Good people are going to become harder to find. And the competition for the best people will continue to intensify. Service/quality improvement will significantly enhance your image as a preferred employer. In fact, *you can't improve Third Ring service without a lot of attention to building employee satisfaction and commitment.*

Doing It Right the First Time

Top performing organizations invest a level of time and energy in the hiring and selection process that astounds the average manager. It is not unusual for them to put their candidates through six to ten interviews with the managers and team that the person would work with if hired. These interviews serve two purposes. Obviously they give the organization a broad look at the candidate's suitability, especially their "fit" within the culture. (That's one of the reasons for colleagues being involved in the process.) Second, they give candidates plenty of time to eliminate themselves if they realize that the organization is not the kind they want to be part of. Richard Pascale, consultant and author of *The Art of Japanese Management,* has studied the characteristics of top performing organizations and how they maintain their strong and distinct cultures. Hiring and selection are their key tools: "The company subjects candidates for employment to a selection process so rigorous that it often seems designed to discourage individuals rather than encourage them to take the job."

The costs (mainly time) of rigorously screening are high. But what are the costs of hiring the wrong people? Let's consider just the costs of turnover. How much does it cost you to rehire and retrain because a new employee stayed only a few months or years? How much management time is lost rehiring and retraining? What's the impact on your service/quality levels if new employees aren't suitable for, or don't care about, providing Third Ring service? What does it cost you to have positions sit vacant because the last person in that job didn't work out?

Turnover is just one of the many costs associated with not hiring right the first time. Starting with the right raw materials is a critical element in building a high service/quality culture. Often overlooked and delegated to personnel or human resources departments, hiring is an essential strategic area for executives and managers in top organizations. Tom Peters says: "The task of transforming raw recruits into committed stars, able to cope with the pace of change that is becoming normal, begins with the recruiting process per se. The best follow three tenets, unfortunatcly ignored by most: (1) spend time, lots of it; (2) insist that line people dominate the process; and (3) don't waffle about the qualities you are looking for in candidates."

OFF TO A STRONG START

You've hired well. You've chosen the best-qualified candidates who not only have the right skills and personal characteristics, but they also embody your service/quality values. It took a while to get to this point, but they are now ready, willing, and eager to contribute. You and your managers, as well as the new recruits' coworkers, are excited about the people you have gone through such an exhaustive process to choose. Given these circumstances, you would likely feel that an extensive training and orientation program would be well worth the investment.

That's how hiring and orientation go hand in hand. If you're just hiring warm bodies, it's not worth spending a lot of time orienting and training them, especially since they probably won't be around for very long. The irony of this is that they won't be around for very long because you weren't selective in hiring them and didn't do much to get them off to a good start.

A strong orientation program not only ensures that your new people are given a better chance to be successful, but it applies additional pressure to hire the right people in the first place. Although turnover is much more expensive than an in-depth training and orientation program, the investments of timc, salaries, and other costs arc much more visible in the latter. Therefore, managers will be more careful about who they select as candidates for these substantial investments.

Orientation Starts with the First Interview

Many managers don't consider the hiring and selection process as part of orientation. Yet that's where candidates gather their first impressions about the values and priorities of the organization. An extensive selection process that focuses on values as the final and largest hurdle (experience, skill or education, and personal characteristics being the first) sends these clear signals to the job candidates and to everyone else in your organization:

- We don't hire just anybody. You are one of a select few.
- Our values aren't just pretty words on the wall.
- This is an important job. You are an important person.
- The quality of your work will be every bit as important as "making the numbers."
- We're planning on a long-term relationship.
- We're careful about who we hire because we work hard to invest in and support your success.

Would you like your people to feel this way?

Characteristics of Effective Orientation Programs

Solid orientation programs have many elements, but two basics stand out in the best organizations: the quality of the program, and the involvement of line management. Industrial psychologists Kenneth Wexley of Michigan State University and Gary Latham of G.P. Latham found that it is critical to do orientation right the first time: "Poor orientation programs can be financially draining to the organization because they can reduce effectiveness for the employee's first few weeks on the job and this can contribute to dissatisfaction and turnover." In an experiment at Texas Instruments, several groups of new employees went through an orientation program while other similar groups did not. A year later those employees who had been well oriented had learned their jobs faster and had higher productivity and lower absence and lateness than those employees who hadn't been formally oriented.

142

Wexley and Latham also found that "orientation training should be the joint responsibility of training staff and the line supervisor." Because it's such an excellent opportunity to reinforce the organization's vision and values, executives for top service/quality performers are often involved in the orientation process as well. Any way you look at it, training and orienting new recruits is far too critical to be glossed over or delegated away. It is a prime strategic opportunity to instill your values and priorities.

PROMOTION, DEMOTION, AND DISMISSAL

Although promotion, demotion, and dismissal are covered in the Systems cylinder (Chapter 14), they are strongly linked to hiring and orienting. Your systems and practices in these areas send strong signals of your true values.

Take a hard look at who's getting promoted in your organization and why. If you're promoting the supervisor or employee who beats up on internal and external customers, then service/ quality is *not* a key value in your organization. It may be a goal or even an ideal, but it is not a real living value. In the early eighties, Terrence Deal and Allan Kennedy first expressed the emerging awareness that every organization has its own unique patterns of "the way we do things around here." In their book, *Corporate Cultures: The Rites and Rituals of Corporate Life*, they make this critical point: "Too many companies are promoting the wrong people and sending conflicting signals through the corporate culture. . . . [An organization] must promote people who embody key values of the business if it is to be successful."

Dismissals and demotions are management's fault. They are usually the result of poor selection, ineffective orientation and training, and weak management coaching. Deal and Kennedy say that to a manager concerned with the cultural signals his or her actions send, "a firing is a catastrophe. It should never happen . . . if the employee fits with the culture." Or as Peter Drucker puts it, "To blame the failed promotion on the promoted person

— as is usually done — is no more rational than to blame a capital investment that has gone sour on the money that was put in."

The negative ripple effect of a firing or demotion can be enormously costly. Yet not making changes when someone is not able to handle the job sends the wrong signals about what kind of behavior or performance is acceptable. The whole sorry mess is yet another example of the high costs of poor hiring and orienting — of not doing it right the first time.

The key question is what are people dismissed or demoted for? The answer defines your organization's values. Deal and Kennedy say: "When a firing is necessary, it should not be the end result of poor performance, but of violations of cultural norms. Moreover, when such an event occurs, it demands the personal attention of the symbolic manager to make sure the cultural message of the firing is fully understood."

HIRING AND ORIENTING IN ACTION

- The international service-award-winning airline Wardair (now merged with Canadian Airlines) actively seeks and rigorously selects cabin, counter, and phone employees with extensive airline or hospitality industry experience. Even more than customer service training, their strategic edge has been hiring and retaining highly qualified staff with a strong service orientation.

- The City of Ottawa put together an extensive introductory binder for all employees that outlines their service improvement program and how employees would be involved. It included sections on their vision and values, their improvement plans, as well as their suggestions and reward systems.

- The rule at Rob Ell's family-owned Flintstones Bedrock City theme park in British Columbia: Don't hire grouchy people.

- Before opening Vancouver's Pan Pacific hotel in 1986, general manager Steve Halliday insisted that every potential pot-washer, bellman, and chambermaid be interviewed by a minimum of six people. Steve was the final arbiter on each hiring. Hotel experience was not a necessary qualification;

however, a "bubbly" personality was. Industry surveys show that the Pan Pacific is now the highest-rated hotel in the province. Tourism Vancouver reports that this hotel has become the benchmark against which every other hotel compares itself. And it now establishes room rates for the city as well.

- Sporting Life, a Toronto sporting goods store, ensures that their 50 to 200 salespeople (depending on the season) have had 28 hours of in-store training and two one-hour exams before being allowed to do the job. "We're in business to make money, but we're also in the business to have happy customers," says a supervisor.

- Another Toronto sporting goods store, Old Firehall Sports, has a similar training and orientation program. They won't allow part-time or full-time employees on their floors until they have had a minimum of 25 hours of product knowledge training. They must also pass tests (with a better than 75 percent average) before they're allowed to sell. Sales per square foot continually set Canadian records for their industry.

- At The Achieve Group, once candidates have passed the usual interviews, reference checks, and selection screens on technical ability and relevant experience, we have them go through a values/culture-fit screening. Here the candidate tells us what she or he has done in the past that illustrates our three key values (service/quality is found in all three). The first such screening is usually done by potential cow-orkers, as a group as well as one on one. The team then assesses the "values fit" of the candidate. Clients are often asked to assess the candidate to see how comfortable they would be working with her or him as well.

- A major car rental firm, a theme park, and a number of hotels, restaurants, and others have designed rigorous interview formats (questions, application forms, etc.) and provide extensive training to management staff on hiring front-line staff with service/quality as a major criterion.

Typical characteristics interviewers watch for include: out-going, friendly, cheerful, a "people" person, and helpful.
- When I was general manager of a branch of Culligan, the international water treatment company, filling sales and service positions while maintaining high standards when there were few candidates applying was often a challenge. To make the process work, we started with an initial screening to determine whether to proceed further. If so, next came a strong sell on the job, which included a video and a meeting with satisfied employees. Once the candidates were clearly hooked, the tables were turned and the candidates were put through a rigorous multi-stage screening process. We not only got the best possible candidates by this method, but we made sure we didn't let new people feel that they were hired because we were desperate and no one else showed up.
- Mark Blumes, founder and president of Mark's Work Wearhouse, a national clothing retail chain, feels it's vital that new head office employees — management and clerical — understand their role. During their orientation, he takes them to the window and asks: "Do you see any customers bringing money into this building to us?"

  "Ah, no, we don't," they reply.

  "Well, don't ever forget that! Customers don't pay us for what we do here. They pay for what happens in the stores. That's where the action is. *All of us* at head office are here to serve and support the stores."
- Holland America is a major cruise ship line that consistently holds the industry's coveted five-star service ranking. A key reason for its success is an unparalleled hiring and orientation process. Candidates are chosen only from the hospitality industry (usually top Asian hotels or airlines). They are put through a dozen or more interviews and tests with numerous cruise ship professionals and managers. Successful candidates are then sent to the cruise line's hospitality school for a few weeks. Next, they spend months under the supervision of a senior employee on the line's

flagship. Only after the recruits have been through this extensive process are they considered ready to come into solo contact with customers on their assigned ship.

- Merck, the pharmaceutical giant, is constantly rated number one among the pharmacists and doctors it serves in the fiercely competitive drug industry. Aspiring salespeople must study basic medical subjects for ten weeks and score 90 percent or better on a weekly test to stay in the program. Then they spend three weeks learning how to present Merck's products. The recruits next go on trial for six months in the field making calls with their district managers. This stage is followed by three weeks at headquarters polishing presentation and selling skills. All salespeople must attend periodic medical classes as constant refreshers. Says vice-president Jerry Keller, "Training is our obsession. People who come to us from other companies can't believe we have this kind of program."

COMMON PITFALLS AND TRAPS TO HIRING AND ORIENTING

Abdicating Responsibility
Don't turn hiring over to human resources or personnel professionals. Their expertise can be very useful, but line managers must be heavily involved. They must "own" the hiring process and the new employees it produces.

"Cap in Hand" Recruiting
Avoid appearing grateful or desperate when there are few qualified candidates. Sell the candidate on the job (assuming the fit is right), then turn the tables and encourage the candidate to sell himself/herself (especially where service/quality is concerned).

"Lone Ranger" Recruiting
Don't fail to get broad and extensive input from other managers and the candidate's future coworkers. "Fit" is hard to define; it

takes a couple of assessments from many people on the team. As well, this process sends a clear signal to a candidate about the value of the job he or she is getting and the need for being a team player. It also builds commitment of other team members to helping "our" newly hired candidate succeed.

Inconsistent Promotions

Make the amount an individual contributes to service/quality a key promotion criterion. If managers can get ahead on technical skills while abusing or ignoring internal or external customers, the message of how important service/quality really is to the organization becomes crystal clear.

The Pygmalion Factor

Don't assume that lower-paid, part-time, or particular ethnic groups don't care about doing a good job. People raise or lower themselves to management expectations (documented in organizational psychology as the Pygmalion Effect). Many top service organizations are staffed with part-time kids, employees on minimum wage, and every nationality imaginable. Too many managers blame their employees for the poor service the organization provides. Yet who hires, orients, trains, manages, rewards, supports, strategizes, and markets to these people?

CHAPTER TEN
Skill Development: Building a Firm Foundation

"Our investment in training is a national disgrace. Despite lip service about people-as-our-most-important-asset, we value hardware assets over people, and have done so for the last century."

— Tom Peters

The house plans were outstanding. The architect's drawings were works of art. The materials were ready. They were among the very finest available — unsurpassed quality. The location was superb. It had a panoramic view and stood on firm but easily worked ground. The tools were ready. They represented the very latest in high tech construction equipment. And the builders were there. But — "Hey, Joe, that didn't seem to get those two-by-fours any straighter. Any more ideas? And those bricks don't seem to be lining up either."

That unlikely scenario describes the all-too-common technomanagement approach taken by many organizations to improve service/quality. The latest in technology (computers, equipment, technical procedures) are combined with strong management systems (process controls, quality teams, councils, and steering committees) to form a powerful but limiting combination. Like the house under construction, your improvement plans, materials, and tools may be among the best available. But they must be effectively used.

QUANTITY OF SERVICE/QUALITY TRAINING AND DEVELOPMENT

Tom Peters sees training and development as an issue critical to the survival of North American companies. For years he has been exhorting executives to increase dramatically their training and development investments. He warns, "The Japanese, Germans, and others outspend us wildly on training, especially in-company skill refurbishment and upgrading. In short, our track record is pathetic." Manufacturing expert Richard Schonberger concurs. In his book, *World Class Manufacturing: The Lessons of Simplicity Applied*, he titled a chapter "Training: The Catalyst." He writes, "Western industry must match the prodigious sums the world class manufacturing companies in Japan and Germany invest in it." This is further supported by Japanese consultant Masaaki Imai, who says, "There is a Japanese axiom: 'Quality control starts with training and ends in training.' "

QUALITY OF TRAINING AND DEVELOPMENT

When it comes to service/quality improvement, training can be of the technical, managerial/process, or leadership variety. Many North American organizations do far too little training, and leadership skills are particularly neglected. "What is needed, "as John Kotter, professor of organizational behavior at Harvard Business School says, "is a much larger number of people who have leadership skills, broadly defined."

But what are "leadership skills"? The term is used loosely and incorrectly by many managers and training professionals to describe what are really management theories. "Leadership" is one of the most overused, least understood elements of today's organizational life. And for all the talk about "skill building," pitifully little of it happens.

UNDERSTANDING "LEADERSHIP"

Art McNeil and I wrote *The VIP Strategy: Leadership Skills for Exceptional Performance* to bring to light our experiences working with hundreds of major organizations to improve their effectiveness. To help understand "leadership," we introduced a simple triangle model to show the interplay among the three basic components of any organization: (1) its expertise and supporting technologies; (2) its management planning and administrative systems; and (3) its ability to deal with the human element — leadership. In our triangle, leadership forms the base to show that management systems and technology are built upon the needs of the customers and those serving them or producing the products and services. However, our experience, backed by a growing mountain of evidence, shows that most organizations have this relationship backwards. These technomanaged organizations try to make their customers and employees serve management's administrative systems and technological wonders.

When looking at service/quality improvement, many executives have found a modified version of our triangle to be a useful way to understand the organizational development process:

THE TRIANGLE OF SERVICE/QUALITY

	Technology	Management Systems	Leadership
Focus	Equipment, Products/ Services or Expertise	Administrative Controls	People (Customers & Employees)
Key Elements	☐ Production/Delivery Methods ☐ Information Processing ☐ Automation	☐ Plans and Strategies ☐ Structures and Processes ☐ Audits and Budgets	☐ Vision and Values ☐ Culture/Environment ☐ Behaviour and Habits
Key Words	☐ Research ☐ Science ☐ Machine ☐ Predictable ☐ Precision ☐ Knowledge	☐ Formal ☐ Standards ☐ Rational ☐ Organize ☐ Efficient ☐ Measure	☐ Commitment ☐ Pride ☐ Emotional ☐ Subjective ☐ Change ☐ Creativity
Examples	☐ Flexible Manufacturing ☐ Computerized Services ☐ New Technologies	☐ Statistical Process Control ☐ Quality Teams and Councils ☐ Cost Of Quality	☐ Taking Initiative ☐ Team Leadership Skills ☐ Cultural Change

Since 1982, The Achieve Group and our U.S. associate, Zenger-Miller, have been studying service/quality improvement processes in use throughout the world. We have found that for every successful service/quality improvement effort, there were two or three that produced disappointing results. We also found that whenever disappointing results or setbacks were experienced, the improvement technology was usually blamed. However, the problem was seldom with the improvement system or technology — most approaches are sound. The failure almost always resulted from a *weak leadership skills* base on which these programs were built. The lead Zenger-Miller researcher at the time, Roland Dumas, concluded, "Many organizations have built '1990 high tech' buildings on 19th century foundations. When the structure [service/quality improvement program] wobbles, they ignore the foundation and rebuild."

One extensive 1988-89 study consisted of surveys of more than 1,000 managers and quality improvement professionals combined with focus group interviews with dozens of them. The results showed that 80 percent of outside training expenditures went for technical training and installing new management systems such as Cost of Quality. Less than 20 percent of the training dollars spent went to developing leadership skills up, down, and across the organization.

However, when participants in the study were asked to identify where most of the blocks to service/quality improvement were, the ratio was almost exactly reversed: 80 percent of the problems were related to management leadership, support, and involvement, and 20 percent were related to technical skills. Dumas says, "We have found repeatedly that there are foundation skills, general leadership and interpersonal, that consistently make or break a quality effort. Through the process of elimination, the problem eventually comes home as a leadership issue. *That systems need to be integrated and led emerges as the long-term lesson.* Introducing new systems and technologies when people don't have the fundamental skills is a prescription for disaster."

FOUNDATION SKILLS FOR
SERVICE/QUALITY IMPROVEMENT

The Service/Quality System contains three skill cylinders critical to effective implementation of the entire effort. Chapters 11 to 13 outline these skill cylinders as well as providing examples and common pitfalls. The outlines are just the tip of the iceberg. Here's a brief overview of these crucial cylinders:

- **Personal Service/Quality Skills** — These essential interpersonal skills determine how effectively everyone in the organization works with each other. Strong personal skills provide the vital lubricant to deal with the high friction caused by an intense drive to higher service/quality. Working with new technologies, strategies, and systems demands skills to work effectively, to communicate clearly, to provide mutual support, to seek and accept help when needed, and to channel emotions.

- **Service/Quality Coaching Skills** — The energy available for service/quality improvement, especially Third Ring enhancements, is determined to a large extent by the atmosphere in the workplace. And that atmosphere is largely determined by the immediate supervisor. Executives can be strongly committed, customers well listened to, and solid improvement plans to implement strategies can be rolling out. But not much will happen if enough employees are turned off by the way their contributions are managed. *All* levels of management need to strengthen their ability to make clear what's expected and to follow up, to praise good performance and encourage new ideas, and to correct behavior problems without belittling people.

- **Service/Quality Team Skills** — It's *impossible* to improve service/quality without extensive use of teams. Task forces, quality teams/councils/circles, steering committees, and implementation groups are used broadly. But bringing people together doesn't make them a team. Research shows that groups are only as effective as their leader is skilled in leading them. Most executives, managers, and supervisors need to increase dramatically their team leadership skills, including promoting group goals, structuring effective team decision making, helping others contribute effectively, and leading meetings smoothly.

UNDERSTANDING "SKILL" DEVELOPMENT

Organizations that want to improve leadership abilities have basically three routes to choose from. The first approach is inspirational. Here organizational members are "turned on" to service/quality improvement through some combination of motivational speakers, videos, books, audio tapes, or newsletters. Strong vision/values along with generous amounts of recognition and celebration help keep enthusiasm and improvement efforts high.

The second approach is based on knowledge or theory. It is the process a vast majority of quality improvement systems/technologies use to try to bring about change. Here, participants are taught the methods to be used, the reasons they work, and what steps are required. This teaching is commonly done through case studies (video, written, and in-person), lectures, group discussion, exercises, computer models, books, application testing, and a host of related teaching methods.

The final behavior-changing route is skill-based. Here the focus is on behavior. In this case, participants are (1) introduced to a set of "key actions," (2) shown examples (usually on video) of the skill being used, (3) given an opportunity to practice the skill with a real situation they face on their job, and (4) given feedback for reinforcement and improvement.

Most organizations say they want to develop leadership skills but then use a theory- or knowledge-based approach to accomplish this goal. It simply doesn't work. No amount of traveling on the wrong road will get you to the right destination. And knowledge-based approaches are clearly the wrong road to skill development. Participants can learn *about* leadership skills. They can even get a good idea of what strong personal, coaching, or team leadership looks like. But no matter how exciting, stimulating, challenging, thought-provoking, insightful, well-researched, or well-designed your development program may be, it will not change behavior if it is knowledge-based. Participants may learn which leadership skills need developing and why. But they won't develop the skills or learn how to put them into action. How comfortable would you be on a plane if the pilot had just graduated from a theoretical course but this was his first time actually in a cockpit?

There is a well-researched and proven approach to skill building. It's called behavior modeling. Two training experts writing in *Training* magazine conclude: "The data is overwhelming: Programs that use behavior modeling technology in their design have a better success rate with respect to transfer of skills to the workplace." Behavior modeling has at its heart the four-step process described above as the third approach to changing leadership. It's simple and it works.

BUILDING A FIRM SKILL FOUNDATION

Following are the building blocks to effective long-term skill-development efforts. For more details, see *The VIP Strategy* and *The VIP Leadership Action Planner* (Clemmer and McNeil, Key Porter Books).

Make All Training Line-Driven and Delivered

I'm not suggesting you exclude training professionals. On the contrary, *effective* human resource development managers can do much to ensure your training investments are sound. But they can't "own" the process. When that happens, training becomes a series of classroom experiences unconnected to your organization's real world. Unless and until you, your managers, and your supervisors practice what your training programs teach, you may as well not waste everyone's time and the organization's money. In far too many organizations, leadership skills, well developed in the classroom, are counteracted by inconsistent executive and management behavior. (In fact, that kind of futile effort only makes participants even more cynical about management's hypocrisy.)

The best way to keep training relevant is to have managers deliver it. A growing number of organizations are taking this approach, often under the guidance of their training and development professionals. The manager as trainer has numerous advantages:

- Line managers are put on the spot to practice what they preach.
- A much larger number of participants can be included in shorter period of time.
- Teaching pushes managers to master leadership skills.
- The signals that skill development is important are loud and clear.
- Managers are in a much stronger position to provide follow-through and coaching on the job.
- The human resource development group stays close to, and better serves, its internal customers.
- Any useless theory or "nice to know" concepts are quickly cut out by busy managers who have time only for what's relevant and useful tomorrow morning to improve service/quality.

Use Your Training Effort to Communicate Your Vision and Values

Here is yet another reason to have senior-level managers involved in planning and delivering your training. William Cone, manager of professional development for Hughes Aircraft, points out: "Through training your employees you can have a greater degree of confidence that the work will progress through a pattern you designed." In his book, *Managing an Organization*, Theodore Caplan adds another view of the strategic role training can play in the hands of an astute executive: "Because the importance of training is so commonly underestimated, the manager who wants to make a dramatic improvement in organizational effectiveness without challenging the status quo will find a training program a good way to start."

Reach "Critical Mass" to Change Your Culture
It is far better to train everyone in a few core skills than to give them smatterings of disjointed training. The concentration of energy and peer pressure will move the boundaries of "normal" behavior in your organization.

Train Early and Often
Make sure new employees and newly promoted management staff get lots of training as soon as they assume their new positions, when those new habits and values are forming. Shape them now to fit the culture you are trying to mold.

Make Sure Your Training Is Building Bigger Fishtanks
The common goldfish is one of a few species that will grow to fit the environment it is raised in. A small fishbowl keeps the fish living there small. A large tank or fish pond produces much larger fish. The same is true of employees. They will be contained or grow to the size of the environment they live in, the expectations that are set for them, the responsibilities they are given, and the training they are provided with. What's the size of your training fishtank?

Increase Your Training Budgets and Make Them Sacred
Top performers do lots of training in good times *and* bad. If you truly want to change your culture, you need a consistent, integrated skill development process that you will stick with through thick and thin until you've changed behavior patterns throughout your organization. Half-heartedly throwing some money to the training department or running an on-again, off-again development program won't take you very far down the road to high service/quality. And it will *never* put you on the route to strategic culture change.

CHAPTER ELEVEN
Cylinder Five: Personal Skills

*"Businesses in general spend too little time training
and motivating their frontline employees, whom they
treat as the lowest workers on the ladder."*
— "Pul-eeze! Will Somebody Help Me?"
in *Time* magazine

Employees hold the balance of power when it comes to delivering high service/quality. That's not to say they are responsible for it. Ultimately management — through its vision, values, strategies, systems, and support — is responsible. But employees make the thousands of small decisions that put those grains of sand on the mediocre or outstanding sides of your organization's service/ quality scale. That's especially true of Third Ring service. It can *only* be delivered voluntarily by committed front-line employees. They decide the outcome of each of the moments of truth they alone deliver.

INFLUENCING AND SUPPORTING
FRONT-LINE PERFORMANCE
Two factors particularly determine how employees manage your organization's moments of truth:

- **Organizational Environment** — Your organization's "cultural norms" (what is seen as normal or desirable behavior by the majority of people) play a major role in determining whether employees will improve service/quality or let it deteriorate.

- **Internal Support** — In top service/quality organizations, management actively serves those on the front delivery or production lines. A major source of this front-line support comes from the use of the internal customer-supplier relationship chain. This simple concept can set off a powerful service/quality ripple throughout your organization. John Opel, chairman of the board of IBM, says: "Everyone in IBM has customers, either inside or outside the company, who use the output of his or her job. Only if each person strives for and achieves defect-free work can we reach our objective of superior quality."

THE INTERNAL CUSTOMER-SUPPLIER CHAIN

The internal customer-supplier chain begins by getting each individual and team in the organization to identify its internal customers. (Leading off this exercise is a great way for management to signal its strong commitment to service/quality.)

Next comes the clarification of those customers' Second Ring expectations. The only way to do this is to *ask them*. For this step, sound customer listening is needed. Don't allow people (especially management) to fall into the "we-know-what-our-customers-need" trap. A critical component of this step is to clarify expectations. A number of internal customers' expectations may not be attainable. But it is vital that internal customers and their suppliers come to some agreement on what the internal standards should be in each relationship, and when the "supplier" will meet them.

The last step is for individuals and teams to develop ways to delight their customers by exceeding their expectations. When delightful service/quality is passed along a strong internal chain, it is delivered to your external customers.

A similar process is repeated for internal suppliers. Each team determines who its internal suppliers are. It then negotiates expectations and standards with them. This chain ultimately works its way back to external suppliers. Top service/quality providers all have rigorous and demanding supplier-management processes in place. These supplier-management systems place more emphasis on service/quality than price. This emphasis constitutes a major change in the purchasing habits of the typical play-one-supplier-off-against-another-and-keep-their-pencils-sharp North American organization.

The internal customer-supplier relationship, as part of the upside-down organization chart, demands that managers view their jobs in a non-traditional way. As the American Society for Quality Control says, "The job of management is to make sure that the links between [internal] customers and suppliers — links that make up the service process — are given top priority." Without that kind of management support, the internal customer-supplier chain pulls apart.

PERSONAL SERVICE/QUALITY SKILLS

The strength of the internal customer-supplier chain depends heavily upon the strength of personal service/quality skills all across the organization. There are two parts to personal service/quality skills. The first set of skills forms the base. These are the technical or job skills that each employee needs to deliver the basic product (First Ring) of their job or function. The second set of skills deals with the personal leadership skills that are used in the Second and Third Rings, whether dealing with internal or external customers.

In the Service/Quality System, we focus primarily on the personal leadership skills component. That's not to exclude technical skills. Without technical skills, service/quality improvement is impossible. However, to get the most out of their technical abilities, people need strong personal leadership skills.

Personal leadership skills include the ability to communicate effectively, to plan, to negotiate, to resolve issues, to build strong relationships, and to be part of a team. Traditionally, responsibility for managing these functions has rested with management. Employees were paid to do what they were told. In other words, "You're a pair of hired hands. Check your brains at the door in the morning."

But today's complex technologies have transformed even the simplest jobs into more demanding positions. A growing number of employees are their organization's experts in those jobs. And that dramatically changes their role. For one thing, employees must deal with broader organizational and interdepartmental issues, since managers are no longer experts in every process and function. Increasingly, managers must rely on their people for expertise.

Industry Week's executive editor, Perry Pascarella, devotes extensive sections of his book *The New Achievers* to the topic of management-employee participation. He builds a strong case for the role of skill development in making these new approaches work: "Many people are not in the right frame of mind for participation and involvement. In fact, the prospect can be downright frightening, especially if you lack the skills for dealing with others, for prioritizing problems, and solving problems in new ways." Perry says that more than 90 percent of employees say they want to try more participative approaches. But "all this is new for many workers and will amount to nothing if the company does not provide training in problem solving, information gathering and analysis, and functioning effectively within a group."

The massive movement to participation, collaboration, and involvement simply can't happen without solid teamwork. Although a team's effectiveness is most heavily dependent upon the skills of its leader, building a strong team out of weak individuals is like pushing a large rock up a steep hill. It can be done, but it's hard work. Developing strong personal service/quality skills within each team member not only teaches everyone how to contribute to the team's effectiveness but also gives team members the confidence to contribute effectively. When strong team members are led by an equally skilled team leader, the gains are breathtaking.

A key cluster in the personal skills set is what John Kotter calls "relational." As chair of the Organizational Behavior and Human Resources Management Area at the Harvard Business School, Kotter has spent years studying how managers, professionals, and front-line performers get things done through working with others. His sixth book, *Power and Influence*, devotes a chapter to "overcoming resistance and gaining cooperation without formal authority." As Kotter explains, these skills are often overlooked: "Over the years, I have encountered literally hundreds of examples of capable people underestimating, to their detriment and the detriment of their organizations, how much others they depended on in lateral relationships would resist cooperating with them on something or how able they would be to resist."

How are your relational skills? *How do you know?* Have you asked your internal customers lately? What are you doing to strengthen these skills? And how about your employees'?

UNDERSTANDING PERSONAL SERVICE/QUALITY SKILLS

A series of smaller skill areas make up this skill cylinder. In Achieve's Service/Quality Culture Readiness Audit, these are grouped within clusters of related skills. As you read through the clusters, rate on a scale of 0 to 100 how close these outlines come to describing your own, your managers', and especially your employees' behavior:

First Cluster: Works Effectively
- uses all available resources to get the job done
- knows the expected results of each new task
- assembles necessary materials before starting a task or task segment
- accepts change and helps new procedures work smoothly

Second Cluster: Communicates Clearly; Helps Others Do the Same
- helps others — especially the quiet ones — speak up at meetings
- provides facts and ideas at meetings
- helps keep meetings focused on the topic and purpose
- asks others for their reactions to the information given

Third Cluster: Provides Positive Mutual Support
- lets others know when they've done a good job

- makes people feel good about their work
- shows interest in the ideas and opinions of others
- shares ideas with others

Fourth Cluster: Seeks and Accepts Help When Needed
- asks for help as soon as he or she needs it
- allows others to help get the job done better
- keeps others informed of what's going on
- lets others know about problems and conflicts early on

Fifth Cluster: Constructively Channels Emotion
- keeps control of own anger and disappointment
- avoids letting own emotion get in the way of reaching results on the job
- deals with negative situations in a positive way

In addition to these five clusters of skills, two clusters of customer and work process skills complete this cylinder. Both these additional skill clusters overlap with, but also lay the foundation for, the Team Skills cylinder (Chapter 13).

The customer skills cluster helps managers and employees develop their ability to (1) clarify customer expectations and to (2) resolve customer dissatisfaction when things get off-track and expectations aren't met.

The work process cluster includes such nuts and bolts as (1) solving quality problems, (2) tools and techniques for solving quality problems, as well as (3) participating in service/quality problem-solving sessions. Also included are the skills and techniques of (4) analyzing work processes to find opportunities for improvement.

PERSONAL SERVICE/QUALITY SKILLS IN ACTION
Following are a few examples of some of the skills of this cylinder in use. As we discussed in the last chapter, however, skill development is more than just knowing what the skill looks like. Skills are developed primarily through practice and feedback.

- A division of Northern Telecom, the major data communications manufacturer, found that front-line employees who received training in personal leadership skills acted more independently and took up far less of their supervisors' time. For example, by learning how to give each other direct feedback, employees resolved issues and differences between themselves, rather than gossiping, bickering, or tattling to management. Observed a delighted manager, "They do a better job, feel better about themselves, and communications have opened up considerably."

- A large hospital used personal leadership skills development to get employees more involved in problem solving and decision making. The effort improved service/quality in two ways: first, it sent a tangible signal on the expanding role and responsibilities employees were to have; second, it gave employees the interpersonal skills they needed to work together more effectively.

- The University of Manitoba uses local actors to fake symptoms so that medical students can practice and be rated on their bedside manner. This training is part of the medical school trend to teach doctors how to treat patients as human beings, not just organisms to be repaired.

- By building her personal leadership skills, an order analyst at NCR Comten was better able to coordinate the entire ordering process. With her newly found confidence, she organized a meeting with her peers from seven departments. Among other things, they decided to circulate information about the availability of parts before the shortages showed up in the process. As a result of this and other initiatives, there is a new willingness to work together as a team.

- As a result of a personal leadership skills program delivered by managers to telephone operators of Bell Canada, service levels improved, and so did morale. Pilot results were so encouraging that the program was rapidly expanded. "We

find the operators now feel more valuable as employees,"
explains the operations manager. "And the managers leading the training sessions have also learned a great deal about
communicating with their staff."

- As part of a long-term drive to increase teamwork for higher
service and productivity, a small telephone company built
the personal leadership skills of project clerks, coordinators,
and clerical staff. As a result, these "non-leaders" began
taking leadership action. They took the initiative to improve
what they could in their jobs and with those on their team.
The impact on team effectiveness was summed up by a
manager: "Team efficiency increases greatly if members
have the right kind of skills to be team players."

- A large municipality found that employees who had partici-
pated in a personal leadership skills program were more
willing to take on new work. They also organized their work
more effectively, had better listening skills, and were eager
to discuss suggestions for improvement.

- The transport and work equipment department of Ontario
Hydro was able to meet sharply increased demands for its
internal service by developing all employees' personal leadership skills. Understanding, communication, and cooperation among various functions in the department improved
significantly. Comments the department manager, "Our
mechanics, accountants, and engineers can now talk to one
another. We couldn't have handled our increased workload
without increasing staff if we hadn't developed those skills."

- The Canadian division of the Japanese multinational Mat-
sushita Electric (Panasonic) used personal leadership skills
development to strengthen its Total Quality Control process. It found that employees were better able to participate
in meetings, resolve issues with others, get their points
across, give feedback, and work as team players.

COMMON TRAPS TO DEVELOPING PERSONAL SKILLS

Knowing vs. Doing
Don't assume that employees have the operational and interpersonal skills needed to enhance service/quality once they understand what needs to be done. Many solid improvement efforts have been badly weakened by a skills foundation that was not firm. Inspiration and knowledge are vital, but they are not the whole equation.

One-Day-Workshop Wonders
A firm, lasting skill-development foundation is not built in a day or two. Sustained behavioral change comes from repetition, practice, and feedback, all supported by strong management follow-through. This is not the stuff of quick fixes and miracle cures. It takes at least six to eight personal skill-building sessions before behavior begins to shift.

Misguided Mentoring
Be very careful about turning training and orientation of new employees over to the veterans in those jobs. Your new employees may not be learning the habits and practices you want to see developed.

Management Duplicity
You can't put training in place to "fix the front line" and then do nothing about management's weak leadership skills. Not only is this dishonest but it's also wasteful. People just aren't that stupid. If they see that supervisors, managers, and executives are not practicing the skills and techniques the employees are being taught, they'll get the message: "Be a good little student, jump through the hoops, get your nice diploma, put the books back on the shelf . . . and get back to the real world."

166

CHAPTER TWELVE
Cylinder Six: Coaching Skills

"Coaching isn't an addition to a manager's job; it's an integral part of it."

—George Odiorne,
How Managers Make Things Happen

During the eighties, the management landscape changed dramatically. The degree of your service/quality improvement depends largely on how well your organization deals with these changes:

- Employees expect — and in many cases now demand — more participation and involvement. They need to have their hands, heads, and hearts connected in the workplace.
- Front-line performers, particularly knowledge workers, increasingly control your organization's processes. Management supplies the plans, tools, and skill development opportunities, but employees decide how effectively they will all be used.
- Good people will continue to be harder and harder to find. It will be extremely hard to replace your best ones. Your organization's performance will increasingly depend on retaining and motivating your solid performers.
- The accelerating speed of technological change and growing complexity of internal customer-supplier relationships means employees need to become part of management. You can't possibly supervise all the coordinating, checking, mea-

suring, customer listening, system adjusting, problem solving, issue resolving, and communicating that goes on in high performing organizations.

NEW MANAGEMENT METHODS

Obviously, management's role needs to grow and change. As Babe Ruth once said, "Yesterday's home runs won't win tomorrow's ballgames." Management approaches that worked under earlier, far different conditions will not work today.

One of the pivotal positions in today's employee-focused organizations is that of the first-level supervisor. Harvey Miller, co-owner of Quill Corporation, says, "The front-line supervisor is probably the strongest motivating or demotivating element of all." And it's easy to see why. To many employees, their immediate supervisor is "management." Probably more than 90 percent of the contact an average employee has with any manager is with her or his supervisor.

As employees' roles and expectations shift, the front-line supervisors' roles and responsibilities must also evolve. What their role will ultimately be is unclear. Some believe that the whole concept of supervision is as outdated as the quality control inspector's position. They point to impressive results from leaderless groups and self-directed work teams. These show that, when given the latitude and skills, employees are highly effective members of the extended management team.

Supervisors may indeed disappear one day, although most organizations are not ready for that radical a change. However, in many organizations, the supervisor's role has undergone a dramatic change. Peter Drucker says, "No job is going to change more. . . . And few people in the work force are less prepared for the changes. . . . We need a stronger, more confident, more responsive firstline supervisor." What are those changes? Brigham Young University professors Gene Dalton and Paul Thompson's landmark research in career transitions pinpoints the critical supervisory pressure point: "Probably the most fundamental shift that must take place . . . is a change in their relationships with others. . . . For many, this is a difficult and sometimes impossible transition."

FROM CONTROL TO COMMITMENT

So how should a supervisor's relationships with his or her employees change? Harvard Business School professor Richard Walton sees the traditional command-and-control approach inherited from the military and Frederick Taylor giving way to the "commitment strategy" where "control and lateral coordination depend on shared goals, and expertise rather than formal position determines influence." He concludes, "The new breed of supervisors must have a level of interpersonal skill and conceptual ability often lacking in the present supervisory work force." This view is supported by Ernesto Poza in his study of strong U.S. factories: "Their [supervisors'] role in creating more efficient and competitive factories was significant. Whenever I observed one . . . I saw a leader, a trainer, and a team developer — not a driver."

It's not hard to see why coaching skills are so important. Service/quality improvement demands a broad-based collective effort. You and your management team will never do it alone.

That means boosting performance levels and pulling teams together. It means nurturing, developing, and especially empowering employees to take on greater responsibility for delivering Third Ring internal and external service. It means setting new standards of accountability and following through to sustain momentum. It means encouraging and rewarding improvement efforts to maintain high levels of "volunteerism" and energy. It means taking quick and firm corrective action when people or plans get off-track. And it means making sure that individuals and teams get feedback on their performance to maintain the process of continual improvement.

UNDERSTANDING SERVICE/QUALITY
COACHING SKILLS

There are three clusters of service/quality leadership skills in Achieve's Service/Quality Culture Readiness Audit. As you review each one, use that 0-100 rating scale to do two assessments: first assess how well your supervisors as a whole do in these areas, then rate your personal skill levels. Of course, you are the worst person to determine your own level. A far more accurate picture would come from asking that group of internal customers who report to you just how good a coach you really are. Why not start improving your customer listening by asking them for this feedback?

Remember, knowing isn't doing. Assessing and understanding coaching skills is only the first step to building them. But, as Henry Mintzberg of McGill University School of Management concluded from his often-cited research in *The Nature of Managerial Work*: "Leadership, like swimming, cannot be learned by reading about it." To improve or develop a skill, you need to identify the key actions of that skill, see good examples of those key actions, practice them, and then get feedback on your application of them.

The three clusters are as follows:

First Cluster: Makes Service/Quality Standards Clear and Follows Up

- describes clearly what needs to be done
- sets a follow-up time to check on things employees have agreed to do
- follows up on how well earlier problem-solving worked
- works with people having problems to help them improve
- explains fully when things need to be done a certain way

This cluster is at the heart of performance management. A big part of the skills in this cluster have to do with holding someone reporting to you accountable for doing what you've both agreed he or she would do. A theoretically simple and effective way to do this is the MBO (Management by Objectives) process popularized by Peter Drucker decades ago. It is a powerful approach: get agreement on the objectives to be achieved for the next month or quarter, and follow up to make sure they are reached, taking corrective action as necessary. Unfortunately, this approach is much easier to understand than to put into practice — yet another example of the difference between knowing and understanding what needs to be done and being able to do it.

In "Why MBO Fails So Often," Joseph Leonard of Miami University in Oxford, Ohio, says, "Research shows that [its] potential has not been realized and, further, that MBO fails more often than it succeeds." He has found that the primary reason for the failure of this sound approach is, once again, problems with implementation. Specifically, managers often lack the coaching *skills* (not knowledge or will) to make MBO approaches work. One of the most crucial skills is giving effective feedback. Leonard says: "Continuous feedback is a prerequisite to making the MBO process work. Face-to-face communication provides the most effective feedback."

Feedback is a fundamental element of good coaching. And yet most employees get only small doses of it. Gary Jonas, chairman of University Research Corporation, is right on with this remark: "I'm still waiting for an employee to complain that he or she has received too much feedback from his supervisor." In *The New Achievers,* Perry Pascarella writes: "Numerous studies in recent years have shown that workers want recognition for their skills and accomplishments, feedback that tells them when they have accomplished something that someone else values, some 'say' in the decisions that affect their work, and the opportunity to develop new skills or acquire new knowledge." The feedback most employees get is inconsistent and often of the "gotcha" variety. How strong are your performance management and feedback skills? *How do you know?*

Second Cluster: Praises Good Performance; Open to New Ideas
* expresses appreciation for the work employees do well
* notices the good things employees do
* receives suggestions from employees in a positive way
* asks for employee suggestions on how to solve problems
* makes employees feel good about their accomplishments and contributions to the organization

171

"Open to new ideas." Every manager in existence not only mouths the importance of this but claims he or she is actually looking for better ways to do things. However, as with many management platitudes, the saying doesn't match the doing.

Probably the most often-repeated management cliché in existence is "our people are our most important resource." Funny way to treat such a "precious" resource. The second most repeated phrase is some variation on the importance and primacy of customers. ("Our customers pay our salaries," or "The customer is Number One.") Funny way to treat the "boss."

And no doubt the third most worn-out management declaration is that good old standby, "the open-door policy." Every manager in the Western world stands up and boldly swears allegiance to it. "My door is always open," he or she proclaims. And maybe it is. But beyond many of those open doors sit managers with closed minds. Their words say one thing, their *actions* say, "If I want any of your bright ideas I'll give them to you." A manager who behaves as though the best ideas come from managers, specialists, and professionals has no place in an organization that's serious about service/quality improvement. The same goes for the many dishonest managers who ask for ideas (through suggestion systems, surveys, meetings, speeches, and the like) and then do nothing with them. Many of these characters don't even have the courage to tell their people what they plan to do differently as a result of the feedback or input they said was so important. Often that's because the answer is simple — they will do nothing.

The Essence of Coaching

> *"The main thing is getting people to play. When you think it's your system that's winning, you're in for a big surprise. It's those players' efforts."*
> —Bum Phillips, coach, New Orleans Saints

The very notion of coaching employees to higher performance levels is heretical to many managers. Raised in the command-

and-control days, many of these "two-by-four managers" believe that getting employees to do a better job means using rules, directives, power, and manipulation, and, when "they just won't do as they're told," heavy amounts of discipline and punishment — as if they were dealing with a bunch of spoiled three-year-olds.

Thankfully, that archaic view is falling out of favor. The supervisor or manager who nurtures and develops his or her people to higher performance levels is proving to be much more effective in the long run. In other words, he or she is a good coach rather than the boss. In their book, *A Passion for Excellence*, Nancy Austin and Tom Peters describe management's emerging coaching role: "Coaching is the process of enabling others to act, of building on their strengths. . . . To coach is to facilitate, which literally means 'to make easy' — not less demanding, less exciting or less intense, but less discouraging, less bound up with excessive controls. . . . Coaching is face-to-face leadership that pulls together people, . . . encourages them to step up to responsibility and continued achievement, and treats them as full-scale partners and contributors. . . . Every coach, at every level, is above all a value-shaper. . . . Perhaps surprisingly, the more elbow room a company grants to its people, the more important on-the-job coaching becomes."

Nurturing and developing others is at the heart of coaching. Patricia Carrigan, a GM plant manager, sounds the alarm: "We have to get people excited about using their talents or we'll end up going down the tube together." Part of that effort involves helping people to take more initiative and responsibility to improve service/quality. In effect, to make them leaders, regardless of their formal position. Consumer advocate Ralph Nader says that "the function of leadership is to produce more leaders, not more followers." To manage your organization's thousands of daily moments of truth, you must have an army of committed, turned-on "employee-leaders." There is no way for management to manage it all alone.

The Manager as Chief Cheerleader

Recognition and celebration is such a key element in every top service/quality organization that it has its own cylinder (Chapter 15). Tom Peters says simply, "Celebrate what you want more of." The use of recognition, encouragement, and positive feedback is so fundamental to effective coaching that *without it there is no coaching.* Period.

Ken Blanchard devoted a large section of *The One-Minute Manager* to "catching people doing things right." He finds that recognition is at the heart of leading others effectively. But once again we run into the knowing-isn't-doing trap. It's a rare manager who won't agree that recognition and encouragement are critical elements of his or her job. But painfully few of those good intentions are translated into daily actions. As Blanchard says, "Good thoughts in your head not delivered don't mean squat."

There are a number of reasons that managers at all levels do such an abysmal job of recognizing and encouraging their people. The biggest reason of all is *they're not sure how.* It is, yet again, a skill issue.

Managers' lack of comfort with "catching people doing things right" is masked in a variety of ways. Charles Garfield's nineteen-year research into the characteristics of more than 400 peak performers identifies recognition as a crucial element of how those at the top of every field of endeavor work with others to support their efforts. He explodes a popular excuse made by those managers who give much less recognition than the best ones do: "Want to ruin a team? Want to ruin an organization? Set up this kind of value system: the mature professional doesn't need positive feedback. That's why we're paying you. We don't have to tell you you're doing well, we expect it. However, if you make an error, eighteen copies of an essential reprimand memo go to all levels of management. Your mother gets a copy, your first grade teacher gets a copy. In fact, we drop them from a blimp over your neighborhood. . . . You can't destroy an organization better than that."

Without lots of recognition, celebration, and encouragement, energy will fade, and your improvement journey will grind to a halt. You and your managers need skill development to increase your recognition-giving confidence and competence as well as getting the habit. *Are you developing those skills?*

Third Cluster: Corrects Behavior Without Belittling People

- focuses on specific problem behavior rather than calling names or attacking personally
- prepares and thinks through what to cover in problem-solving discussions with an employee
- remains calm when initiating problem-solving discussions with employees

Many traditional managers see the world as black and white when it comes to dealing with employees who are off-track. On the one hand, they think they can be tough and hard-nosed and maintain high levels of platoon-sergeant discipline. Public ridicule, harsh punishment, and take-no-guff approaches characterize this world. The alternative, traditional managers believe, is the "country club" style of management. This approach is more concerned with relationships and "love thy neighbor" than with getting the job done. It's a soft, easy-going environment where customers and employees are treated like kings — and where performance slips. Where seldom is heard a negative word — and things fall through the cracks. Country-club management is unproductive and will eventually kill any organization, argue traditional managers. And they are right. Those kinds of unbalanced organizations do struggle. "See," retorts the traditional manager, "that's why I have to use my trusty two-by-four. It may not be pretty, but it gets the job done. After all, business is business. Management is not a popularity contest."

That either/or view of correcting behavior or performance problems is a cop-out. The most effective organizations are filled with managers who have mastered the skill of holding people accountable to tough, uncompromising standards or goals while maintaining their employees' self-esteem.

175

Effective service/quality coaches make clear what's expected and follow up. They emphasize the positive and look for ways to recognize and reward the behavior they want more of. Good coaches draw out and act on other people's improvement ideas. And when things get off-track, as they inevitably will, strong coaches know how to step on toes without messing up anybody's shoeshine.

All this requires skills. Skills that don't seem to be present naturally. *How are your skills?*

SERVICE/QUALITY COACHING SKILLS IN ACTION

Following are examples of managers practicing their service/quality coaching skills:

- Through vastly improved coaching skills, Ottawa's OC Transpo, a large urban transit organization, was able to reduce grievances by 40 percent and arbitration cases from seventeen to zero over a two-year period. As a result of a dramatically improved internal environment, customer service measurements also improved.

- Toronto's York University found that its managers were either jumping too hard on employees' performance problems or letting situations drag on until it was too late to resolve them. Both extremes damaged service/quality levels. By improving coaching skills, managers learned how to deal more effectively with their employees' performance problems. Managers' own performance expectations are now linked to the skills they've developed.

- After a Calgary oil company's managers developed their coaching skills, it was noted that they were working out problems with employees earlier. They also offered reinforcement more effectively to employees and to each other.

- When a head nurse at Toronto East General and Orthopaedic Hospital developed her coaching skills, patient satisfaction ratings increased. Also, staff turnover decreased, resulting in a more fully staffed and stable group. "Before I improved these skills, I'd become upset, lose my cool, and jump on people," reflected the head nurse. "I have now learned how to better convey my points and concerns to the staff."

- A large health center found that improving management's coaching skills reduced absenteeism, which in turn improved service by ensuring more consistent availability of qualified staff.
- An international packaging and printing company trains middle and senior managers to deliver their coaching skills development program to first-level supervisors. "We look for high-potential fast-track managers, regarding this as an important developmental tool for them," says the program's coordinator. Results have been better teamwork among supervisors and with their managers. The culture is now shifting from orders, rules, and regulations to participation, reinforcement, and commitment.
- Many top service/quality providers, such as Bell Cellular, are strengthening their coaching by adding sections to performance reviews like: "Was this person involved in the service/quality improvement effort? Did he foster and promote it? Did she set objectives? Were these objectives accomplished?"

COMMON PITFALLS AND TRAPS TO DEVELOPING COACHING SKILLS

Confusing "What" and "How"

Because this trap snares so many organizations wanting to develop their skills, it bears repeating: don't confuse inspiration and knowledge with skills. Even if your supervisors, managers, and executives want to provide better coaching and know what it looks like, this doesn't mean they can deliver it. Skill building demands a development process that provides how-to steps and relevant models or examples with plenty of practice and feedback.

The Experience Assumption
Too often it's assumed that supervisors and managers already
have coaching skills simply because they have managerial experience. Using ineffective approaches many times doesn't lead to
higher service/quality. As the legendary Green Bay Packers
coach Vince Lombardi once said, "Practice does not make perfect. Only perfect practice makes perfect." Make sure you and
your managers are practicing the right things.

Underdevelopment
Many organizations throw a few one-day-wonder workshops at
their service/quality performance coaches. The effect is usually
about as high as the investment made. Sometimes it's better to
do nothing than to provide weak development experiences in
small doses.

Cutting Out the Coaches
Don't fail to involve your front-line supervisors/managers in
planning and delivering your service/quality improvement strategies. Since service/quality coaching is vital to harnessing the
vast energy available for improvement, this group's involvement
and commitment is critical to your success.

Failing to Coach the Coaches
Research overwhelmingly shows that not following through with
on-the-job coaching after skill-development sessions can result in
failure rates as high as *87 percent* at applying the new skills to the
job. So who's coaching your front-line coaches? If you don't train,
hold accountable, and reinforce your executives and managers
who provide this crucial support, only a small amount of your
development investments will take. Just as your moments of
truth are only as strong as the weakest link in your internal
customer-supplier chain, the quality of the coaching your employees receive is only as strong as your executive-to-supervisor
coaching chain.

Executives Not Leading by Example

This is the single biggest reason coaching skills are not developed throughout an organization. Ensure that your executives practice the coaching skills preached by your development program. Supervisors and managers will imitate those at the top. If merely paying lip service to coaching skills got an executive to the top, why would his or her management staff give it much more attention? If executives are "too busy" to participate in developing their service/quality coaching skills, don't waste everyone else's time. Drop the whole skill development program and prepare to slow or even abandon your service/quality improvement journey.

CHAPTER THIRTEEN
Cylinder Seven: Team Skills

"We know we need better teamwork; the question is how to achieve it. The usual method is exhortation. But this approach has failed us time and time again."
— Robert Daniell, CEO, United Technologies Corp.

Teamwork is at the very center of outstanding service/quality. Study after study confirms that top performing organizations use a great number and variety of small groups to develop innovative solutions to service/quality problems, to build commitment to improvement, to communicate more effectively up, down, and across the organization, to draw out the full contributions of large numbers of people, to guide and direct the service/quality journey, and much more.

The path to stronger teamwork is a difficult one, but the terrain should look familiar by now. Just as putting together a winning professional sports team involves pulling a number of elements together, a lot of ingredients go into successful teamwork. How good are the recruits you're putting on the team? Is there a well-developed game plan? How well is it understood? How strong is the commitment to the plan? What kind of environment is the team operating in? Are systems aligned to support winning or to provide bureaucratic controls for management?

ONE MORE TIME: TEAM SKILLS PROVIDE
A FIRM FOUNDATION

One of the major ingredients in strong teams is the *strength of the leaders*. Back in the sixties, Norman Maier of the University of Michigan did some groundbreaking research on the factors contributing to group performance. After dozens of experiments with ineffective and effective groups, with strong and weak teams, and with creative and less creative groups, he concluded that *the primary determinant of the team's success was the skill of the person leading it*. This finding jibes with more current research undertaken by Janice Klein from Harvard Business School and Pamela Posey from the University of Vermont. They discovered that "teams left to run their own shows often lacked direction. Team members didn't have the skills to solve many of the technical problems that arose and found it hard to get functional support. Many team members also balked at evaluating and disciplining their peers. At first the problems were ascribed to inexperience. But as time went on and teams matured, managers and workers had to admit that the old adage still holds, 'Every team needs a coach.' "

We continually find that the extent to which managers see and capitalize on opportunities to bring teams together is in direct proportion to their degree of team skills. When managers can confidently reach for their team-leading tools and techniques to rally people around a problem or plan, they do so often because it works so incredibly well. As Koichi Tsukamoto, president of Wascoal Corporation in Japan, says, "One step by 100 persons is better than 100 steps by one person."

But when their team skills are weak, managers resist the group approach. Meetings, which are frequent and well used in most top service/quality organizations, are avoided. As one frustrated manager put it coming out of yet another marathon meeting, "Perhaps hell is nothing more than an enormous conference of those who, with little or nothing to say, take an eternity to say it."

In the traditional (generally struggling) organization, "heroic management" reigns supreme as employees stand by and watch the weak manager fight all the fires alone. (Ironically, many weak team leaders believe that frequent meetings are a sign of weak management!) Solutions to problems are initiated by management — as are the rescue efforts, because employees, on whom the plans depend for success, never owned them in the first place.

I'll never forget a meeting I had with the general manager of a mid-sized computer company. He was extremely frustrated because his many attempts to bring his senior management group and their management groups together into a solid team had failed. He recounted all that he had done: wilderness retreats, team-building exercises, restructuring the organization around decentralized groups. "We even wrote a manual on the need for teamwork and how to make it happen," he lamented. But teamwork wasn't happening. Further investigation revealed the reason: the general manager and his managers knew the whys and wherefores of team leadership — they could almost wax poetic on the virtues of group dynamics — but they didn't have the *skills* to put their good intentions into action. And since they didn't see the need to go through the time-consuming process of developing those skills, they didn't. And the teams didn't come together any better over the next year — about the time the general manager was fired.

Service/quality coaching and team skills are inextricably linked. You really can't have one without the other. In *Managing for Excellence*, David Bradford and Allan Cohen explain one way the two skill areas merge: "At the same time that the manager works to develop management responsibility in subordinates, he or she must develop the subordinate's ability to share management of the unit's performance." And that happens most effectively by pulling individuals together into a cohesive team. But, they warn, "neither willingness to accept responsibility nor ability to do so are automatic and instant." In other words, everyone can benefit from skill development. Because skill development lays such a firm foundation for the entire service/

quality improvement effort, these three cylinders are often the starting point.

DEVELOPING EFFECTIVE TEAM SKILLS MEANS REDEFINING MANAGEMENT ROLES

Just as we saw in the Coaching cylinder, team skills will be effective only if aspiring managers rethink and redefine their traditional command-and-control role. It is so obvious, but managers seem to need constant reminding: *You can't manage (command, demand, structure, order, control) your way to teamwork. You can only lead a group of people to pull together as a team.*

Pulling a team together requires a leader who can take a less directing, more facilitative approach. The manager must move out of the spotlight and empower and assist the group to take over. The words of Chinese philosopher Lao-tzu express the kind of leadership that makes top performing teams effective: "When the best leader's work is done, the people say, 'We did this ourselves.' "

The idea of turning over power and credit to the team is threatening to many traditional managers. That's at least one of the major reasons (right up there with lack of skills) that so many managers do such a bad job of leading groups. In *Peak Performers*, psychologist and performance researcher Charles Garfield writes, "The five most misunderstood letters in the center of that word — power — call for a clear understanding of what 'empowerment' means. It does not mean giving away your strength to someone else like Samson to the Philistines. On the contrary, peak performers discover time and again that releasing the power in others, whether in co-workers or customers, benefits them in the long run. In developing, rewarding, and recognizing those around them, they are simply allowing the human assets with which they work to appreciate in value. The more they empower, the more they can achieve, and the more successful the whole enterprise becomes."

183

UNDERSTANDING SERVICE/QUALITY TEAM SKILLS

Again drawing from Achieve's Service/Quality Readiness Audit, following are the four main clusters of skills found within the Team Skills cylinder. Each of these clusters represents a series of related skills that might take from four to eight or more practice sessions to strengthen.

As you review each cluster, again use the 0-100 rating scale to assess how effective your organization's team leaders are in that skill area. Then go back and rate yourself, even though you are not the best person to rate your own skills. Go ahead. Ask your internal team customers (people in the groups you lead) to give you feedback on this critical service/quality improvement skill.

First Cluster: Promotes Committed Action on Group Goals

- makes certain that solutions are agreed upon by the group
- sets priorities and schedules action steps
- encourages discussion about innovative solutions to problems

Getting a group of diverse people with conflicting interests and varied backgrounds to pull together is a big part of what team skills are all about. Any manager can get a group of people to consent, especially if they report to him or her. But it takes a skilled *leader* to get a group to truly be *committed*. Winston Churchill put it this way: "Parliament can compel people to obey or to submit, but it cannot compel them to agree." Strong team leaders get groups to agree to work together to put the *group's* plans into action.

A fundamental group goal that the team leader must get everyone committed to if the improvement journey is to be successful is *focusing their team on quality*. Team members need to know "what does quality mean to me?" and "how does it affect my job?" Everyone must be convinced that improvement is worth the effort, especially if this direction is new or your organization has a history of changing directions or making bold but empty declarations.

Weak Team Skills: Uncertainty and Participative Games
Many team leaders leave their groups hanging at the end of a meeting. Consensus, commitment, and even action are left in a state of suspended animation. Team members wander out unclear what's to happen next. As each then goes off to do his or her own thing, subsequent meetings and firefighting actions are needed. Chris Argyis, of the Harvard Graduate School of Education, describes this all-too-familiar situation and one of the main reasons for it: "Because the executives [trying to avoid interpersonal problems] don't say what they really mean or test the assumptions they really hold, their skills inhibit a resolution of the important intellectual issues. . . . Thus the meetings end with only lists and no decisions. . . . People's tendency to avoid conflict, to duck tough issues, becomes institutionalized and leads to a culture that can't tolerate straight talk." Sounding familiar?

As participative management has become more popular in recent years, some astute managers have decided that they had better play the game to get in on "the team stuff" and all its benefits. And that's been their undoing — playing the participative game. These manipulative managers see participative management as one more lever to be pulled, another string to be yanked. They put on a participative act, unsupported by personal development of team skills or habits. They might, for example, bring people together to "decide" on a course of action that they have already set. The transparency of this kind of "participation" soon becomes evident to all. So as the manager pretends participation, his or her group members pretend commitment.

Second Cluster: Structures Effective Team Decision Making
- sets criteria to select topics for group problem-solving sessions
- makes sure that an objective problem-solving statement is written down before moving ahead

- makes suggestions to the group about methods to approach problems
- gets agreement on ways to monitor progress and evaluate outcomes

The main function of service/quality improvement teams is to identify and solve problems that inhibit higher performance. Yet in many organizations, team members and their leaders get only little or useless training. With little training, teams often plunge boldly in to develop the right solutions to the wrong problems. And the approach they use is to jump in with both feet, fur flying, hoping to emerge with a solution. As Hungarian mathematician George Polya noted, "Success in solving the problem depends on choosing the right aspect, on attacking the fortress from its accessible side." Too many groups attack problems they don't fully understand from whatever angle they happen to be facing.

The "trained" team leaders are too often given a process that is long and cumbersome. It may work well with Lone Ranger engineers solving complex technological problems, but it can easily tie a group of front-line problem solvers up in knots.

That's not to say that problem-solving or problem-prevention (like process control) approaches need to be simple. What's critical is that whatever process is used, it must be clearly understood by everyone involved and geared to the dynamics of people working in groups. Most approaches are neither.

Effective problem solving brings us back to the other three skill clusters in this cylinder. If the group leader is weak in those other skill areas, even a strong, well-understood problem-solving process will falter.

There are three primary reasons employees need to be heavily involved in problem solving all across your organization. First, they are the experts in the jobs and processes that most directly affect your service/quality levels. Their insights into and understanding of what does and doesn't work are far greater than those of most managers and outside experts. Second, employee involvement is the number-one way to foster commitment to your organization and its goals. Today, employees want much more out of their jobs than just a paycheque. They want to make a real contribution to a meaningful cause (such as service/quality improvement). In *The Plateauing Trap*, Judith Bardwick writes, "Nothing creates more self-respect among employees than being included in the process of making decisions." Third, your employees are the ones who will implement the solutions decided upon, especially those involving Third Ring enhancements. As we said in earlier chapters, if they help plan the battle, they won't battle the plan.

Third Cluster: Helps Others Contribute Effectively
- asks questions that draw others into the discussion
- clarifies what others say to make sure views are understood
- avoids talking too much and does not prevent others from contributing
- listens to others' ideas

Far too many meetings of, say, six people are not meetings of six people at all. Rather, they are meetings of three people with three spectators. So why are they all there? If they all had something to contribute, the leader was responsible for drawing it from them, but failed to do so. If not, why waste their time?

To practice this skill cluster is to be truly a facilitator. Once most managers master these skills, their view of what constitutes strong team leadership is altered forever.

When the group leader is also the participants' manager, there is a delicate balancing act to be performed between facilitating the group discussion and unwittingly issuing management directives. George Odiorne of the University of Massachusetts explains the dilemma: "There's a law of administration which I'd suggest holds true in almost every situation. That is, if the boss presents his solution first and asks for opinions about it, a vote of approval will follow almost every time."

A key to getting everyone to contribute fully is to manage diversity. Harvard's John Kotter explains: "People who have studied decision-making processes have often observed that diversity and interdependence are essential ingredients in fostering original ideas. If there is only one person involved in a decision-making situation (no interdependence), or if the group of individuals involved all think pretty much the same way (no diversity), the breadth of information brought to bear on a problem is almost always narrow in scope. When a number of people are involved, and when they have different perspectives, more information gets into the process often because more conflict develops. The conflict forces people to stop and think and look for ways to resolve it."

Of course, if it's not well managed, conflict can quickly wrench a team apart. Whether conflict helps or hinders the team's effort to improve service/quality depends, to a large extent, upon the team skills of the team leader. Editor and publisher Dagobert Runes puts his finger on one of the keys to managing team diversity and conflict: "Handle people with gloves, but issues, bare-fisted."

Fourth Cluster: Leads Meetings Smoothly
- organizes the way to approach issues at meetings
- keeps the meeting moving
- quickly moves to discourage personal conflict between group members
- waits to state personal views or opinions until others have had a chance to speak

The only explanation is ignorance. Managers just don't know any better, or they would make sweeping changes. In a lot of ways it's like the Cost of (poor) Quality: When you don't know how much waste there really is, you blissfully carry on wasting.

I'm talking about the unbelievable waste of time and energy that is allowed to pass for meetings in so many organizations. If managers were allowed to waste their capital assets the way they waste human ones, heads would roll. Andy Grove, president of the fast-growing high tech firm Intel Corp., puts it into perspective: "It's estimated that the dollar cost of a manager's time, including overhead allotted to it, is around $100 per hour. A meeting attended by ten managers for two hours thus costs the company $2,000. . . . Yet a manager can call a meeting and commit $2,000 worth of managerial resources on a whim. If that meeting is unnecessary or so poorly run it achieves nothing, that's $2,000 wasted."

And too many of those meetings are poorly run. A survey conducted by the New York recruiting firm Robert Half International found that executives considered nearly a third of meetings a waste of time. When you look at how much time you spend in meetings, that's a lot of wasted time! A number of studies put the amount of time managers spend in meetings as high as 40 percent. And with the growing trend to broader participation and involvement in service/quality, not only will managers' meeting time increase but employees' time will rise dramatically as well. Once meetings were considered an interruption of one's work. Today, meetings (formal sessions with agendas, impromptu gatherings with agendas generated on the spot, one-on-one get-togethers, "coffee conferences," and so on) are becoming the job itself. And if a third of those meetings are ineffective, we're talking about a waste of salaries, benefits, and other staff overhead on a grand scale.

Meetings Are a Microcosm of the Culture
Cervantes wrote, "By a small sample we may judge of the whole piece." Meetings are but a small slice of the manager's mini-culture. Taken together, an organization's meetings paint a picture of the whole culture.

Take a look at your meetings. What do they say about your team skills and culture? Who attends them? How do you split the airtime within the group? How much diversity is encouraged? How is conflict handled? What process do you use for problem solving? Do you draw contributions from the whole group? *How do you know?*

SERVICE/QUALITY TEAM SKILLS IN ACTION
- Team skills helped Dow Chemical manage its quality improvement effort more effectively. "Meetings start and finish on time. Everyone participates. Diversity is encouraged but managed in a constructive fashion so it's not

disruptive. Specific assignments with clear completion dates are made and accepted."

- A major manufacturer implemented team skill training from the CEO down to supervisors. The results were improved meeting effectiveness, better teamwork, and improved levels of internal service. Comments the corporate controller: "Our management style is now much more organized with more participation from our engineers."

- CEO Will Barrett and his key executives at Avco Financial Services were trained as instructors in the company's service/quality team skills development program. As part of a multi-year effort that dramatically improved service/quality — and profit levels — every employee became part of a Quality Team led by a trained leader. Barrett reflects on the successful process: "We took a group of managers who had been 'bosses' their entire career and turned them into facilitators. They discovered, through the use of these new skills, what a tremendous wealth of talent we have."

- After developing their team skills, the systems group of the Royal Bank of Canada changed their approach to serve their internal customers better. For years, they would spend a week at a time in a branch reviewing operations and then making recommendations to branch management for improvement. By learning how to organize and lead groups, systems professionals began helping branch staff identify and improve their own operations. Not only did better problem solving result, but also commitment to — and implementation of — solutions improved dramatically.

- A large food-products manufacturer had all management staff from the vice-president of manufacturing to first-level supervisors participate in a team skills development program. The skills formed the base of an extensive quality enhancement drive. They found that improving team skills resulted in more effective meetings within shorter time frames; clearer roles, responsibilities, and action-planning follow-through within quality improvement and management teams; greatly improved communications among different levels of management; and higher degrees of participation and teamwork.

- GM's Oshawa Plastics Plant found that support staff and professionals significantly increased their contributions to improving quality when they developed better team skills. Equipment, tool, and process engineers, office staff, and hourly electrical technicians were shown how to organize and lead groups and to use a step-by-step group problem-solving process.

COMMON PITFALLS AND TRAPS TO DEVELOPING TEAM SKILLS

What the Top Orders the Middle to Do for the Bottom

One of the key factors determining the skills of all management staff is the team leadership skills of senior management. Accustomed to using their technical or management system skills (inner ring), most senior managers' team skills are — to put it gently — rusty. Numerous organizations have proven that developing the skills of executives in this vital area has a profound and lasting impact on service levels.

Confusing Structure and Skills

Don't assume that bringing groups of people together under a team leader produces teamwork. Far too many groups are a loose collection of individuals, not a team. Research indicates that the single greatest factor in producing teamwork is the skill of the team leader. Such skills are seldom inherent in organizations; they need rigorous, systematic development.

Dangerous Assumptions and Shaky Foundations

Far too many strong teams are built on shaky skills. Weak skills are a major cause of the failure of many Corrective Action Teams, Employee Involvement Groups, Service/Quality Task Forces, and Quality Circles.

Reverting Under Pressure

The truest test of teamwork, involvement, and participative management is when the crunch is on. If you and your manage-

191

ment team revert to command-and-control management, your credibility may be shot. That doesn't mean you have to give up your prerogative to make the tough decisions that go against popular opinion. People want you to show that leadership strength — when it's called for. But how you go about it makes all the difference in the world. As much as possible, gather broad input and give people a chance to have their say. Once you've made your decision, reiterate the reasons for it and solicit the support of others.

A Weak Top Management Team

Get your own house in order. It's amazing how many executives run around spouting off about the need for teamwork when their own executive team doesn't pull together. In "Twelve Actions to Build Strong U.S. Factories," Ernesto Poza says, "Top management that works effectively as a team sends strong signals down the organization that there is a commitment to the team concept and a flatter structure." Don't be hypocritical. Your people aren't blind.

CHAPTER FOURTEEN
Cylinder Eight: Systems

*"Early decline and certain death are the fate of
companies whose policies are geared totally and
obsessively to their own convenience at the total expense
of the customer."*
— Ted Levitt, editor, *Harvard Business Review*

This cylinder covers enormous territory. It also plays a major
role in determining whether your service/quality improvement
efforts will pay off or be tangled up in red tape.

The basic issue is simple. For whose convenience is your
organization designed? If you're anything like 90 percent of
North American organizations, your employees and customers
would shout in unison: "You're designed for the convenience of
you and your management team." In other words, you're both
hard to do business with and hard to work for.

But you've said you want to put the upside-down organization
chart into practice to improve service/quality on the front lines.
You've said you believe that managers should serve their internal
customers. You've said customers should define what's in each of
your organization's Three Rings of Perceived Value. You've said
that employees need more support and empowerment to improve service/quality. And you've said sweeping changes may be
needed to rebuild your culture around the customer and those
serving them.

Having said all that, you must now align your systems and controls to support your service/quality improvement drive. At the very least, you need to ensure they aren't getting in the way.

WHERE'S YOUR FOCUS?

Quality guru W. Edwards Deming was not a prophet in his own land. But after the Second World War, he quickly became one in Japan. As the Japanese struggled to rebuild their industrial base and establish world markets for their goods, Deming played a key role in helping them implement the strategy they used to dominate their competitors. One of Japan's highest corporate honors today is the Deming Prize for outstanding quality.

Meanwhile, back in North America, domestic markets were exploding while world markets were expanding. In 1946, North America accounted for half the world's Gross National Product. Just keeping up with demand became the biggest challenge during the fifties, sixties, and into the early seventies. Since North American companies owned most of the world's technology, customers flocked to our shores. In such a heady environment it was hard to fail. We deluded ourselves into thinking we were smarter and faster than the rest of the world.

As revenue growth rocketed upward year by year, Peter Drucker and others turned the attention of executive and business schools toward the development of modern management methods to prevent the phenomenal growth from also driving up costs and reducing profits through inefficiencies. And because well-educated, affordable labor was plentiful, managers looked for ways to squeeze as much efficiency from people as possible. Most companies could pretty much call the shots, picking and choosing who could have the privilege of working for them and under what conditions.

But times have changed. North American managers in both the public and the private sectors no longer have guaranteed revenue growth. And those in the shrinking pool of employees are less grateful for a job. Times have changed, *but many management systems haven't.*

Now in great demand in North America, Deming grows increasingly frustrated with how slow managers here are to update their approaches to compete in today's radically different world: "Western management has too long focused on the end product — get reports on people, productivity, quality, sales, inventory. It is necessary that management shift the focus to management's responsibility for the source of quality and service, namely, design of product and service and of the management systems that turn out the product and service. These systems include people! Management in the Western world [has] for too long been driving the automobile by keeping an eye on the rear view mirror."

Peter Drucker concurs. Many managers took the new systems to extreme command-and-control lengths. And while things were going pretty much their way, it worked. But in today's new world, many of those control systems have moved from an asset to a liability. They are getting in the way. They are like the gills on a fish that has been thrust upon dry land. Organizations must change their systems and controls, or else prepare to face the consequences.

SUPPORTING OR STIFLING THE FRONT LINE?

In order to align systems for service/quality, organizations need first to focus on their customers' needs. Then they must design systems that support those who serve these needs. *Management's needs come third.*

But that rarely happens. As Peter Drucker says, "So much of what we call management consists of making it difficult for people to work." In *The Changing World of the Executive,* he devotes a chapter to managing "the knowledge worker" (which every employee becomes in an intensive service/quality improvement drive): "Perhaps the most important rule — and the one to which few managements pay much attention — is to enable the knowledge worker to do what they are being paid for. Not to be able to do what one is being paid for invariably quenches whatever motivation there is."

So what are you telling your people they're being paid to do? If you're serious about heading down the service/quality road, you're telling them they are being paid to improve the organization's performance. Are your control systems helping or hindering this effort? Karl Albrecht finds that the answer to this question is quite often negative: "Many service problems are caused by nonsensical or irrational policies, procedures, or rules that prevent employees from responding quickly to customers' needs."

RECOVERY, SPONTANEITY, AND THIRD RING SERVICE

As you try to move your front-line people out into the Third Ring, your systems are critical to the success of the effort. Even if you hire the most capable and motivated people, train them and their managers well, and provide plenty of rewards, your management systems and controls could severely cripple their best efforts. You may be sending them out there handcuffed and shackled. *Put a good performer up against a poor service/quality support system and the system will win nine out of ten times*. In many organizations, the service/quality being provided is *in spite of*, not because of, management systems and controls.

In *Service America!*, Karl Albrecht and Ron Zemke report that when British Airways launched their successful Customer First improvement effort, they started with customer listening. The big surprise for BA was the customers' concern about "recovery" and "spontaneity." "Recovery" describes an organization's ability to recover the customer's confidence and loyalty after something goes wrong. BA's Donald Porter explains what's meant by "spontaneity": "Customers were saying, 'We want to know that your front-line people are authorized to think. When a problem comes up that doesn't fit the procedure book, can the service person use some discretion — find a way to jockey the system on the customer's behalf? Or does he or she simply shrug their shoulders and brush the customer off?'"

That raises the issue of autonomy. If you want your front-line people to provide consistent Third Ring service, they need to be given some latitude to do so. The systems and controls need to be user-friendly and supportive. To make it work, you substitute command-and-control with skills and strategies that are developed in concert with your people on the front lines.

TAKE A LOOK AT YOUR KEY SYSTEMS

One of our clients identified 48 operating systems that affected their service/quality. Let's examine some of the common ones:

- **Promotions and Job Assignments** — Who gets the plum jobs? For what kind of behavior? If you answered, "For good performance," what does that mean? Is it making the numbers, being a good bureaucrat, or years of showing up for work on time? Where does service/quality fit into the picture? If it's not a *key* criteria in your promotion and job assignment activities, it's not a value in your organization.

- **Performance Evaluations and Compensation** — If you don't hold people accountable for, and reward them for, service/quality improvement, it won't happen. And make sure managers and support employees (accounting, Management Information System, human resources, etc.) are accountable for their levels of internal service/quality to the front line.

- **Planning Systems** — As objectives and goals are set, ensure that *measurable* service/quality improvements are at the top of the lists. Service/quality improvement must be a key result area for *everyone* in the organization.

- **Technology** — The American Society for Quality Control says, "Automation can help improve quality — or it can be the source of errors, delay, and frustration. Your success will be in direct proportion to your emphasis on quality." Technology can be a potent competitive weapon, depending on how it's used. The PIMS data base led the Strategic Planning Institute to conclude, "A company can improve its relative performance by advancing its technology faster than its competitors or by doing a better job than competitors in coupling technological advances to evolving customer needs." Coupling technology to customer needs is the key here. Make sure that the *first* question asked by *every* group considering technological changes is, "What's the effect on our customers?" Don't let "gee whiz" technology make management's life easier at the expense of your customers or your front-line deliverers.

- **Telephone Systems** — This is one of the most visible and neglected pieces of technology. So long as management's needs are met, upgrading the system or training people to use the current system better is often a low priority. Are you paying a high price for the frustration and chaos caused by telephone problems in your organization? *How do you know?*

- **Invoicing** — Ninety percent of companies have an invoicing system that is not user-friendly. In fact, it may as well be written in a foreign language as far as most customers are concerned. But of course it's convenient for the accounting department.

- **Organizational Structure** — Do your customers need a copy of your organization chart to deal with you? Are they bounced from one department to another? Are you structured around your products and services, around your management system, or around your customers? Do your customers think you're easy to do business with? What would your employees say? Ask them.

- **Feedback and Measurement** — This is a critical area that has its own cylinder (Chapter 17). Feedback and measurement systems focus the organization on those elements management considers the most essential for monitoring. Service/quality becomes real only when it is high on this list.

- **Policies, Procedures, Rules, and Regulations** — Take a long hard look at this area for two critical points: first, are your rules wrapping your front-line people in red tape and inhibiting their performance, and second, what messages are your policies sending about how much you trust your employees and how smart you think they are? How does that affect their "volunteerism"?

- **Memos, Reports, and Proposals** — Someone once said that when an organization gets over a few hundred employees, it's capable of generating enough paperwork to keep everyone busy for a year without any contact with the outside world. Declare war on this white noise. If the paper that's being shoveled around the organization isn't helping to improve service/quality, get rid of it. Who's asking for all this stuff, anyway? I'll bet it's *not* your customers or front-line people.

- **Planning and Budgeting** — As you prepare strategic plans and operational budgets, what role does service/quality improvement play? *All* your plans and budgets should be shaped to exceed your customers' needs. That starts with making sure your front-line staff get what they need to do the job.

TOWARD ALIGNED SYSTEMS

- Quality award winner Xerox Canada's "Leadership through Quality" process aligns performance reviews and promotion practices with customer satisfaction and quality improvement. One of the key factors in deciding promotions is the degree to which the candidate is a service/quality role model.

- When I checked in on my second visit to the Westin Hotel in Calgary, I was asked only to verify and sign the already completed registration slip. Their computer system had all my registration information from my last stay there six months earlier.

- Four Seasons Hotels are going even further. They are installing a computer system to track information on each guest's preferences. This system will allow each hotel in the chain to know whether the guest likes a nonallergenic pillow or prefers a particular kind of tea.

- Bramalea Ltd. computerized all the inspection and service-call reports for its newly constructed homes. Service representatives can now instantly get an update on repair work when customers call to report a problem or check on progress. Says former president Ken Field, "It has really turned into a major source of information and pleasure for customers." The system also allows Bramalea to monitor its various subtrades and identify which people or groups are consistently doing the best and worst work.

- A number of managers are finding that simply asking employees, "What systems hinder high service/quality delivery?" can quickly identify major bureaucratic barriers to improvement.

- GE's Answer Center has a data base of more than 750,000 answers, which its service reps have instant access to when on the phone with a customer. The system also allows the rep to identify the closest "good" dealer. These dealers are rated on their customer satisfaction index. Since many of the calls to the Answer Center result in further purchases, these referrals provide incentive for dealers to keep their customer satisfaction ratings high.

- To avoid the telephone runaround all too common with government and large companies, the Georgia office of Consumer Affairs introduced the Tie Line. Local and incoming 800 number phone lines have a call-bridging capability. When consumers' questions or complaints can't be answered by the Tie Line counselors, they are bridged directly to whomever can best help. The counselor then stays on the line to ensure that the consumer gets the help he or she needs.

- B.C. Tel set up Dumb Rules and Dumb Forms committees with a senior executive on each one. The committees' mandate is to seek and destroy all those bureaucratic rules and forms that are no longer useful but never fade away gracefully on their own.

- Area managers at B.C. Tel have declared that no one will be promoted unless he or she improves his or her customer service.

- The City of Calgary established a one-call system for taxpayers seeking information. Once a call is received, the caller is "escorted" through the system by the counselor taking the call. The counselor ensures that the caller gets to talk to the person who can answer the question or provide the service being sought.

• Xerox Canada revamped its invoicing system after finding out what customers thought would serve their needs better.

• "The biggest waste of time in many companies is reports," declares Chrysler's George Butts. "Everybody's writing reports. They send a copy to Joe, they send a copy to Ray, they send a copy to me. Secretaries wind up spending most of their time filing these dumb pieces of paper. Why do we need those reports? We reduced our reports 25 percent in this company. We're killing all the 'white noise' we can find."

• Federal Express's customer information system tells customers the exact status of a particular package within 30 minutes of the inquiry, or their money is refunded. Fred Smith, chairman and CEO, says, "Most customers understand that problems can occur. What they won't forgive is a lack of information, or having a problem handled poorly."

• By better tuning in to its customers, the City of Ottawa discovered that the existing snow removal notification system was inadequate. The sign directing drivers not to park in the area didn't state when snow removal crews would begin work. Sometimes the operation didn't begin until 24 to 36 hours after the snowfall. By this time, disbelieving drivers had parked their cars on the streets. This situation resulted in delays, towed cars, and angry customers. Working with front-line operators, the snow removal system was revised to mark sections for plowing within a specific 12-hour period. And drivers kept the streets clear. This solution meant fewer disruptions for the city crew, fewer towed cars, fewer angry customers and fewer city councilors to be appeased, and substantial savings.

COMMON PITFALLS AND TRAPS TO ALIGNING SYSTEMS

Rank Has Its Privileges
Executive parking spaces, washrooms, dining rooms, and other perks send elitist messages. These "little extras" carry an enormous cost in lost corporate energy. They convey a traditional organizational hierarchy with executives on top and employees and customers at the bottom. Are they really worth the price?

Responsible But Not Accountable
Telling people that improving service/quality is a key part of their job and then not holding them accountable makes the whole effort look superficial. Ensure that service/quality goals are part of managers' annual objectives and hold them to it. When service/quality goals become formal objectives, they become real.

Bureaucratic Bramblebushes
Unless you prune out old, dysfunctional systems, they will choke off the potential that your newer ones might have to offer. *You must have a process for identifying and changing management systems that hinder rather than help improve service/quality.* The best people to streamline your systems are those using them — if you *really* believe in the upside-down organization chart. Ask them, "What's the dumbest things we do around here?" "What management systems or controls get in the way of delivering high service/quality?"

Creating Turf Warfare
A sure prescription for bureaucratic backbiting and empire-defending is to delegate the task of pruning systems. Removing policies, changing procedures, eliminating reports, reducing requirements, or dropping duties can be extremely threatening. Only senior management can cut through the bafflegab, double speak, and "not my form, you don't" defensiveness.

202

Not Practicing What You Preach

Make sure you're part of the solution, not the problem. Take a long hard look at your own habits. How many reports and memos do you generate or ask for? Get constant feedback on this to keep you honest.

Management-Directed Systems

If it makes your life easier or satisfies your command-and-control urges but inhibits service/quality improvement, you are paying a high price for that convenience or comfort. The effect a system has on your internal and external customers should be your *first* consideration.

CHAPTER FIFTEEN
Cylinder Nine: Reward and Recognition

"The most neglected form of compensation is the six-letter word 'thanks'."

—Robert Townsend,
author and corporate-turnaround specialist

The deceptive thing about having a cylinder for motivation is that it sounds as though there are a few techniques or magic buttons to push that will inspire your people to stellar performance. It isn't so. In fact, motivation is a byproduct of an organization's culture or total environment. Just as a gardener never really grows anything, a manager doesn't motivate anybody. Rather, a gardener starts with the right seed (carrot seeds won't produce tomatoes), gets it started in the right conditions, makes sure it has the best nutrition and growing conditions, pulls out the weeds, protects it from frost, and doesn't keep pulling it up to see how it's doing.

However, assuming that service/quality vision, values, skills, systems, technology, processes, marketing, and other factors are strong, a number of approaches can be used to give an organization that turbo-boost that moves it from good to out-standing performance.

A study by the National Science Foundation concludes, "The key to having workers who are both satisfied and productive is motivation, that is, arousing and maintaining the will to work effectively — having workers who are effective not because they are coerced but because they are committed. Of all the factors which help to create motivated/satisfied workers, the principal one appears to be that effective performance be recognized and rewarded — in whatever terms are meaningful to the individual, be it financial or psychological or both."

It's just more common sense: *what gets rewarded gets repeated.* But again, common sense is not common practice. Managers too often declare they want more service/quality improvement and innovation but instead reward good technomanagers or those who make their numbers. Employees whose energy and commitment are so desperately needed are left wondering what's in it for them.

When the Science Foundation study is compared with another one cited by former McDonald's vice-president Bob Desatnick, it's easy to see why most organizations may have the will but not the corporate energy to improve service/quality: "A recent national poll of thousands of workers asked, 'If you were to improve service quality and productivity, do you believe you would be rewarded accordingly?' Only 22 percent said yes. As a consequence, 75 percent of the workers reported they deliberately withhold extra effort on the job. *Imagine the potential impact on customer service!*"

METHODS OF REWARDING AND RECOGNIZING

There are two basic ways of rewarding and recognizing employees in order to encourage and reinforce the kind of behavior your organization needs to drive it to higher service/quality. The first is financial: how contributions are financially recognized. The second is non-monetary: how people are provided with those all-important psychological pay-offs (their "thanks pay").

Financial Rewards

"We can improve our service by paying more attention, and more money, to the people we hire," declares Alvin Burger, founder of the highly successful pest control company "Bugs" Burger Bug Killers. The debate over the role money plays in motivating people has raged for years and shows little sign of being conclusively settled. What is clear, though, is that the perceived lack of money or undercompensation for doing a job is a demotivator. It is also clear that a remuneration system will improve service/ quality only if it is tied to performance. Zemke and Schaaf report that the National Science Foundation examined 300 studies of productivity, pay, and job satisfaction. They found that motivation, productivity, and job satisfaction are markedly higher when pay is linked to performance. One study they reviewed looked at 400 companies and found that going from "no measurement of work" to a "work measurement and performance feedback system" raised productivity an average of 43 percent! By using both performance feedback and incentives, productivity rose an average of 63.8 percent.

The Science Foundation's work is corroborated by a study of employee views of pay for performance done by the Public Agenda Foundation. They found that almost two-thirds of employees would like to see a better connection between performance and pay. And more than 70 percent felt that *work had deteriorated* because there was no connection between pay and performance.

Top service/quality providers routinely include their employees in bonus programs. These programs may take the form of cash awards, profit sharing, employee stock option plans, and gain sharing (programs such as Scanlon, Rucker, or Improshare split the savings generated from suggestions or productivity gains). As Sony chairman Akio Morita explains, these approaches are one of the reasons Japanese companies have become such formidable competitors: "Sometimes American companies use employees to make money for the management. That's why management gets a great bonus. . . . In Japan we don't pay bonus [only] to the managers. We pay bonus to the employees because if we make a profit, we want to have them enjoy it together with us."

Be Careful of What Performance You're Paying For
If you don't already have a carefully crafted (but simple and easy to understand) compensation system that links pay to individual, group, or organizational performance, you're missing a key piece

206

of the improvement puzzle. But be careful of the kind of performance you reward. As with all operational activities, financial
rewards need to be aligned around the customer's, not management's, needs and priorities. Ron Zemke explains: "Incentives
should help emphasize legitimate customer satisfaction. An incentive program that subordinates an organization's long-term
relationship with the customer to consideration of an individual's
selfish, short-term gain — whether that individual is a frontline
salesperson, a stockholder, or a highly placed executive — is a
dangerous narcotic."

However, paying well and linking pay to performance does not
automatically lead to higher service/quality. There are plenty of
examples of well-paid employees and managers who are not well
motivated. The public sector and large, wealthy companies (such
as utilities and oil companies) have many such people. The
problem is not necessarily with the individuals. Often it is a sign
that management has failed to provide critical non-monetary
incentives. Making this point in the *Wall Street Journal*, Robert
Kelley of Carnegie-Mellon University writes, "High pay does not
equal good service, and, as McDonald's has shown, low pay need
not result in poor service. . . . High-quality service depends on
high-quality management."

Recognition

This is the most inexpensive, easy-to-use motivational technique
available to management. Yet the degree to which this essential
service/quality improvement tool is underused by most otherwise intelligent managers is bewildering. As we work with top
performing organizations and those aspiring to be, the two
groups might as well be on different planets in their approaches
to recognition, celebration, hoopla, and sincere thank-yous.
Comparing the companies highlighted in *In Search of Excellence*
to average — mediocre — organizations, Tom Peters and
Robert Waterman report, "The volume of contrived opportunities for showering pins, buttons, badges, and medals on
people is staggering at McDonald's, Tupperware, IBM, and

many of the other top performers. They actively seek out and pursue endless opportunities to give out rewards."

We all crave appreciation for our contributions. Logically, doing good work should be its own reward. We should not need the approval of others to increase our sense of worth and self-esteem. But we're not creatures of logic. And a vast majority of us tie our self-esteem, and the subsequent motivation to excel further, to the positive strokes we get from others, especially our bosses and peers. George Blomgren, president of Organizational Psychologists, says, "Recognition lets people see themselves in a winning identity role. There's a universal need for recognition and most people are starved for it."

Recognition Types and Approaches

The thousands of ways effective managers recognize solid performance can be broken into three main categories: (1) individual recognition programs; (2) team recognition and celebration; and (3) personal one-on-one "thanks" or "way to go's."

1. Individual Recognition Programs

> *"I'm just a plowhand from Arkansas, but I have learned how to hold a team together. How to lift some men up, how to calm down others, until finally they've got one heartbeat together, a team. There's just three things I'd ever say:*
> *If anything goes bad, I did it.*
> *If anything goes semi-good, then we did it.*
> *If anything goes real good, then you did it.*
> *That's all it takes to get people to win football games for you."*
>
> —Coach Paul "Bear" Bryant

Tom Peters finds that "well-constructed recognition settings provide the single most important opportunity to parade and reinforce the specific kinds of new behavior one hopes others will emulate." Davidow and Uttal found that "companies that provide superior service use a wealth of motivational programs to keep employees' energy flowing. . . . At companies that are fanatic about service, and where employees have frequent, intense contact with customers, managers seem to invent programs constantly."

There are a multitude of ways to recognize contributions to service/quality improvement. By doing so often, consistently, and with fanfare, you clearly signal what kind of behavior is most valued. *This recognition encourages what was rewarded to be repeated.*

But don't wait for people to do things perfectly. As Ken Blanchard suggests, you will get more tries and eventually much better results by at first rewarding people for doing things approximately right. Don't set the standards too high to begin with. As performance improves, you can move the goal posts further away.

Following are just some of the ways individuals can be publicly recognized for their contributions (your own list is limited only by your resourcefulness):

- certificates, citations, and plaques for achieving improvement goals
- employee-of-the-month/week/day for above-average improvement efforts or results
- mention in an internal or customer newsletter story (this is also solid internal/external marketing)
- picture and write-up in local newspaper
- picture and write-up on a bulletin board in a high-traffic area
- special privileges
- honors or awards presented with fanfare by senior management at special events such as celebrations or thank-you banquets
- special meetings with or visits from senior management
- status symbols such as rings, tie or lapel pins, better office, parking space . . .
- a hall of fame for top performers

- public praise
- promotions, title changes, increased responsibilities
- publicly announced raises and bonuses
- a night on the town for the achiever and spouse or friend
- sports or theater tickets
- gift certificates
- company products or services
- catalogue program of prizes "bought" by earning award points
- company-paid vacations
- trips to customer locations
- attendance at, or being featured in, industry or improvement conferences
- special job assignments or project leadership

2. Team Recognition and Celebration

Given the increasing importance of teams, group recognition becomes a vital way to energize the team. Organization development consultant Cathy DeForest, co-author of *Transforming Leadership: From Vision to Results*, explains, "Celebrating provides a way to nourish the spirit of an organization as well as create a moment in time when a glimpse of a transformed organization can be seen and felt. Organizational celebration is a way, a process, of honoring individuals, groups, events, achievements, the common and extraordinary life within an organization in a meaningful, and often festive manner."

Group recognition is often more effective than individual recognition, which can actually reduce teamwork. Charles Garfield outlines how that can happen: "Want to destroy a team? A great way to do it is to reward only the leader. So, he's up there getting a plaque from the CEO and the troops are in the front row planning his assassination." The delicate balancing act is to reward both individual initiative and team efforts without having one overshadow the other. Tom Peters suggests that you "make sure that most of the awards go to teams of people, not individuals."

Here are just a few of the ways teams can be recognized:

210

- a meal is served (or cooked) by senior management to thank the team for achieving a goal, completing a project, exceeding performance levels, etc.
- doughnuts are brought in to congratulate a team for passing a milestone
- special meals in the cafeteria with balloons and streamers, where senior managers pass out accolades, thanks, awards, bonuses, etc.
- charts or posters show group progress
- pictures of successful groups are posted along with articles on their improvement accomplishments
- successful groups present their accomplishments to senior management
- groups are featured at industry or technical conferences
- groups are given trips to suppliers or customers
- plaques, pins, trophies, certificates are handed out to top performing teams
- members receive exclusive T-shirts, pen sets, calculators, etc. with a "winning" slogan or team name
- senior managers drop into team meetings to say thanks for a job well done

3. Personal Thanks or "Way to Go"

"I can live for two months on a good compliment."
—Mark Twain

The legendary steel executive Charles Schwab once said, "I have never seen a man who could do real work except under the stimulus of encouragement and enthusiasm and the approval of the people for whom he is working." As we discussed in the coaching cylinder (Chapter 12), personal recognition and praise are essential. Though the fanfare of public recognition adds sparkle, sincere, well-expressed appreciation given personally by a manager goes a long way as well.

Following are some of the ways to practice the dying skill of personal recognition and thanks:

- personal thank-you notes
- a simple, sincere thanks for successful completion of a task. Electronic Data Systems founder H. Ross Perot advocates rewarding workers "while the sweat is still on their brow."
- following your praise with a congratulatory letter in the employee's file
- a note or special card sent to the employee's house
- returning an employee's memo or report with your hand-written notes complimenting the quality of the work
- personal notes of appreciation included with birthday, anniversary, or Christmas cards
- passing along complimentary comments made by others, especially senior managers
- making a special point to repeat the positive feedback given during your quarterly performance appraisals
- sending a note to the employee's significant other at home complimenting the employee's work and thanking the significant other for his or her support

EXAMPLES OF REWARDING AND RECOGNIZING FOR SERVICE/QUALITY

- The distribution division of the rapidly growing Domino's Pizza holds an annual Olympics to recognize key service/quality skills. Local and regional competitions decide who will go on to compete for $4,000 in cash prizes or lavish vacations. The fourteen areas of competition include veggie slicing (emphasizing quality and quantity of vegetables, sanitation, and appearance), traffic management (routing and coordinating team members and their trucks), dough making and catching, store delivery, driving, loading, and maintenance. As well, accountants compete not only on their bookkeeping skills but also on their interpersonal and phone skills. The judges are the Domino franchisees who are the customers of this group.
- American Express, Campbell Soup, and other top performing organizations have used their annual financial reports as vehicles for recognizing and reinforcing contributions to

service/quality improvement. These reports are usually full of team and individual pictures and short explanations of how the contributions helped to fulfill the organization's strategies and move it toward its improvement and financial goals.

- When commissioner Ron Contino of New York City Sanitation Department was invited to a conference to speak about its award-winning service/quality improvement program, he was offered airfare, expenses, and an honorarium. He asked instead that he be allowed to bring along one of his front-line people to participate in the presentation. As he said, "After all, they initiated the improvements, not me. I was only a cheerleader."
- B.C. Tel recognizes good internal customer service with the People's Choice Awards. These awards are given to the managers identified by employees as the most help to them in their delivery of service/quality (the upside-down organization chart in action). The company also holds "operator appreciation days" for front-line performers and their families.
- In Security Pacific National Bank's Circle of Excellence Awards program, the 300 winners are nominated by branch personnel and supervisors for final judging by headquarters. The winners enjoy an annual gala dinner, a "surprise" night out when the winners are announced in each branch, and special status as a Circle of Excellence member.
- Paul Revere Insurance developed a program based on the number of ideas each of its 125 "Quality Teams" implemented, or their annual financial worth. The awards are: Bronze — ten certified ideas or $10,000 in annual savings; Silver — twenty-five certified ideas or $25,000 in annual savings; Gold — fifty certified ideas or $50,000 in annual savings. The awards consist of gift certificates for $10 to $40, presented by a senior executive. Winners are also highlighted in internal publications and receive bronze, silver, or gold lapel pins. Cash awards go to the Most Valuable

Team, the Most Valuable Player, and other categories at a year-end gala celebration.

- American Express has more than 100 recognition and reward programs. Each year the financial powerhouse holds an annual Great Performers banquet in New York for its top front-line people.
- Campbell Canada developed stickers with a picture of the "Campbell Kid" that said "Thanks For A Souper Job." These were used by managers to show appreciation for good work.
- When a complimentary letter is received at Walt Disney World, the individual's supervisor is notified, it goes into the employee's personnel file, and the letter (as well as the person mentioned) is featured in the company's weekly newsletter.
- POI Office Interiors has a Caught You Caring program. This consists of circulating notes of recognition among managers, employees, etc. saying thank you for reinforcing Third Ring service efforts.
- At The Achieve Group, we asked a particularly happy Client to attend a national meeting. Roses were presented to each member of the Achieve team who stretched to help this Client. The Client added her own accolades. Pictures were taken for our newsletter.
- The City of Calgary provided an Academy Awards-style gala to announce the winners of individual and team service/quality awards. The winners were given plaques and awards along with a hot air balloon ride with mayor Ralph Klein, and their pictures appeared in the local papers.
- A growing number of companies are basing management bonuses on customer satisfaction indices and employee morale levels.
- Construction superintendents vote on the "Tradesman of the Year" at Bramalea Ltd. These non-staff suppliers are then lavished with prizes and recognition.
- *The Service Edge* newsletter reports that Northwest Air-

lines chose 300 of its frequent flying customers as "phantom customers" to hand out tickets to the airline employees they come in contact with. Blue "congratulations" tickets could be redeemed by employees for free plane tickets. Red "sorry" cards didn't need to be reported, but gave feedback when the employee was off-track. Comments vice-president Brent Baskfield, "The important thing is it's non-punitive. The passenger can slip the employee a red card and the manager never knows about it. It's just a poignant reminder. And it involves the customer in improving service."

- As a regional manager for Holiday Inns in Tennessee, Drew Diamond initiated a highly successful non-monetary program. Each guest was given a book of coupons to present to employees who provide outstanding service. As the coupons came in, the manager would seek out and praise the employee for his or her efforts. Within a few months, service ratings jumped while employee absenteeism and tardiness fell.

- A home building firm names streets in its housing developments after top performing employees.

- To make sure no praiseworthy efforts go unnoticed, Transco Energy in Houston has quarterly "bragging sessions." Individuals and teams are invited to stand before management and present their accomplishments.

COMMON REWARD AND RECOGNITION PITFALLS AND TRAPS

Random Recognition
Don't leave recognition to chance; set up a formal, disciplined system for generating rewards, hoopla, and celebration at all levels and in all divisions. As well, make sure your managers' coaching skills are strong so they are confident and competent enough to give plenty of recognition. Ensure that recognition and rewards are also a critical factor in all performance evaluations.

And to keep others from thinking that those who get recognition or special honors are management's favorites ("How did you suck up for that award?"), use peer review, customer feedback, and objective measures. And make sure the criteria are well understood by everyone.

Thankless Executives

If there's any one reason that managers do such a poor job of showing appreciation, it's this: their senior managers take them for granted and give them little to no appreciation. Recognition, celebration, and hoopla is contagious. Are you a carrier?

And senior executives who attend the first few reward/recognition events must not then be allowed to get bored with it all and stop coming. Recognition programs need constant attention and must emanate clearly from on high.

Phony Flattery

Employees also quickly catch on to "I'm doing my recognition thing now." Managers who won't practice and develop their cheerleader or catching-em-doing-things-right skills shouldn't have people management responsibilities.

Jelly Bean Motivation

This phrase was coined by motivational expert M. Scott Myers to describe that empty praise that congratulates and thanks people for something that hasn't been done. It's "keep up the good work" from a manager who has no idea what work was really done. Ken Blanchard advises, "Feel free to praise, but praise specifically. By continually flattering people for no good reason, they'll come to expect applause, even when they are doing slipshod work." Tom Peters adds, "Too many random congratulations only serve to devalue the truly earned ones. What managers must do is give more thought to just what kind of performance *does* earn applause, and then applaud it — loudly, sincerely, frequently."

Tinsel and Trinkets

Recognition can't make up for paying people peanuts (which, as the wag said, only attracts monkeys). Formalized recognition programs can also reveal those managers who see employees not

216

as partners to be listened to and involved in running the organization but as chattels to be exploited and manipulated.What messages are you sending?

Front-Line Fixation

Don't focus just on front-line servers who have the heaviest customer contact. Employees who "serve the servers" are also vital links in the service/quality chain, and they too need to be energized by recognition and rewards.

Big Bangs

A few mega-rewards to your superstars will have far less pay-off than a large number of smaller rewards distributed broadly. Top performing organizations set up recognition and reward programs that create many winners and recharge as large a number of individuals and team members as possible.

CHAPTER SIXTEEN
Cylinder Ten: Team Tactics

"No matter how high or how excellent technology may be and how much capital may be accumulated, unless the group of human beings which comprise the enterprise work together toward one unified goal, the enterprise is sure to go down the path of decline."

—Takashi Ishihara, president,
Nissan Motor Co.

There's certainly nothing new about employee involvement. The problem, as Robert Waterman points out, "is getting non-Japanese managers to buy into it." Back in the forties, Allan "Mogie" Morgensen found in his consulting work with General Electric and other large companies that it was possible to increase the workforce's output by as much as *50 percent* by involving employees. One of the basic principles underlying his successful consulting work was — "the person doing the job knows far better than anyone else the best way of doing that job and therefore is the best person fitted to improve it."

One company that has benefited from employee involvement in a big way is Ford. Higher product-quality levels and innovative, market-responsive designs continue to fuel market-share growth at this revitalized giant. Past CEO Philip Caldwell explains the impact of involving employees: "The magic of employee involvement is that it allows individuals to discover their own potential

— and to put that potential to work in creative ways. . . . People develop in themselves pride in workmanship, self-respect, self-reliance, and a heightened sense of responsibility.''

The power of employee involvement is echoed by Jack Mac-Allister, CEO of "Baby Bell" US West. He reflects on a visit to a service improvement team that had been newly empowered to make whatever changes were needed to improve local service: "The energy in that room almost blew me out. I literally could not sit in that chair. . . . Here was a group of people who had been empowered to think. The atmosphere alone was bringing out the very best they had in them.'' Adds Walter Fallon, chairman of Eastman-Kodak, "You can't drive a good work force 30 percent harder, but we've found that we could often work 30, 50, or even 150 percent smarter.''

HELPING TO PLAN THE BATTLE

Not only will employees be far less inclined to battle a plan they have developed, but it is far more likely to be the most effective tactic for improving service/quality within their processes or department. That's because front-line employees are the experts. They know the job.

Catching errors at the source, and doing it right the first time: these vital elements to service/quality improvement point to the need for implementation to be tied to decision making. Traditional managers don't see the world that way. Instead, they believe that management's job is to set the course and the employee's job is to follow those directions. Robert Waterman explains the shortcoming of that old-fashioned approach: "Carrying out a decision doesn't start after the decision; it starts with the decision. Figuring out how to get something done is just as important as deciding what to do.'' So why aren't employees more involved in decision making? Waterman points to one of the reasons: "We are so busy grandstanding with 'crisp decisions' that we don't take the time to involve those who have to make the decisions work.''

PARTNERSHIPS AND TEAMWORK

Enabling employees to make improvements calls for a strong partnership with management and a high amount of teamwork among employees, departments, and management.

As you start to work on this vital service/quality improvement cylinder, you must build carefully on the skills base and organizational environment you now have. IBM's James Harrington advises, "In most cases, it is best to structure the team participation process around your present management system and, as the employees' capabilities increase, expand the first-line manager's span of control to offset the decreased work load that has resulted from the additional decisions being made by the employees."

A number of team tactics can improve service/quality, though most of the variations are combinations of four basic configurations:

Quality Circles

These are generally small groups of employees who meet voluntarily to solve problems within their department. Usually these problems directly affect the group's output. The Quality Circle meets regularly and frequently until the problem is solved. At that time, the circle is either disbanded or defines a new problem to work on. Quality Circle meetings are often led by a facilitator from elsewhere in the organization rather than by the department supervisor or manager.

Quality Circles began the North American movement to team improvement approaches in the early eighties. However, they are rarely used in their original form today. A 1985 study by the consulting firm A.T. Kearny found that of the 80 percent of Fortune 500 firms who had started Quality Circles since 1980, some 83 percent had abandoned them within eighteen months of kicking them off.

Serious limitations were discovered by many of those organizations. Chief among the problems were poor management support and spotty implementation success rates. Another equally important reason many Quality Circles failed is that they were

220

run outside the organization's day-to-day operation. Since they developed outside the functional management system, they were not considered part of the "real job."

Department Improvement Teams

These are quickly becoming the most widely used form of service/quality teams. Department Improvement Teams bring together all employees to identify improvement opportunities and to implement the strategies decided by the group. Since its members are the source of the department's output, they are in the best position to analyze, improve, and monitor the department's processes and service cycles.

One significant benefit of energized Department Improvement Teams is the positive influence of peer pressure. James Harrington explains, "When the department is being measured as a team, the people begin to help and police those who detract from the total performance, thus increasing quality and output. ... The department improvement team [also] allows informal group leaders to influence management in setting targets, performance standards, and activity planning. ... In making the informal leader part of the improvement process, management obtains a very strong ally who in some cases has a significant influence over the employees."

Process Improvement Teams

These teams are composed of cross sections of experienced front-line employees, professionals, and often managers from different departments. Together they solve system problems and improve production, delivery, and support processes that cut across functional lines. Known under such names as Service Improvement Teams, Quality Improvement Teams, Task Forces, or Corrective Action Teams, this participative approach is growing in popularity as more managers come to realize the limits of traditional, hierarchical organizations.

Segmented, departmentalized organizations often create artificial walls that have little to do with customer needs or work flow. Our traditional vertical organizations with their top-down organization charts were designed for management rather than customer convenience. They made things easier, neater, and more controllable. But they often went against the flow of work, which crisscrosses departments through the internal customer-supplier chains.

Process Improvement Teams often begin by developing a flow diagram of the process under study and establishing measurement points and feedback loops. They then identify improvement opportunities and put action plans in place. Their role shifts to monitoring and reporting process results and changes, while looking for further improvement opportunities.

Work Cells

Work that involves many people and departments can be difficult to control. No one is really accountable or responsible for the output of the process. On top of that, ownership and commitment to the process is lowered. To counteract these problems, a growing number of organizations are restructuring work teams to be more autonomous in the production or delivery process. Team members are trained to build most or all of the product, or to take care of the customers inside their own unit, with minimal support from others in the organization.

Work cells contribute greatly to decentralizing and delayering the bureaucracy that inevitably blossoms forth when an organizational unit grows beyond a few dozen people. "Chunking" organizations and work processes into their smallest pieces as close to the front line as possible simplifies operations. The resulting simplification and visibility of the work reduces the number of steps and people involved. That drops error rates and puts customers closer to people who can take immediate action to respond to their needs.

Increasingly, manufacturers are finding that when they give a team full responsibility for building a complete component, or even an entire car, quality improves, morale soars, and productivity jumps. This approach means breaking the traditional assembly line into "mini-factories" throughout the manufacturing plant and pulling teams together to manage the work cell.

Service organizations are now taking similar approaches. By moving order or claims processing, accounts receivable, customer inquiries, or account administration to local offices, employees and customers form closer relationships. And as local service providers control more of the administrative processes, they are able to respond more quickly and to correct problems that would have become lost in the old centralized bureaucratic maze.

ESTABLISHING THE ENVIRONMENT FOR SUCCESSFUL SERVICE/QUALITY TEAMS

As happened with Quality Circles by the mid-eighties, there are signs that the rising popularity of service/quality teams is leading organizations to install them in environments that aren't yet ready to sustain them. For the majority of organizations embarking on the service/quality improvement journey, this cylinder is the wrong place to start. Before launching improvement teams, it is necessary to establish the environment and managerial/leadership skills to support the effort. Tom Peters says: "We don't want for evidence that the average worker is capable of moving mountains — if only we'll ask him or her, and construct a supportive environment."

Cultural factors can influence just how effective service/quality team tactics will be in your organization. As you review some of the key factors discussed here, rate your organization's readiness (your people are the best ones to make this assessment):

Trust
James Harrington declares, "Without a strong feeling of mutual trust and respect, it is difficult if not impossible to get the employees to identify problems and solve them." "We-they" gaps (between management and employees, departments, etc.) are found in all too many organizations. These must be bridged before service/quality teams will have any chance of success.

Partnerships

If employees are to build strong partnerships with their internal and external customers, they must share a strong sense of common purpose with management. Building that partnership begins with management's view of its employees. Chairman of Pitney-Bowes, Fred Allan, offered this insight: "It is probably not love that makes the world go round, but rather those mutually supportive alliances through which partners recognize their dependence on each other for the achievement of shared and private goals. . . . Treat employees like partners, and they will act like partners."

Developing Autonomy

Trust and partnerships are born of looser management reins. If you say, "We trust you to run this organization together with us" and then use an autocratic or even consultative approach, your true degree of trust will be evident to all.

But autonomy doesn't happen by wishing it were so. Rather, it comes through skill development and focused leadership. Robert Waterman explains, "It's the kind of leadership that encourages, nurtures, nudges, supports, and inspires people everywhere in the organization. It's a leadership that offers direction, but doesn't pretend to know all the answers. At some very important level it is counting on the totality of individual initiative to be a lot smarter."

Team Skills

It's a continual theme — the coaching and team skills of your supervisors, managers, and executives play a major part in determining the kind of environment that your service/quality teams will operate within. John Young, president of Hewlett-Packard, says, "Where quality teams at HP have been successful, managers have been closely involved. They used quality teams as a resource for accomplishing their business objectives. And they practised what they preached."

224

Improvement Plans and Structures

Successful service/quality teams are seldom isolated or random anomalies. Rather, their activities are connected to a larger structure and planning process.

GETTING SERVICE/QUALITY TEAMS STARTED

Once the environment for service/quality teams is well established and the structure and plans are in place, your teams will need a clear focus, improvement tools and techniques, as well as the skills to use them.

Focusing Service/Quality Teams

To energize and pull people together, team members need a solid grounding in the following areas:

- **Why Improve Service/Quality?** — Team members should know why the organization needs to improve. Even more importantly, they should have a clear understanding of the personal benefits of improving service/quality.
- **Who Are Our Customers?** — Starting with external customers, teams should trace back the customer-supplier chain to show where their own activities fit. Departmental improvement teams then identify their external or internal customers as well as clarifying their key expectations.
- **The Three Rings of Perceived Value** — By applying this model to their departmental and personal activities, team members will begin to see the organization from their customers' point of view. As Achieve's Mark Henderson observes, the Three Rings model helps people to look at an organization from the outside in (the way customers do) while beginning the improvement process from the inside out.

Tools and Techniques

Successful service/quality teams use a number of approaches to get a handle on what needs to be improved and how best to make those improvements. Here are some of the more popular ones:

- **Flow Charts** — These are most often used to analyze work processes. Teams begin by agreeing where the process they want to improve starts and ends. They then prepare a flowchart that shows all the steps, decision points, and feedback loops in the process.

- **Analyzing Service Sequences** — Rob Ell introduced a useful approach, called storyboarding, for teams concerned with improving their moments of truth. Building on Disney's method of laying out each step sequentially in a cartoon or amusement ride, the team lays out the steps as experienced by the teams' customer. Restickable Post-it Notes are used to increase the team's flexibility in moving steps, customer groupings, expectations, action ideas, and so forth around the board as the team brainstorms and plans for improvement.

- **Establishing Monitoring and Measurement Methods** — At first, this vital step shows whether the work process or service sequence is missing, meeting, or exceeding expectations. As the team implements improvements, monitoring and measurement provide the feedback that allows everyone to see how effective the changes have been and where further improvements could be made. Checksheets, run charts, diagrams, interviews, and questionnaires are some of the common methods used. Data collected is visible and accessible to all team members and anyone else who can contribute (internal suppliers, management, customers) suggestions, support, or action to keep the scores moving upward.

- **Identifying Improvement Opportunities** — By comparing the work processes or service sequences against customers' expectations and data feedback, opportunities for improvement are listed. The service/quality team then might choose the best opportunities on the basis of highest payback, visibility, probability of success, or link to the organization's other improvement activities.

- **Problem Solving** — To decide what steps will most likely

capitalize on the improvement opportunities, service/quality teams often use this process:
1. Describe the problem
2. Determine the cause or causes
3. Choose a solution
4. Plan action steps and follow-up

   The common techniques used within these problem-solving steps include: scatter and fishbone diagrams; control, pareto, and planning charts; brainstorming; rating; ranking; and nominal group process. The techniques chosen depend upon whether at that point the team wants to expand its thinking, gather information, or organize information.

- **Recording and Reporting Results** — Team logs and action plans are used to monitor follow-through. These are often the starting point for the next team meeting. They also provide a record for the team, management, or the steering committee and a way to review progress and look for achievements to recognize and celebrate.

The Skills Foundation

Strategies, tools, and techniques are useless without the skills to use them effectively. Robert Waterman says: "Companies can be thought of as bundles of skills, capabilities, and competencies. One of the main differences between two companies, even in the same business, is the difference in their collective skills."

Service/Quality Teams are only as effective as their environment and skills. James Harrington warns, "We can provide the team members with the most sophisticated problem-solving and process-control tools, but if we haven't taught them to cooperate and respect one another, it is to no avail."

EXAMPLES OF TEAM TACTICS

- George Weyerhaeuser, president of the forest products, paper, and real estate giant, Weyerhaeuser Company, says, "Because of our quality improvement efforts, hourly workers, working as teams, are now able to do much of the planning and control formerly imposed upon them, and they are doing it better."

- Crouse-Hinds, an electrical construction materials manufacturer, has re-structured its Scarborough, Ontario plant into work cells. Each cell is completely responsible for the production of particular components. Work-In-Process inventories have dropped as quality and productivity has risen.

- Northrop Corporation's Aircraft Division has used quality teams very successfully for a number of years. Bev Moser, vice-president for commercial operations, says, "During the two years we've emphasized that it is *us* rather than *thee* and *me*, the cost of the 747 unit we're delivering to our customer went down 50 percent."

- A big part of the rise to world dominance of many Japanese companies can be traced to the quality advantage they achieve through employee involvement and quality teams. Toyota started using these approaches back in the fifties. Now they receive 500,000 employee proposals per year, which produce $230 million in savings.

- At Motorola, improvement teams reduced the amount of lost gold in a production process, to save over $3 million per year.

- When improvement teams at Hewlett-Packard focused on their order processing, they dropped the average days outstanding from 62 to 54 and saved $150 million per year.

- In their intense focus to drive down their COQ (Cost of Quality), IBM improvement teams have accomplished: a tenfold improvement in large accounts-receivable delinquencies and an 85 percent reduction in customers' time on invoices; a reduction of distribution-center inventory errors from 30 percent to 0.08 percent; and, through analyzing its processes and establishing a feedback system, a drop in the rerun rate of information support by 50 percent and central processing unit time by 30 percent.

- John Psarouthakis' thriving business specializes in buying and turning around floundering manufacturing companies.

He relies on plant workers for help to improve the operation. One auto-parts maker he bought had an operating margin of less than 1.5 percent. Working with its employees, he boosted that margin to 8.5 percent within a year.

- When Ford set out to design the Taurus, they assembled a team from all steps in the overall process — from design through assembly to marketing. The team spent years visiting assembly plants, major suppliers, the Service Managers Council, and insurance companies. They amassed thousands of ideas. But they paid particular attention to the 1,400 suggestions from Ford employees, *especially those who would build the cars.* The result was an award-winning car with very low defect rates and production costs.

- When Dow Jones, owners of the Wall Street Journal and other media companies, decided to install a printing press, they were told by the vendor that it would mean a six-week period of repeated plant shut-downs. An operations team of employees developed a process that had the machinery operating within *six days.* They have since improved the installation process so that it can be done over a weekend with *no* downtime.

- At GM and Toyota's joint manufacturing venture, NUMMI, employees are extensively involved in running the plant through improvement teams. Despite below-average levels of automation, the plant quickly became tops in productivity of all GM's plants. Their absenteeism and grievance rates are also among GM's lowest. And the cars produced in NUMMI's plant are among the highest-quality cars built in North America.

"Workers who were once supposed to shut up and take orders are now encouraged to use their brains. A team of hourly and salaried employees figured out how to reduce from 52 to 30 the number of parts in the rear floor of Cadillacs and big Oldsmobiles. That squashed

the number of stamping presses used from 93 to 10 . . .
annual savings: a dazzling $52 million."
    — Fortune, "The Task Facing General Motors"

COMMON TEAM PITFALLS AND TRAPS

Jumping the Gun

Eager to begin enjoying the benefits of involving service/quality teams, too many organizations are plunging ahead before they're ready. A nurturing environment, supportive structure, all built on a solid skills foundation, must first be in place before work on Team Tactics can begin. This cylinder is often phase two or even three of a long-term improvement plan.

Underinvesting in Tools, Techniques, and Training

When the incredible results achieved by high performing service/ quality teams are reported, what's often missed is the amount of investment that management has made to equip those teams. *A direct and positive correlation exists between the results obtained and the amount of training and retraining given to the team members and their leaders.*

In Another World

Improvement teams can't function outside the system. Team Tactics are not separate "programs" to make a few changes around the fringes; they change the way work is done in the organization. Supervisors, managers, and executives must be held accountable for the success of improvement teams within their area or under their guidance.

Baffling Boundaries

Improvement teams need clear mandates and parameters; otherwise they will just spin their wheels needlessly or overreach their jurisdiction. Management needs to make it very clear that the partnership they are ready to build is a dynamic relationship that will include greater and greater management responsibility to service/quality teams as they strengthen and develop.

This is the way top performing organizations are able to stay so lean — keeping managerial and professional overheads down while increasing flexibility and customer responsiveness.

Backroom Boys (and Girls)
Improvement teams should always begin with a focus on the external customers' expectations and trace the line back. One of the best ways to do that is to make frequent visits to the teams' customers. Another excellent way to stay customer-focused is to get as many customers on the improvement team as possible. This step is *vital* if the team's focus is on serving internal customers.

Weak Rewards and Recognition
A key performance criteria for all managers, but especially senior executives, must be the amount of recognizing, celebrating, and rewarding they lavish on improvement teams who are making progress. The service team log, action plans, and other such documents give managers all the information they need to "catch people doing things right." If your organization is to sustain the momentum for the long improvement journey, this reinforcement *must stay at the top* of management's To Do lists. It's a key source of team energy.

CHAPTER SEVENTEEN
Cylinder Eleven: Measurement

"Service quality can be measured. It is important to do so; because if you don't measure it, you won't improve it."

— "The Strategic Management of Service Quality," *PIMS Newsletter*, The Strategic Planning Institute

What gets measured gets managed. Unless, and until, your organization puts "hard" accountability around the "soft" issues of service/quality (especially Third Ring service), you will see very little long-term change. In his book *The Improvement Process*, James Harrington writes, "Measurement is absolutely essential to progress." Ron Zemke also found measurement to be at the center of the success enjoyed by the companies he and his researchers studied: "Far from leaving anything to chance, the Service 101 establish clear, customer-oriented performance standards throughout their organizations and then constantly and meticulously measure performance against those standards."

Technomanagers have no trouble with the idea of performance standards and measurement. In fact, their organizations are brimming with them. But they are sophisticated (read, complex) measures of the wrong things. Proud of their bottomline focus, technomanagers pay exclusive attention to results instead of to the processes that produce those results. And that, paradoxically, leads to lower results. Technomanagers spend more time counting and splitting the beans than figuring out how to grow more or keep them from spoiling.

The financial measures and systems that were so helpful in bringing order, control, and efficiency to the explosive economic growth of the fifties, sixties, and seventies are now choking service/quality improvement. In *Relevance Lost: The Rise and Fall of Management Accounting,* Thomas Johnson and Robert Kaplan report that a growing number of experts are concluding that "cost accounting is the number-one enemy of productivity." Tom Peters brings the problem into focus: "Our fixation with financial measures leads us to downplay or ignore less tangible nonfinancial measures, such as product quality, customer satisfaction, order lead time, factory flexibility, the time it takes to launch a new product, and the accumulation of skills by labor over time. Yet these are increasingly the real drivers of corporate success over the middle or long term."

It's by effectively measuring and managing the processes both to increase your customers' perceptions of value and to reduce your costs of poor quality that your financial results will show winning scores. In fact, solid service/quality measures act as an early warning system to whatever your bottomline results are. Once you've isolated your key service/quality indicators and are closely monitoring them, they will help you see in advance what your organizational results will be; whether, for example, revenues are likely to move upward and costs head south, or the other way around.

TYPES OF SERVICE/QUALITY MEASURES

The many service/quality indicators can be divided into two main groups: external and internal measurements. Effective external measures assess customers' perceptions of the service/quality levels provided. These let you see whether you are hitting the First, Second, or Third Rings of Perceived Value. They also help you track your customers' rapidly shifting standards and expectations and plot new strategies and directions.

Internal measures deal with the quality side of the service/quality equation. When employed effectively, they establish a monitoring system that enables your organization to manage the many processes that join to produce the First Ring products or services that are the reason for your organization's existence. These controls also extend to the processes that support delivery of the organization's Second and Third Ring service.

Where to Start?

"We use the customer as the quality control inspector of the company."

—Harry Cogill,
Xerox Canada

As obvious as it may seem, many organizations going flat out to improve fall into the trap of rigorously measuring the service/quality results that are important to *them* or that they *think* their customers care about. This trap is especially tempting to many process-control approaches used by quality control/assurance professionals.

What to measure and where to start is simple: *Start with those things your customers consider important.* In other words, your customers' (not your own) perceptions of what constitutes high service/quality must be at the center of your improvement strategies and measurements. For this reason, this cylinder is closely tied to customer listening (Chapter 7). You can't effectively measure your service/quality results unless you have been listening to your customers and know what's important to them. Otherwise you could find yourself setting up measurements on product or service dimensions your customers don't care about.

The best service/quality providers couple their endless listening with customer measurements of how they're doing. ("You said turnaround time is a top priority. How would you rate our organization's turnaround time?") It becomes a continuous loop.

Find out what your customers' changing needs are from as many angles as possible and then have them measure your effectiveness at meeting or exceeding their expectations.

What Do Customers Most Care About?

Texas A&M marketing professor Len Berry has worked with market researchers to develop universal measurement systems for customer service. From the focus groups and survey research work they've done in a variety of industries, they developed five statistically derived factors they call ServQual:

- **Reliability** — the ability to provide what was promised, dependably and accurately.
- **Assurance** — the knowledge and courtesy of employees, and their ability to convey trust and confidence.
- **Empathy** — the degree of caring and individual attention provided to customers.
- **Responsiveness** — the willingness to help customers and provide prompt service.
- **Tangibles** — the physical facilities and equipment, and appearance of personnel.

Whether these ServQual factors capture what is important to your organization's success is a question only your customers can answer. The big question is, *are you asking them?*

Outside-In Measurement Systems

In keeping with the upside-down organization chart, service/ quality measurement starts at the top with customers and works its way in, or down the organization. Each step in the multitude of service/quality delivery processes, and each link in the many customer-supplier chains, is a potential measurement point. But if you were to apply that many measures, you would be joining the herd of managers who are, to use *Megatrends* author John Naisbett's words, "drowning in information but starved for knowledge." *The key to effective measurement of service/ quality is a small number of simple measures that channel the organization's energy and focus on the strategic areas with the highest potential return.*

So who determines what those key strategic measures should be? Management leads off that process by deciding just what business the organization is in (Reason for Being), what the core values or timeless priorities are, what the long-term strategies and short-term goals will be, and what resources will be invested to do the job. High-performing managers almost universally make those decisions in partnership with the customers they serve and the people who will make it happen.

Inevitably, that means those at the top of the organization — your front-line employees — working together with your customers ultimately determine the measures that will monitor delivery of the organization's service/quality vision and strategies as well as customer needs and expectations throughout your organization. From their research on how the best service/quality companies operate, *Fortune* reports, "These companies monitor service at every level including internally, because workers who treat one another well serve customers better. Successful companies listen to everyone in the distribution chain — dealers, distributors, retailers — as well as the fellow who carries the package home."

To do as many things as possible right the first time, you need to go back in the production chain as close to the source as you can get. IBM's James Harrington advises, "It is essential that measurement points be placed close to the activity being performed. Ideally the measurement point should be part of the activity." He illustrates the value in at-the-source measurement by citing a few computer industry studies: "Hewlett-Packard [found] that a defective resistor costs $.02 if thrown away before use. It costs $10 if they find it at the board-assembly level, and hundreds of dollars if it is not detected until it reaches the customer."

Indicators, Symptoms, or Measures?

The following questions are a few of those that top performers use to measure service/quality. Like a body's vital signs, the answers are potential indicators of health or illness. Getting to the source of the problem may require more detailed diagnosis, testing, and monitoring in specific areas.

To decide which measurements make the most sense for your departments, teams, divisions, or your entire organization to use, ask your customers or front-line servers what's the most important. And keep in mind the enormous costs of poor quality many of the items on this list represent for you.

- How many customer complaints do you receive? (How many more haven't bothered to complain?)
- How many error-free orders are processed?
- How many on-time deliveries are made?
- What is your back-order rate?
- How long does it take you to process and ship an order?
- How long do callers wait on "hold"?
- How many items are out of stock at any given time?
- How much merchandise is returned for refund?
- How many credits do you issue? And for what reasons?
- How many accounts receivable are outstanding?
- What is your rate of warranty claims?
- How frequently do technicians have to redo work or repairs?
- What are your inventory levels?
- How many calls does each employee answer or make?
- How often are deliveries made incorrectly?
- How often do customers call you for clarification on the use of your products or services?
- Do you use the feedback from your field service or sales representatives to chart trends?
- What are your yield rates?
- How frequently are your systems or production lines down?
- What is your accident rate?
- How often does work have to be redone or reprocessed?
- What are your scrap rates?

EXAMPLES OF SERVICE/QUALITY MEASUREMENT

- At Avco Financial Services, a special task force was created to devise tools to measure quality. It took twelve people three months to develop their field quality index. The index has hundreds of components, including yardsticks such as customer retention, delinquency, and receivables. Among other monitoring techniques is an ongoing "Tell Us If You Love Us" customer poll run by branch offices, and a periodic president's survey mailed directly to customers.

- Ford is now using customer service ratings called QCP (Quality-Commitment-Performance) to determine which dealers are allowed to expand to new dealerships and lavish awards at annual gala recognition events upon those who score well. These ratings prod the dealers and the company into listening to customer concerns, identifying problems, developing solutions, and keeping track of follow-through. Many dealers are starting to compensate sales and service people on their individual or team customer-satisfaction ratings.

- "We believe as a company that the customer is going to judge us from a lot of different viewpoints," says Lucy Iovinelli, assistant vice-president of quality assurance for American Airlines. "That's why we hold our 60,000 employees to dozens of standards, and check performance constantly." For example, reservation phones must be answered within 20 seconds, and 85 percent of all flights must take off within five minutes of departure time and land within 15 minutes of their scheduled arrival time. Pay and promotion are linked to service/quality performance. Passengers are surveyed regularly.

- Travel Related Services does transaction-based surveys of personal cardholders to determine how a customer feels about a single contact with American Express. Trends are noted and used for employee feedback. American Express will follow up more than 20,000 transactions a year to see how customers rate the service they received.

- A large U.S. bank developed 700 measures of operational quality throughout all aspects of the bank. The performance levels of 14,000 employees are shown on weekly charts and reports. Thirty percent of a manager's bonus is based on how well expectations are met. Downward trends must be explained and accompanied by solutions.

- As part of a computer company's call-back program, professional interviewers call each customer to clarify expectations about the relationship with its customer service engineers, and to check on work performed. Future service is then tailored to each customer's need.

- Senior operations managers at Diners Club (the credit card company) developed a battery of statistical standards for service delivery, such as the speed of answering customers' phone calls. The company surveys customers after they have had a contact with the organization and correlates the data with its quality service indicators.

- A restaurant printed a brief customer survey on the back of its checks. Customers who complete it receive a small discount on their total.

- A national car rental agency returns a coupon for one day's free car rental to any customer who completes and mails back a customer survey.

- Measuring is one thing; doing something about it is another. At Honeywell Bull's customer service division, the logistics distribution organization makes it a point to visit all customers who rated their spare parts support as poor or marginal.

- Sewell Village Cadillac in Dallas, Texas, has built a thriving business and gained international attention for their obsessive attention to continual service/quality improvement. Measurement has long been a cornerstone of their efforts. For example, a computerized system was installed to inform customer service representatives ("lot lizards" at most dealerships) which cars to bring from the lot. The time it took to deliver the car to the customer was tracked and posted for all to see. Within a short time, average elapsed time dropped from four and a half minutes to two. Believing measurement is critical to improved service/quality, Carl Sewell says, "We measure everything we can think of in this dealership, and we share everything we measure."

- Bramalea Ltd. uses outside market research firms to vist customers in their new homes and review a list of ratings and gather comments on the perceived quality of the home and follow-up service. This feedback goes to each manager and department involved. It is also studied closely by senior management to glean ideas for future products or enhancements.

- BC Tel has an outside research firm do a monthly series of customer interviews and surveys to track customer satisfaction levels. This data is used for performance discussions, problem solving, and celebrations/recognition.

- Domino's pays 10,000 "mystery shoppers" to buy 12 pizzas throughout the year and evaluate the company's service/quality. Managers' compensation is based partly on these ratings.

- Becton Dickinson Canada used classical process control techniques to further reduce the number of pinholes in its surgical gloves. Statistical measures were charted daily for all to see. An improvement team used fishbone diagrams and problem-solving techniques to narrow in on potential causes of pinholes. The manufacturing process was adjusted, quality trends charted, manufacturing adjusted, and so on, until quality exceeded the original goals.

- To meet their commitment to a 48-hour error-free turnaround, Deluxe Check has a different color of order form for each day. For example, Tuesday's is orange. Says a plant manager, "At 4:30 on Wednesday, I don't want to see any orange around here."

- "The manufacturing people at both Motorola and Westinghouse have chosen lead-time reduction as a dominant measure; various divisions of Hewlett-Packard and General

Electric have too," says Richard Schonberger in *World Class Manufacturing*. "Lead time is a sure and truthful measure, because a plant can reduce it only by solving problems that cause delays. . . . One by one, top companies are coming to the conclusion that reducing lead time is a simple and powerful measure of how well you're doing."

COMMON MEASUREMENT PITFALLS AND TRAPS

Inside-Out Measurement
Take a hard look at the assumptions your current performance measures are based upon. Do your measures satisfy management's command-and-control paranoia ("snoopervision")? Are they inner-ring or product-focused? Where do your *customers'* needs and perceptions figure into your measurement and feedback systems? If they aren't shaping your *entire* measurement chain, you're destined to wander off-track — and not even know it.

Managing Results
Results are the outcome: they can't be managed any more than you can turn back time. Like a score, they are a historical record of how you did. In competitive sports you improve your score by improving your play in key strategic areas. To know what part of the game needs work, players need specific feedback. To improve service/quality, start by measuring key production processes and delivery steps.

The Measurement Stick
If measures are used as "gotchas" by management, not only will employees look for ways to "sweeten" the feedback, they will be completely uncommitted to improvement. As Ron Zemke says, "When the feedback system doesn't work, it's often because the information gathered is used incorrectly. It has stopped being feedback and become a chore, a threat, or something to be avoided."

Moving Targets

Ensure that consistent measurement systems are used long enough to identify trends. Constant changes not only send inconsistent signals but also make progress tracking impossible.

Playing vs. Coaching

Don't confine results to the executive team. If employees are going to help with (or even care about) service/quality improvement, they need to know the score. Besides, *your front-line staff* should be deciding what to measure, how to measure it, how to record and communicate it, and how to use it. Managers and experts are there to lead, train, and support the players. You can't go out on the field with them.

Slow and Sluggish

Avoid acting too slowly or invisibly on feedback gathered. Completing surveys and providing "how are we doing" input leads people to expect signs of improvement. It's a major turn-off to feel that the whole activity was an exercise in futility.

CHAPTER EIGHTEEN

Cylinder Twelve: Marketing Strategies

"Fifty percent of Japanese companies do not have a marketing department, and 90 percent have no special section for marketing research. The reason is that everyone is considered to be a marketing specialist."
—Hirotaka Takeuchi, Harvard Business School

The marketing cylinder is the last of the twelve for a reason: you must first drive up your service/quality levels before you start broadcasting to the world how great you are.

Dizzy Dean, former professional baseball player, reportedly said, "If you've done it, it ain't bragging." As you and I know from too many painful experiences as customers, lots of companies do far too much empty bragging. In many companies, the service/quality program is directed by marketing and public-relations specialists who lie to the organization's customers. Being astute observers of which way market preferences are blowing, marketers are aware that service/quality has become one of the issues in most purchasing decisions today. So they work with senior management to capitalize on that trend and design clever marketing campaigns to lure customers with promises of unsurpassed quality, fast and friendly service, and the like.

In a *Wall Street Journal* article entitled "Service with a Smile? Not by a Mile," Jim Mitchell writes, "The message of the commercials is 'We want you!' The message of the service is 'We want you unless we have to be creative or courteous or better

243

than barely adequate. In that case, get lost!' " As Rob Ell is fond of saying, "Service/quality is often the first thing promised and the last thing delivered."

But today's customers are less gullible. They've been burned too often. That's why word-of-mouth has become a principal source of information concerning buying decisions today. But word-of-mouth is not just you telling two friends, who tell two friends, who tell two friends. Today, word-of-mouth is growing in complexity and sophistication. User groups, buying networks, consumer and industry associations, consumer and industry trade publications, and consumer complaint advocates, bureaus (such as the Better Business Bureau), and protection groups are cutting through the advertising hype.

To the many organizations who are long on talk but short on action, today's environment of lightning-quick customer net-working and communications is a threat. To the few organizations *perceived in the marketplace* to be providing high value through superb service/quality, it's an opportunity to continue taking market share while maintaining their premium prices. The rich get richer.

CHANGING THE PERCEPTION OF YOUR SERVICE/QUALITY

Steve Estridge, CEO of Temps & Co., says, "Presenting an upbeat face to the public does wonders for the way people perceive your business." The $64-million question is, how do you present that upbeat face to your public?

In typical hurry-up North American fashion, many managers try to buy that image through advertising and public relations. Although top performers are often heavy advertisers, that is not how they developed their service/quality images. Top performers did not get to the top with promotion and marketing leading the way.

The surest way to present that upbeat face to your customers is through your people. They manage the moments of truth. They raise or lower the perceptions of service/quality that your customers hold of you. The venerable Peter Drucker puts it this way: "Marketing . . . is the whole business seen from the point of view of its final result, that is, from the customer's point of view. Concern and responsibility for marketing must, therefore, permeate all areas of responsibility."

It has been said that war is too important to be left to the generals. The same can be said of marketing. *Marketing service/quality cannot be left to marketing specialists.* The most effective service/quality marketing happens when front-line people are provided with the environment, tools, support, training, and confidence to act as ambassadors for your organization. In its fledgling years, IBM's motto was Service Sells. They spent an enormous amount of their limited time and what few resources they had to get *everyone* to understand and act on the basic premise that if they weren't serving the customer directly, they had better be serving someone who is. At Disney, *every* employee in *all* parts of the organization is very clear about the value and primacy of Guests with a capital *G*.

The long-term effect of IBM, Disney, Four Seasons, 3M, and other major-league performers' single-minded, relentless focus on top service/quality has been the development of sterling reputations that no amount of marketing dollars could ever buy. And their ability to increase, or even maintain, their market share is dependent to a large extent upon how well they compete in a crowded service/quality-sensitive international marketplace. If they fail to continue briskly along in their service/quality improvement journey, they will surely be overtaken by changing customer expectations or by nimbler, more responsive competitors. Sure, marketing will help them build their business base. But ultimately the quality and desirability of their products and services will determine their fate.

So belly up to the mirror. Where has your marketing focus gone? How true are the service/quality claims you're making? What kind of ambassadors or marketers are your front-line people? How much more does it cost your organization to attract new customers than to keep the ones you have? What kind of "marketing" are your customers doing behind your back? (Review the research in Chapter 1 on customer turnover.) *How do you know?*

MARKETING'S DOWNSIDE: MANAGING SERVICE/QUALITY EXPECTATIONS

It's one thing to get customers in the door; meeting their expectations is another thing again. In fact, the cruel irony is that a growing number of exemplary service/quality providers are trapped by their own success. Their customers expect miracles every day. Exceeding expectations (Third Ring) becomes a gargantuan challenge.

But you should have this problem! However, you do have to be concerned about managing expectations — especially if you've been marketing service/quality as a way to attract or retain customers. The dilemma is that you could be providing some of the highest service/quality around, but if your customers expect more from you, for whatever reason, you could end up with fairly low customer satisfaction ratings.

Here are some ways you can keep expectations within reach:

- Be very careful of the promises you make in your advertising, sales, marketing, and public-relations activities.
- Make it a personal and ultimately an organizational habit to promise a little and deliver a lot.
- Make sure everyone can clarify her or his expectations to her or his internal customers so the chain isn't weakened.
- Train your sales force and then make it a corporate strategy to go after only those market niches whose expectations match your delivery capabilities. All sales dollars are not equal. Some customers come with expectations that you can't meet or that will prove to be very expensive to your organization. Besides, you want only those customers who want, appreciate, and will pay for the levels of service/quality you've decided to offer.

THE BEST-KEPT SECRET

On the other hand, service/quality is in the eye of the beholder. It doesn't exist until it is perceived to exist. Many public or internal organizations who serve captive customers may offer high levels of service/quality, but their customers may not know how good they have it. The high service/quality may be taken for granted.

We often counsel our public-sector Clients to put a public relations person on the steering committee (we'll discuss this further in Chapter 19) to ensure that the good news of improvement progress gets out. Internal providers can do a lot to market their achievements by getting a few of their customers on their steering committee. But be careful that opinions of the high service/quality your organizations delivers are not just your own. Establish a basis in fact for this conclusion by comparing your organization to a number of others or by working with a few lead customers.

MOST EXAMPLES OF MARKETING ARE EMPTY PROMISES

Look around you. There is no shortage of companies cleverly marketing service/quality. Probably half of all ads have the words *service* or *quality* in them somewhere. The shortage is of organizations whose people actually deliver Third Ring service. How's your organization doing? A high score in service/quality advertising and marketing coupled with low scores in the other cylinders is a recipe for disaster.

Ultimately marketing is an important piece in the entire improvement puzzle. But if you're like 95 percent of organizations, you need to work hard in the other cylinders before you worry about this one.

COMMON MARKETING STRATEGY PITFALLS AND TRAPS

Intentions vs. Capabilities
Don't kid yourself and lie to your customers. They'll take their revenge in painful monetary ways.

Marketing Outside In
Although external service/quality marketing can help give your organization an image to live up to, it works only when employees

feel they are connected to the marketing effort and are partners in the improvement process. Any campaign to raise external customers' expectations *must* have its start with internal marketing if it's to be effectively followed through by employees and made real.

Raising Your Own Barriers

Don't fail to recognize how marketing service/quality to customers can make things tougher for your organization. Competitors or other agencies may respond with higher service/quality as well (or at least with similar claims). Customer expectations will also rise. All this underscores the need for *continuous service/ quality improvement* that goes well beyond slick marketing campaigns.

In the long term, it's often more effective to sneak past your competitors with an intense service/quality improvement effort that keeps customers coming back and doing your marketing for you.

CHAPTER NINETEEN
Charting Your Service/Quality Journey

"There is nothing more difficult to take in hand, more perilous to conduct, or more uncertain in its success, than to take the lead in the introduction of a new order of things."

—Niccolo Machiavelli,
Florentine statesman and philosopher

A man took his son for entrance to Hiram College. "Can you arrange a shorter course for him to get through quicker?" asked the father. The college's president, James Garfield, replied, "Oh, yes. He can take a short course; it all depends on what you want to make of him. When God wants to make an oak, He takes a hundred years, but He takes only two months to make a squash."

There are no shortcuts on the service/quality journey. Some routes may be shorter and less difficult than others, but there's no avoiding the fact that the pathway to high service/quality is a long, unending, tough trip. That's why so many organizations start with great expectations and grand plans only to drift off-track and peter out. Identifying your destination is easy. Getting there is hard. Here's how John Fisher, senior vice-president of Bank One Corporation, puts it: "Getting a service quality improvement effort started in a big way and keeping it rolling is the major issue. Such a gigantic effort is required to overcome inertia that the size of the problem becomes its own roadblock. It is not just a matter of saying, 'OK, people, let's smile and use the

249

customer's name.' Genuinely improving the quality of service is an everlasting effort. It's like switching from breathing air to breathing water."

MANAGING OR MUDDLING YOUR SERVICE/QUALITY JOURNEY?

"The only things that evolve by themselves in an organization are disorder, friction, and malperformance."

—Peter Drucker

Imagine taking a caravan of hundreds or even thousands of untrained and inexperienced people on a long journey with no plan, no one in charge, no logistical support, no structure to keep everyone informed, weak communication links to assess and update progress, no navigational instruments, and no map. Sheer madness? You bet!

But before you scoff at the stupidity of such an absurd scenario, look at your own service/quality effort. How much of it is good intentions, dreamy destinations, and a "let's get at it" sort of enthusiasm? Is your executive team focused on how the organization's key issues and values frame the whole effort? Do you have a navigator for your journey? Are the roles and responsibilities of executives, managers, supervisors, and front-line performers clear? Is there a structure to support the improvement efforts of those at the top of your organization? Are you getting regular readings of the progress made? Are your people well trained in traversing the unfamiliar terrain confronting them at every turn? Are the leadership skills in place to take you where you need to go? How effective are your information-gathering and communication processes? *Do you have a detailed plan providing a well-understood map for all travelers?*

Managing your service/quality improvement journey may not be easy, but it is certainly do-able. The researchers and writers at *Fortune* magazine came to this conclusion in their study of "companies that serve you best": "North American managers have learned to improve the quality of their products enormously

250

in recent years. The champions of customer pampering show that organizations can improve service with similar common sense management tools."

CHARTING THE COURSE AND BUILDING COMMITMENT

The Service/Quality System is no more than continual improvement of the twelve cylinders. But it can't all be done at once. So where do you start? What is the best firing order for your cylinders?

Although there are rules of thumb, there is no right way to implement service/quality improvement for all, or even any two, organizations. Each implementation effort is unique to that organization. And within an organization, each department, section, or division often calls for a slightly different implementation sequence.

Even if there was a right way to improve the cylinders, dropping that plan on the organization would be the wrong way to proceed. That's because consensus and commitment are so vital to the success of the whole effort. The plan would be management's, or even worse, an outside consultant's.

The details of each implementation effort differ widely, yet the steps, roles, structures, planning, and momentum maintenance of those organizations showing the most service/quality improvement usually follow the approaches outlined in this chapter.

FOCUSING MANAGEMENT

As we discussed in Chapter 6, service/quality improvement starts at the top. Delegating it instantly moves it down the organization's list of priorities. *Unless and until the executive team has brought service/quality into focus for the organization, your best efforts will never be anything more than training.* And that means your culture is not going to shift noticeably.

The best way to get your executive team singing off the same sheet of music on the service/quality issue begins with an executive retreat — ideally, a three-day session away from the office in a peaceful setting. Getting away to a relaxed environment gives the team uninterrupted time to reflect, learn, under-

251

stand each other's perspectives, and focus on the service/quality issue.

EXECUTIVE RETREAT AGENDA

The agenda for the executive retreat needs to be tailored to the team's needs. However, a number of steps are common to most retreats. The tailoring comes in the emphasis given to particular areas.

Day One
The Service/Quality Revolution
The team assesses just how critical service/quality improvement is to the organization's future. (See Chapters 1 and 2.)

What Does Service/Quality Mean?
Participants learn that quality is more than product, that customers define service/quality, and that employees play the pivotal role in the whole effort. (See Chapter 3.)

Deadly Service/Quality Improvement Assumptions
The team looks at the erroneous assumptions it holds and makes sometimes painful readjustments. (See Chapter 4.)

Assessing Service/Quality Strengths and Weaknesses
The team takes a quick look at the twelve cylinders, and each participant scores the organization's current "compression rating" within each cylinder. (See Chapters 6 to 18.)

Day Two
Clarifying Core Values
Two or three unchanging, bedrock beliefs *shared by the team* are identified. These preserve the strengths of the past and determine the focus for the future.

Reason for Being
The team establishes a short, appealing "rallying cry" that will galvanize the organization into unified service/quality improvement action.

Vision of the Preferred Future
The executive team paints a picture of how the organization will look in two to three years.

Walking the Talk
The executive team sets plans to signal the vision and values through their personal behavior. They also establish how they will get feedback from customers, employees, and each other on how well they are doing.

Cylinder Analysis
To begin to understand the magnitude of the issues and changes required within each cylinder, executives familiarize themselves with their highest-priority cylinders. They move on to analyze what in their organization contributes to and inhibits higher performance in that cylinder. They then identify ways to improve the cylinders studied.

Implementation Planning
- They review pitfalls and traps they may encounter. (See pages 267 to 269 at the end of this chapter.)
- They discuss the structure of their improvement effort. (See the rest of this chapter.)
- They assess their commitment by considering the questions in Chapter 20 (pages 271 to 273).
- They chart the course. The executives set the direction of the effort. They choose or verify the coordinator and clarify his or her mandate.

Day Three
This is a skill-building and planning day. Executives practice selected coaching or team skills. They also get an overview of the skill development sessions to be given to the rest of the organization and how they can reinforce and support that effort.

ROLES

Corporate Coordinator

A key role in the Service/Quality System is the corporate coordinator, or, as James Harrington calls this person, the "improvement czar." The corporate coordinator is usually a full-time position in any organization of more than a few hundred people. He or she reports directly to the CEO or most senior executive of the organization.

Here are the main functions of the corporate coordinator:

- Advise and assist line managers and service/quality teams in their improvement efforts
- Plan, design, and carry out service/quality orientations for managers and employees
- Help managers select implementation assistants and facilitators
- Provide or arrange for coaching, training, networking, and other support for implementation assistants and facilitators
- Prepare internal marketing materials
- Provide internal and external auditing, measurement, listening, and other feedback tools, and provide consulting support in their use
- Act as secretary and primary staff support resource to the Corporate Steering Committee
- Act as consultant to implementation assistants and their Local Service/Quality Councils
- Write the Corporate Service/Quality Improvement Plan based on the direction and input of the Corporate Steering Committee
- Plan and organize celebrations and recognition activities for line managers to reward their individual contributors and performance teams
- Establish and arrange training programs to support implementation of the improvement plans
- Champion and provide consulting support on the twelve cylinders

254

Coordinators can fall into a number of traps, though we have found that three seem to be particularly tempting and are especially deadly. These are:

1. Usurping leadership from line management. Line managers and front-line performers *must* own and implement service/quality improvement as an integral part of their jobs. The coordinator is a staff support person, *not a manager.*

2. Coordinator in the spotlight. Once the coordinator becomes the hero who takes credit for the effort's success, ownership of the program (no longer an operating process) is just around the corner.

3. Coordinator reports too low in the organization. If this effort is not given a high profile and made the personal concern of the most senior executive in the division, department, ministry, or company, it will quickly move down everyone's list of priorities.

Coordinator Selection and Training

Given the pivotal role played by the corporate coordinator, putting the right person in this position is one of the most significant variables to the success of the improvement effort. The executive team must give careful consideration to choosing who will fill this critical post. We have seen successful corporate coordinators with various backgrounds. Where coordinators come from in the organization is not as important to their success as their personal characteristics and perspectives.

Following are some of the most critical attributes. Since they describe an ideal candidate and it is unlikely any one person has all of them, the executive team must decide which carry the most weight and then assess their candidates against that profile. The coordinator should be:

- A true champion (whom Peter Drucker defines as "a monomaniac with a mission") of, and zealous believer in, service/quality improvement
- An acceptable choice to managers and front-line performers
- A person with extensive experience in the organization or

its industry

- A capable manager of large-scale, strategic processes involving many groups and people
- A person able to stand firm with the executive team when giving difficult feedback or advocating new strategies
- A high performer who quietly exemplifies the organization's values
- A successful manager who is available full-time and has no other duties or responsibilities for eighteen to twenty-four months (at which point someone fresh may be brought in to guide the process)
- A good sideline coach or offstage director. In other words, she or he thrives on helping others become successful without needing public applause her or himself. (However, senior line managers need to pay special attention to recognizing successful coordinators.)

Few coordinators are able to step into their new role without training and coaching. Those who have tried find they spend their first three to six months educating themselves before they can even begin to provide any real support inside their organization. Coordinators can get themselves and their organization up and running much more quickly by participating in training that will help them steer their organizations around the many potholes that can seriously damage and even stop progress on the service/quality improvement journey.

Coordinators benefit most from training concentrated in these areas:

- The roles of corporate coordinators, implementation assistants, facilitators, and line management
- Measurements of service/quality levels and processes
- Preparation of a comprehensive improvement plan (often an underrated and hastily done task)
- Ways to track and communicate successes and failures, and to make recommendations
- Techniques for conducting follow-up and networking

activities
- Examples from the experiences of other coordinators and the executives they report to and support
- The strengths and weaknesses of the techniques and approaches of the most widely followed service/quality gurus
- A long-term improvement framework and an inventory of skill development sessions for employees and managers
- The complex issues involved in cultural change and how managers can successfully manage the process

Chief Executive or Administrative Officer (CEO/CAO)

"The leader's role is most important at the moment of crisis, when the issue is in doubt. Then the leader must be visible. He must inspire confidence and impose calm and order."

—Caesar's *Commentaries*

Although the corporate coordinator plays a pivotal role, her or his long-term success and the success of the entire service/ quality improvement effort rests most heavily upon the shoulders of the leader of the organization. The CEO/CAO must be squarely and visibly behind the effort if it is truly to become a cultural change and not just another training program.

Here's the role of the CEO/CAO or senior manager. He or she should:

- Actively and visibly champion and lead the process at every possible opportunity
- Chair the Corporate Steering Committee
- Provide adequate resources and support to make sure this critical journey is not underfunded or understaffed
- Shelter the process and its champions from the bureaucrats who are threatened by it and will resist or try to kill the changes it produces
- Live and strongly signal the core values at the center of the improvement effort
- Ensure that there are extensive annual reports and plans

- Hold line managers accountable for service/quality improvement activities and results

The CEO/CAO or senior manager relies heavily on the support and assistance of the corporate coordinator. He or she is the CEO/CAO's hands and feet working furiously behind the scenes to maximize the effect of the CEO/CAO's work to drive the service/quality improvement process. A good coordinator stage manages or provides direction from the wings to the CEO/CAO. The CEO/CAO is the one on center stage with the supporting cast of managers. In many ways, a good coordinator is also the conscience of the CEO/CAO.

STRUCTURE

Corporate Steering Committee

The service/quality improvement effort must model the approaches and techniques it is advocating. That means from day one, you need to ask for extensive input on the planning process. The best way to build a broad base for consensus and commitment is through a Corporate Steering Committee.

The role and mandate of the committee varies from one organization to another. Here are some examples of the functions performed by many steering committees:

- Provide input to, modify/refine, and approve the improvement plan put together by the corporate coordinator to ensure that adequate financial and human resources are available to orient, train, and support all areas of the organization for the first two- to three-year implementation period
- Develop the principles, policies, and guidelines that frame the improvement effort (e.g., mandatory participation, service/quality team parameters, amount and type of involvement)
- Review and approve the role, mandate, and improvement plans of Local Service/Quality Councils and their implementation assistants
- Become ambassadors, champions, and communicators of

the improvement process and its key messages
- Coordinate cross-functional initiatives such as Process Improvement Teams that cut across a number of departments or areas
- Help managers, employees, and improvement teams establish priorities
- Work with the CEO/CAO and the senior team to resolve system problems that hinder service/quality improvement
- Track and measure the effect of the improvement process through the corporate and local efforts
- Act as a focal point for successes and difficulties so all parts of the organization can more effectively learn and readjust their efforts
- Publish an annual report that pulls together a comprehensive record of all accomplishments
- Develop and aggressively manage a reward and recognition program that celebrates successes, makes "heroes" of high performing individuals and teams, and broadcasts these accomplishments inside and outside the organization

Ideally the Corporate Steering Committee should have no more than ten or twelve people. It is chaired by the CEO/CAO or senior manager with the corporate coordinator acting as secretary. Other members include representatives from management, human resources, and public relations/communications. Customers should eventually be included as well, especially if the improvement effort is focused on serving internal customers. Front-line performers should also be represented, since they hold many of the keys to implementation and can keep the committee grounded in the real world.

Local Roles and Structure
This is where improvement happens. The Corporate Steering Committee may develop ambitious plans, but their implementation happens at the local level.

Each local department, region, or division should have its own Local Service/Quality Council, improvement plan, and implementation assistant. The role of line managers and implementation assistants is similar to the CEO/CAO and corporate coordinator, except the local people manage the tactical details and work directly with the front-line people who make it happen. The implementation assistant is usually a part-time position filled by a strong performer with many of the same characteristics identified in effective corporate coordinators. This position is more of a hands-on role. Implementation assistants often administer audits, communicate the effort's objectives, progress, etc. directly to front-line performers, actively market the improvement effort, and work with line managers to remove blocks and empower improvement teams. The implementation assistants work closely with, and often take some direction from, the corporate coordinator. However, the implementation assistant reports to the most senior local manager and takes his or her ultimate direction from the Local Service/Quality Council.

A role unique (and vital) to local organizations is the facilitator. Facilitators conduct skill training and are usually supervisors or senior employees. Sometimes they are human resource professionals. The number of facilitators depends on the size of the local organization and the scope and speed of the local improvement plan. With most improvement plans calling for six to twelve skill development sessions for all front-line performers, and twelve to twenty-four sessions for managers, a number of facilitators are usually needed.

Facilitators provide the training that equips management and front-line performers to put the improvement strategies, structures, and techniques into action. The facilitators help to build the personal, coaching, and team skills that are the foundation of the improvement effort. They usually also conduct orientation sessions and help set up improvement teams with a solid implementation process and tools (e.g., analyzing work processes, problem-solving techniques).

To be effective trainers, facilitators need solid training themselves. They need to develop the skills of group facilitation and instructing adults. Skill-based instructor certification with plenty of practice and feedback is a must to develop a facilitator's ability to develop the skills of others.

Local Structure

Local Service/Quality Councils are similar in make-up and mandate to the Corporate Steering Committee. However, like the implementation assistants, these councils are much more concerned with the implementation details than with the overall direction of the organizational improvement effort.

A prime activity of the Local Service/Quality Council is working with the Service/Quality Teams in their area. The council makes sure these teams have the training, tools, support, and understanding of their role to begin improving local service/ quality. The council then works to remove management obstacles and change technology and systems to help Service/Quality Teams get the job done. Avco Financial Services' Quality Councils "review ideas rejected by management to make sure that no potentially valuable suggestion is turned down because of someone's ingrained idea about how to do things." Local Councils also look for ways to recognize individuals and teams making service/ quality improvements. They communicate and celebrate this progress around the organization.

AUDITS

To plan a journey, you first need to know where you are now. Audits of customers and employees tell you where your organization currently is and what route will most likely take you to higher service/quality.

Many of the customer auditing approaches are covered in the Listening and Measurement cylinders (Chapters 7 and 17). As you map your service/quality journey, the main things you want to know from your customers are what they perceive your current service/quality levels to be and what their expectations are. Closing those gaps becomes your route to higher performance.

Front-line performers and managers are another group that can provide you with invaluable assessments of your current position and directions on what needs to be done to prepare the organization for the improvement journey. Front-line performers can give you an assessment of external service/quality that will be remarkably close to your customers' perceptions. But just as useful is your front-line performers' assessment of internal service/quality. This is often broadened to include an evaluation of the personal, coaching, and team skills base in the organization. When combined with an outline of the kind of culture organizational members would find most supportive and motivational, these assessments can provide a clear map for the route to higher performance.

Internal audits are often begun through surveys. These are most useful if they involve survey participants in feedback and interpretation sessions once the data has been collected and the results tabulated. The worst thing managers or Steering Committees can do is take the data as gospel and begin making decisions on it as it is. Survey participants should begin working with the data within no more than six to eight weeks of completing the questionnaires. This will give managers and committees a much stronger feeling for the areas with the highest potential influence on performance. It also models the involvement your service/quality improvement effort will be using. And it builds commitment to the jointly developed actions your organization will be taking to shift organizational behavior.

In addition to customer and internal audits, your organization should audit its service/quality improvement process once a year. This audit rates the effectiveness of your improvement effort. It is best conducted by an outside party.

IMPLEMENTATION PLANNING

"For when the ancients said that a work begun was half done, they meant that we ought to take the utmost pains in every undertaking to make a good beginning."
— Polybius, Greek historian

Throughout this book I have been stressing the vital components of service/quality improvement. These have included management commitment, leadership skills development, customer listening, measurement, employee participation, teamwork, clear roles, and structure. Also vital to service/quality improvement is a comprehensive implementation plan. Indeed, it pulls together all the other pieces.

It is unbelievable how many otherwise sensible managers set out on their service/quality journey with a map that isn't much more than scratches on a napkin. Vague platitudes, generalities, a bit of training, and a lot of bravado constitute the "plans" of all too many organizations. Karl Albrecht warns: "A customer service program without a driving idea and clear plan for converting it into action at the front line loses momentum very early." Setting out on your service/quality improvement journey without a solid implementation plan is not only bad management, it virtually guarantees that you won't get the organization where you're not sure it's going.

The Corporate Plan

"The man who goes alone can start today; but he who travels with another must wait till that other is ready."
—Henry David Thoreau

Early in the process the corporate coordinator prepares a discussion draft or skeletal plan for the Corporate Steering Committee. This draft becomes the focal point for the committee as it begins the improvement effort. It's not unusual for it to take months of intensive work for the coordinator and steering committee to make the Corporate Plan final. That time is used to gather input and work through the roles, responsibilities, structures, and other implementation details. But as Japanese companies have demonstrated so well, the time invested in the start of the journey pays off with a blistering, relentless pace once the improvement journey begins.

Here's a brief outline of the steps included in the most useful Corporate Plans:

- **Aim** — The purpose and expected use of this planning

263

document.

- **Background** — The reasons that the organization is at this point; what has been done along these lines so far; how this process will integrate with the past; the overarching organizational vision and values; and why it is essential to improve service/quality.
- **Theme** (if used) — Examples: "Service Excellence," "Quality Has Value," "Caring Through Service Excellence," "Quality Is Job 1."
- **Definition of Service/Quality** — How you are going to get everyone talking the same language about a subjective topic.
- **Objectives** — The short-term (one-year) goal and the longer-term (two-to-three year) goals.
- **Implementation Schedule** — Steps to take to improve performance in all twelve cylinders. This schedule is often shown in two stages for each cylinder: the first twelve months, and the following twelve-month period.
- **Structure** — How implementation assistants and facilitators, Local Service/Quality Councils, line managers, and improvement teams work together. And how they will link to the Corporate Steering Committee and Corporate Plan.
- **Accountabilities and Responsibilities** — The responsibilities of the senior manager up to front-line supervisors, performers, and improvement teams, and the way in which everyone will be held accountable for improvement activities.
- **Resources and Budget** — The amount of money and time that will be devoted to the process, and the way it will be allocated.
- **Guidelines and Principles** — A statement of the values or beliefs framing the improvement activities (e.g., "employees hold the key", "participation", "line responsibility"). This section may also include policies or boundaries.
- **Component Sub-plan** — How corporate communica-

tions, rewards, and recognition will be used to keep energy high and momentum maintained. This section also often contains a detailed implementation plan for the extensive training effort central to the success of service/quality improvement.

- **Conclusion and Summary** — An outline of the benefits we expect from the improvement effort and a description of what the preferred future will look like.
- **Appendices** — Tables, charts, statistics, or background material supporting the main body of the plan.

Local Plans

These plans can be as detailed and extensive as the Corporate Plan or simply be a few pages. The Local Plan spins off the Corporate Plan, often following a similar format and using it as the background. The Local Plan focuses on the objectives and project details specific to that area of the organization. It is especially concerned with how *every* employee participates in the improvement process.

MAINTAINING MOMENTUM

Most managers can rouse excitement at the beginning. With fanfare, hoopla, and bold declarations of the new future ahead, it's fairly easy to get all but the most cynical person eager to get going. But the truly determined travelers are separated from the dreamers and talkers as the journey wears on, the going gets tough, and the scenery becomes boringly repetitive. *Maintaining energy and commitment through the long term is critical.*

Momentum can be maintained in several ways. Strong execution of cylinder improvements, especially Commitment (Chapter 6), Internal Marketing (Chapter 8), and Reward and Recognition (Chapter 15), will go a long way toward keeping improvement enthusiasm and activities high.

Bringing the implementation assistants and facilitators together periodically to exchange ideas and experiences will help provide a forum for mutual support and encouragement, training and skills updating, and coordination of activities.

Another tool for maintaining momentum is the annual report. At the end of the first twelve-month improvement period, and each year after that, every Local Service/Quality Council puts together a list of the accomplishments of the improvement teams in its area. If it's being tracked, this list may include a summary of the effects of those improvements on service/quality indicators or dollars saved or reductions in Cost of Quality. The results found in these reports are then used as the basis for rewards, recognition, and celebrations.

The local reports are collected and pulled together by the corporate coordinator to form the annual report. In an intense, far-reaching improvement effort, the effect of pulling together all the progress made by the whole organization can be electrifying. Excitement, pride, and feelings of accomplishment run high as everyone sees just how far the organization has progressed. This energy then sparks interest in the plans for the next twelve months.

How senior executives follow through is also an important element in maintaining momentum. Reflecting on the successful transformation of B.C. Tel, past president Terry Heenan said: "I think that much of our success was because we took a disciplined approach to follow-up. I started my executive meetings by having all of the vice-presidents report on the leadership initiatives they were involved with, and the results they noticed as they lived our values. There is nothing that encourages people more to get things done than having to report on their accomplishments to their boss in front of their peer group."

Another critical element in maintaining the drive for service/quality improvement is measurement (Chapter 17). Remember — *what gets measured gets managed.* When results are visible for all to see and individuals and groups are held accountable for them as well as being rewarded for them, interest in keeping the improvement drive alive is very high. William Weisz is president of Motorola and winner of the highest U.S. award for quality improvement — the Baldridge Prize. Looking back on its improvement journey, he discusses the impact of measurement: "There was a lot of frustration and concern by managers that with all this effort going on, they really were not able to measure the definitive results. Then we crossed that hurdle and began to definitely measure substantive improvement. It was like a snowball. The enthusiasm is higher today than it was in the beginning."

COMMON PITFALLS AND TRAPS TO IMPLEMENTING AN IMPROVEMENT EFFORT

"I think, therefore I am"
Just declaring yourself to be a quality or service organization doesn't make you one. Many an executive has fallen into the abyss that separates good intentions and bold declarations from concrete *action*. Implementation, implementation, implementation!

"Let's pretend"
Speeches, memos, newsletters, videos, slogans, and advertising campaigns can make it look as though things are really happening — for a while. Barry Sheehy says: "Words are not adequate to describe the contempt I feel for leaders who engage in this deception. It's one thing to fool yourself, it's another matter entirely to try to fool customers and employees."

"No one home"
How many successful projects do you know that had no one in charge? Unless and until you appoint navigators (coordinators and implementation assistants) to help managers, individuals, and teams make the service/quality journey, you won't get very far.

"Hurry up — and do it wrong"
We live in an instant-gratification, hurry-up society. Once we set our sights on a destination or goal, we want it yesterday. Preparing for the service/quality journey is critical. And it takes time. But as the top performers continually show us, the planning, training, and preparation pays huge improvement dividends.

"Hurry up — before I get bored"

Far too many executives are looking for that service/quality silver bullet. They would like nothing better than to make a few bold strategic master strokes (reorganize, hire and fire a few key people, run a quick training program, put together a slick marketing campaign) and get on to other things. That's living in a fantasy world. *Service/quality improvement is tough, grinding work over a long time.* Just when you are getting bored with repeating the same old messages yet again, your front-line performers are beginning to think that maybe you really mean it this time. To move on to something "new" is to cause them to say, "Aha! They really were up to their old 'say one thing, do another' tricks again."

"Now I understand"

There's a world of difference between knowing and doing. Understanding the Service/Quality System is not the journey, it is the preparation. The question upon which the future of your organization depends is not what you understand about service/quality improvement, but what are you *doing* about it?

"Let's skip the hard stuff"

Clarifying values and developing skills are hard for many executive teams to come to grips with. Yet these form the base upon which the easier improvement techniques are built. In the race to hurry up and get on with improvements, a weak skills and values base will inevitably throw you off-track.

"Buddy, can you spare a dime?"

Service/quality isn't free, especially as you begin. You can't take a million-dollar trip on a hundred-dollar budget. However, the investments made in service/quality improvement are routinely measured in hundreds or thousands of percentage return — eighteen to thirty-six months down the road.

"Snatching defeat from the jaws of victory"

Just as the results start to come in at the end of the first twelve to eighteen months, the old, highly threatened culture will mount a formidable campaign to halt or reverse the process. This is a crucial time, since critical mass hasn't yet shifted organizational norms to embrace the new service/quality behaviors. Intensive persistence and attention to the original plan is vital at this point, especially from senior management. Once you turn this corner, there is no going back. Your people will then begin climbing aboard in droves. Those who don't will have to be left behind.

CHAPTER TWENTY
Let's End with Your Beginning

"Either do not attempt at all, or go through with it"
—Ovid, Roman poet

You've seen what's involved in improving service/quality. This journey is not for the faint of heart. It would be much easier to do a little "smile training." It's even easier to stay put and do nothing at all.

As you contemplate setting out on the service/quality journey, take a hard look at the level of commitment you and your management team have. If it's low, you won't go far before the potholes, detours, and obstacles bring the whole effort to a slow stall. Service/quality improvement calls for an assault on deeply rooted customs and procedures. It demands that resources be allocated in radically new ways with much heavier customer input. It requires staying power when it appears that the organization's effectiveness is actually decreasing during the difficult transition from the old to the new culture. And the harder you try to turn things around, the louder will be the howls of pain and protest from your own people, especially your middle managers.

Karl Albrecht finds that "only 10-15 percent of organizations are truly willing to make the kind of all-out commitment needed to become service-driven." I think he is too optimistic! Only a tiny fraction of organizations are prepared to pay the price of improved performance — although many are interested. And that means that the rich will continue to get richer, joined by only a few organizations that are making the grueling trek — and enjoying the rich rewards.

ASSESSING MANAGEMENT COMMITMENT

A woman rushed up to famed violinist Fritz Kreisler after a concert and cried, "I'd give my life to play as beautifully as you do." Kreisler replied, "I did."

Are you and your management team ready to embark on the service/quality journey? The following questionnaire will help you determine that. Circle the number that best describes the state of your executive team at the moment. Then add up your score for a grand total.

To gauge your management team's commitment, have each member complete the questionnaire on her or his own and add up the scores to get a composite picture.

To what extent are you prepared to:

	Not At all		Some-what		Abso-lutely
1. Invest a substantial amount of personal and organizational time over a 36-month period in service/quality improvement?	1	2	3	4	5
2. Hold line managers accountable for service/quality improvement as much as for financial results?	1	2	3	4	5
3. Regularly review and reinforce service/quality improvement efforts?	1	2	3	4	5

4. Commit the financial and human resources needed for a full implementation? 1 2 3 4 5

5. Integrate improvement efforts with current strategic and financial planning? 1 2 3 4 5

6. Revise or replace personal or organizational systems or procedures that hinder service/quality improvement? 1 2 3 4 5

7. Bring employees heavily into the improvement planning and implementation process? 1 2 3 4 5

8. Protect the "boat-rockers," "champions," and innovators who upset the status quo with their improvement efforts? 1 2 3 4 5

9. Visibly promote and live a strong commitment to the service/quality vision and core values? 1 2 3 4 5

10. Ensure that coordinators and facilitators have plenty of training and visible support? 1 2 3 4 5

11. Support an orderly implementation schedule? 1 2 3 4 5

12. Repeatedly touch
    everyone in the
    organization to create
    awareness, develop
    skills, set team
    strategies, and reinforce
    success?   1   2   3   4   5

TOTAL SCORE:

If your score was less than 45 points, don't bother packing yet — you're not going anywhere. If you set out now, you'll just strand everyone out in the wilderness and build better cynics for the next time you announce a new destination. You and your management team need to take a serious look at what is blocking your commitment, and work to strengthen it before you say anything to anyone about higher service/quality.

If your score was between 46 and 55 points, you need to be cautious. There may not be enough commitment to take your organization through the long haul. A frank discussion of what is holding back full-scale commitment is needed.

WHAT WE GET IS WHAT WE SEE

"If you don't know where you're going, any path will take you there."

—Sioux proverb

If you and your management team are truly committed to the journey to higher service/quality, you'll need to start with a vision of your destination. Visioning is a powerful tool that's sadly underutilized and often misunderstood. Yet it's clear that the best leaders through the ages have (often unconsciously) used this powerful approach. Let's end this book where you need to begin your journey — visioning your preferred future.

Let's Get Personal

To appreciate the incredible power of organizational visioning, we need to start with a look at the evidence that is piling up from the world of personal performance and development. One of the most extensive studies I know of in this field is the on-going research of psychologist Charles Garfield. He has spent more than twenty years studying over 400 peak performers in various fields. Having been an Olympic weight lifter, Garfield's research began in the world of high performing athletes. In his first book, *Peak Performance: Mental Training Techniques of the World's Greatest Athletes*, he writes: "All peak performers I have interviewed report that they use some form of mental rehearsal in both training and competition."

In the world of sports, visioning has become a highly recognized success factor. James Hickman of the Washington Research Center in San Francisco says this technique is now the most widely applied mental tool in modern sports. Visioning (often called imaging or visualization) provides such an important ingredient to successful athletic competition that almost every major team or competitor, especially at the Olympic level, now uses specially trained sports psychologists to supplement physical training with mental conditioning.

Lee Pulos, sports psychologist at the University of British Columbia, has worked with the Canadian National Women's Volleyball Team practicing visioning during their mental practice sessions. He explains how the technique works: "What athletes have ideally executed in their minds' eye, they will be able to translate into action during practice or competition." He says that they are "laying the proper neurological tracks" with this approach. Olympic gold medalist Bruce Jenner says, "I always felt my greatest asset was not my physical ability, it was my mental ability."

Whether it's golf, baseball, or racket sports, you use visioning every time you play. It's the picture you have of the likely outcome as you step up to the tee, pick up a bat, or get ready to serve. In his book, *Golf My Way*, Jack Nicklaus describes how he has used visioning successfully throughout his career: "First I 'see' the ball where I want it to finish, nice and white and sitting up high on the bright green grass. Then the scene quickly changes, and I 'see' the ball going there: its trajectory and shape, even its behavior on landing. Then there is sort of a fade-out, and the next scene shows me making the kind of swing that will turn the previous images into reality."

The Power of Negative Visioning

Our subconscious mind is neutral. Like a computer, it doesn't censure the commands we give it. It just follows instructions. Too often, when we step up to the ball, the images filling our head and sending instructions to our subconscious are negative. We see all the bad things that could happen. We expect the worst, and our subconscious often delivers what was ordered.

Warren Bennis calls this the Wallenda factor. In their five-year study of leadership, he and Burt Nanus found that visioning worked just as strongly in making our fears come true. The term came from discussions with the wife of Karl Wallenda, father of the famous Flying Wallendas, the high-wire performers. In 1978, Karl fell to his death while traversing a wire in downtown San Juan, Puerto Rico. His wife recalls Karl's deadly visioning: "All Karl thought about for three months prior to it was *falling*. It was the first time he'd ever thought about that, and it seemed to me he put all his energies into *not falling* rather than walking the tightrope."

From their study of more than 90 outstanding leaders in a number of fields, and many more less successful aspirants, Bennis and Nanus conclude: "From what we've learned from the interviews with successful leaders, it became increasingly clear that when Karl Wallenda poured his energies into *not falling* rather than walking the tightrope he was virtually destined to fall."

We all practice visioning each and every day. For most, it entails running a series of things we don't want to happen into our subconscious, which, needing programming, eagerly accepts those as the day's instructions. Day by day, powerful images build up that limit our confidence and our accomplishments. Like the elephant that remains faithful to the tight circle around the stake, even when the chain is gone, we become prisoners of our own negative visions.

One of the fundamental differences that sets outstanding performers apart is their use of positive visioning to reprogram the flood of negative messages society has poured into their brains. Charles Garfield says, "Peak performers, particularly in business, sports, and the arts, report a highly developed ability to imprint images of successful actions in the mind. They practice, mentally, specific skills and behaviors leading to those outcomes and achievements which they ultimately attain."

ORGANIZATIONAL VISIONING

Just as every individual has a vision of the future, every organization does as well. Your organization's vision is simply a collection of everyone's individual vision.

Your organizational vision acts as a magnet. It attracts people, events, and circumstances to it. Another way of looking at visioning is as a self-fulfilling prophecy. What your people believe will happen, they will make happen, often unconsciously.

So the *big* question becomes, what is your organizational vision? Is it what you and your management team want to have happen, or is it a collection of everyone's fears and paranoia? What the majority of your people see, they will work to make reality.

Service/Quality Vision

As you get the organization ready to depart on your long and difficult improvement journey, a positive, compelling vision can go a long way toward providing the energy and enthusiasm your people need to make the trip successful. Many a weary traveler's footsteps have been lightened by thoughts of his or her destination. And by constantly keeping that exciting picture of what your destination will look and feel like in front of everyone, you'll be programming them to help take the organization there. The more powerful and well communicated your service/quality vision, the better it will lift everyone's sights from the many obstacles, dead-ends, traps, and problems immediately in front of

276

you. Any manager can point out all the reasons why performance can't be improved. It takes a strong leader to move people's attention to the future that could be.

To establish your service/quality vision, imagine what your organization's preferred future looks like. As that picture takes shape, help your management team do the same. Put these images together to form a team vision. Now review Signaling Commitment (Chapter 6) and work with your team to change the collective vision of your organization as you begin the improvement journey outlined in this book.

To help you set your service/quality vision, relax, close your eyes, and picture yourself hovering in a balloon over your organization. It is two or three years from today and you have superman/woman eyes and ears. As you look down and listen in, the universe is unfolding as it should for your organization — and it's wonderful! Record your observations as you hear interactions with front-line performers and customers, with managers and their teams, between people all over the organization. And bask in the warm glow of results beyond your wildest dreams. . . .

Bon voyage!

NOTES

Page numbers on which cited material appears are shown in bold face. The following abbreviations have been used in the notes:

IP: *The Improvement Process: How Leading American Companies Improve Quality*, H. James Harrington, McGraw-Hill, New York, 1987.

MBQ: *The Manager's Book of Quotations*, Lewis D. Eigen and Jonathan P. Siegel, Amacom, New York, 1989.

PIMSletter: *The PIMSletter on Business Strategy*, The Strategic Planning Institute, Cambridge, Mass.

PIMSPrinciples: *The PIMS* (Profit Impact of Market Strategy) Principles: Linking Strategy to Performance*, Robert D. Buzzell and Bradley T. Gale, The Free Press, New York, 1987.

PP: *Peak Performance: Mental Training Techniques of the World's Greatest Athletes*, Charles Garfield, Tarcher, Los Angeles, 1984.

RF: *The Renewal Factor: How the Best Get and Keep the Competitive Edge*, Robert H. Waterman, Jr., Bantam, New York, 1987.

SE: *The Service Edge*, Ron Zemke with Dick Schaaf, New American Library, New York, 1989.

SEN: *The Service Edge* newsletter, Lakewood Publications, Minneapolis, Minn.

SQ: *Service Quality: A Profit Strategy for Financial Institutions*, Leonard L. Berry, David R. Bennett, Carter W. Brown, Dow Jones Irwin, Homewood, Ill., 1989.

TC: *Thriving on Chaos*, Tom Peters, Knopf, New York, 1987.

VIP: *The VIP Strategy: Leadership Skills for Exceptional Performances*, Jim Clemmer and Art McNeil, Key Porter Books, Toronto, 1988.

WP: *The Winning Performance: How America's High-Growth Companies Succeed*, Donald K. Clifford and Richard E. Cavanagh, Bantam, New York, 1985.

Introduction
2. "Companies That Serve You Best," Bro Uttal, *Fortune*, December 7, 1987, pp. 98-116; **5.** Ted Levitt, quoted in "Quality: The Competitive Advantage," special supplement, *Fortune*, September 28, 1987.

278

Chapter One

6. E.S. Woolard, Jr., quoted in "The Race to Quality Improvement," special supplement, *Fortune*, September 1989; **8.** Raymond Ablondi, quoted in "Quality Helps Sell, Too," *Industry Week*, April 6, 1987, p. 49/ **9.** "Companies That Serve You Best," Bro Uttal, *Fortune*, December 7, 1987, pp. 98-116; **9.** "Pul-eeze! Will Somebody Help Me?" *Time*, February 2, 1987, pp. 47-53; **10.** "Customers value good repairwork . . ." PIMSPrinciples; **10.** "Would You Buy a Car from This Man?" Thomas Moore, *Fortune*, April 11, 1988, pp. 72-74; **10.** "Will Services Follow Manufacturing Into Decline?" James Brian Quinn and Christopher E. Gagnon, *Harvard Business Review*, November-December 1986, pp. 95-103; **10.** "Poorly Served Employees Serve Customers Just As Poorly," Robert Kelley, *Wall Street Journal*, October 13, 1987, p. 15; **11.** "Disappearance of 'Service With a Smile' Leave Customers Nostalgic and Angry," Patricia Owen, *Toronto Star*, Saturday, May 14 1989, p. 1; **11.** "Pul-eeze! Will Somebody Help Me?" *Time*, February 2, 1987, pp. 47-53; **11.** "Rediscovering the Customer," special supplement, *Fortune*, January 18, 1988; **11.** *Forbes* article cited in SE, p. 5; **11.** SE, p. xvii; **11.** "1987 ASQC/Gallup Survey," *Quality Progress*, December 1987, pp. 13-17; **12.** "Service only road" and "Entering era of" from "The Strategic Management of Service Quality," PIMSletter, no. 33; **13.** "With the PIMS data . . ." from "Formulating a Quality Improvement Strategy," PIMSletter, no. 31; **14.** Spencer Nilson, quoted in "Companies That Serve You Best," Bro Uttal, *Fortune*, December 6, 1987, p. 99; **14.** Retail Council of Canada cited in "Superior Service Is a Must for Retailers, Survey Says," Kenneth Kidd, *Toronto Star*, April 9, 1986; **14.** American Business Conference study found in WP; **14.** *The Customer is Key*, Milind M. Lele with Jagdish N. Sheth, Wiley, New York, 1987, p. 25; **15.** Property and casualty study from SE, p. 9; **15.** PIMS quote from "Formulating a Quality Improvement Strategy," PIMSletter, no. 31, pp. 1-2; **17.** "Competitors that cannot . . ." from "Formulating a Quality Improvement Strategy," PIMSletter, no. 31, pp. 4-6; **18.** *American Banker* study cited in SQ, 1989, p. 5; **20.** John Grocock, quoted in TC, pp. 67-68; **20.** PIMS quote from "The Strategic Management of Service Quality," PIMSletter, no. 33, p. 9; **21.** *Canadian Grocer* study found in David Kingsmill's column "Between Bites," *Toronto Star*, January 15, 1986, p. D2; **22-27.** TARP stastics compiled from various sources (TC; SEN, November 1988, p. 2; "Consumer Complaint Handling in America: An Update Study – Part II," Technical Assistance Research Programs for the United States Office of Consumer Affairs, March 31, 1986; "How Good Is Your Service and, in the Utility Industry, Does It Really Matter?" working paper by John A. Goodman president of TARP, May 1983); **26.** Regis McKenna, "Marketing in an Age of Diversity," *Harvard Business Review*, September/October 1988, p. 93; **26.** GE study cited in "Consumer Complaint Handling in America: An Update Study – Part II," Technical Assistance Research Programs for the United States Office of Consumer Affairs, March 31, 1986, pp. 49-50; **27.** "Leverage in satisfying customers . . ." from "Would You Buy a Car from This Man?" Thomas Moore, *Fortune*, April 11, 1988, pp. 72-74; **28.** Stew Leonard, quoted in SEN, January 1989, p. 5.

Chapter Two

29. Peter Drucker, *Innovation and Entrepreneurship: Practices and Principles*, Harper and Row, New York, 1985, p. 177; **38.** Richard Walton, "From Control to Commitment in the Workplace," *Harvard Business Review*, March/April, 1985; **39.**

David Zussman and Jak Jabes, "Survey of Managerial Attitudes," Faculty of Admin- istration, University of Ottawa, unpublished paper; **41.** Karl Albrecht, quoted in a summary of his book *At America's Service*, July 1988, Soundview Executive Book Summaries, Bristol, Vt.; **46.** TC, p. 87; **46.** Milt Honea, quoted in SEN, November 1988, p. 4.

Chapter Three
50. Ted Levitt, quoted in "Quality: The Competitive Advantage," special supple- ment, *Fortune*, September 28, 1987; **52.** Walter Monteith, quoted in SEN, De- cember 1988; **55.** Regis McKenna, "Marketing in an Age of Diversity," *Harvard Business Review*, September/October 1988, p. 92; **57.** W. Edwards Deming, from an unpublished abstract of his book, *Quality, Productivity and Competitive Position:* **57.** ASQC/Gallup survey cited in SEN, November 1988; **58.** Tom Peters, from a letter promoting his newsletter "On Achieving Excellence"; **59.** Hyatt Hotel study cited in SEN, October 1988; **59.** Gallup poll quoted in SE, p. 4; **60.** John M. Kolesar, quoted in SQ, p. 25; **60.** Alexander Berry, quoted in SQ, pp. 43-44; **60.** IBM analysis outlined in "The Strategic Management of Service Quality," PIMSletter, no. 33; **61.** Buck Rodgers, *The IBM Way: Insights Into the World's Most Successful Marketing Organization*, Harper and Row, New York, 1986, p. 145; **62.** "guest bible misprint" from "Power Is Proprietorship," *Canadian Business*, December 1988, p. 54; **62.** Carol Resnick example from "Hospitality Award Candidates Went Extra Mile, With a Smile," *Toronto Star*, May 17, 1989; **64.** Bryan Sue Example from "Hospitality Award Candidates Went Extra Mile, With a Smile," *Toronto Star*, May 17, 1989; **67.** SE, p. 18; **70.** Bro Uttal, "Companies That Serve You Best," *Fortune*, December 7, 1987, pp. 98-116; **71.** John Naisbett, quoted in "Pul-eeze! Will Somebody Help Me?" *Time*, February 2, 1987, pp. 47-53; **71.** Lewis Lehr, quoted in SEN, November 1988.

Chapter Four
72. "Victories in the Quality Crusade," Joel Dreyfuss, *Fortune*, October 10, 1988, p. 80; **74.** SE, p. 10; **75.** "Companies That Serve You Best," Bro Uttal, *Fortune*, December 7, 1987, p. 108; **77.** John F. McDonnell, from "The Race to Quality Improvement," special supplement, *Fortune*, September 1989; **77.** SE, p. 19; **78.** Karl Albrecht, quoted in a summary of *At America's Service*, July 1988, Soundview Executive Book Summaries, Bristol, Vt.; **78.** Jack MacAllister, quoted in SEN, December 1988, p. 5; **79.** *Total Customer Service*, William H. Davidow and Bro Uttal, Harper and Row, New York, 1989, p. 133; **81.** *Total Customer Service*, page 111; **82.** Albrecht-Zemke and Karl Albrecht, from "Achieving Excellence in Service," *Training and Development Journal*, December 1985; **83.** James E. Burke, quoted in a summary of *Image At the Top: Crisis and Renaissance in Corporate Leadership*, September 1984, Soundview Executive Book Summaries, Bristol, Vt.; **83.** Ken Blanchard, quoted in SEN, March 1988, p. 8; **84.** Bob Grimm, quoted in SEN, November 1988, pp. 1-2; **87.** Richard Davis, quoted in SQ, p. 106; **88.** Lynn Shostack, quoted in SQ, p. 95; **89.** ASQC/Gallup poll and David Kearn, from "1987 ASQC/Gallup Survey," *Quality Progress*, December 1987, pp. 13-17; **89.** ASQC statistics from "On a Silver Platter," American Society for Quality Control, Milwaukee, Wis.; **90.** "Formulating a Quality Improvement Strategy," PIMSletter, no. 31; **90.** Kay Whit-

more and G. Christan Lanzch, "The Quality Imperative," special supplement, *Fortune*, September 29, 1986; **90.** John Young and Donald R. Frahm, quoted in "Quality First," American Society for Quality Control, Milwaukee, Wis.; **91.** Stanley J. Calderon, quoted in SQ, p. 12; **91.** Raymond Larkin, quoted in SQ, pp. 12-13; **92.** TARP studies from "How Good Is Your Service and, in the Utility Industry, Does It Really Matter?" working paper by John A. Goodman president of TARP, May 1983; **93.** John Akers, quoted in "The Renaissance of American Quality," special supplement, *Fortune*, October 14, 1985.

Chapter Five
96. Bro Uttal, "Companies That Serve You Best," *Fortune*, December 7, 1987, p. 97; **97.** Arthur Rock, quoted in *A Kick in the Seat of the Pants*, Roger von Oech, Harper and Row, New York, 1986; **97.** ASQC quote from "Quality First," American Society for Quality Control, Milwaukee, Wis.; **97.** Ron Zemke's comment from SEN, November 1988, p. 1; **97.** Karl Albrecht, from a summary of his book *At America's Service*, July 1988, Soundview Executive Book Summaries, Bristol, Vt.; **97-98.** Michael Beer and ASQC/Gallup, quoted in "1987 ASQC/Gallup Survey," *Quality Progress*, December 1987, pp. 13-17; **98.** W. Edwards Deming, from an unpublished abstract of his book, *Quality, Productivity and Competitive Position*; **98.** Regis McKenna, "Marketing in an Age of Diversity," *Harvard Business Review*, September/October 1988, p. 95; **100.** "Poorly Served Employees Serve Customers Just As Poorly," Robert Kelley, *Wall Street Journal*, October 13, 1987, p. 15; **100.** Benjamin Schneider's research cited in SE, pp. 68-69; **100.** David Bowen's study cited in "Service: A CEO's Perspective," Robert Desatnick, *Management Review*, October 1987; **101.** Herbert Kelleher, quoted in SQ, p. 58; **101.** Jessie McClure example from SE, p. 67.

Chapter Six
105. IP, p. 92; **105.** Ray Boedecker, quoted in *GMP: The Greatest Management Principle in the World*, Michael LeBoeuf, Berkley Books, New York, 1985, p. 76; **106.** James E. Olsen, quoted in "On a Silver Platter," American Society for Quality Control, Milwaukee, Wis.; **107.** The "I" of the Hurricane: Creating Corporate Energy, Art McNeil, Stoddart, Toronto, 1987; **108.** Richard S. Ruch and Ronald Goodman, *Image At the Top: Crisis and Renaissance in Corporate Leadership*, Free Press, New York, 1983, p. 85; **108.** "Chief Evangelical Officer" comment from WP; **108.** James R. Houghton, "Make Quality a Way of Life," *Quality Progress*, August 1987, p. 24; **108.** Walter Kiechel III, "No Word from on High," *Fortune*, January 6, 1986; **109.** Thomas Melohn, quoted in "Quality a Competitive Point of Difference at North American Tool & Die," American Productivity Center, April 10, 1987, Vol. 6, no. 10; **112.** American Airlines example from SEN, November 1988, p. 7; **112.** Bob Small example was given by Ken Blanchard writing in SEN, March 1989, p. 8; **112.** Corning Glass example and James R. Houghton quoted in "The Chairman Doesn't Blink," *Quality Progress*, March 1987, p. 23; **113.** "Paul Revere Group Forges New Approaches in Employee Involvement," by Patrick Townsend, *Personnel Journal*, September 1986; **113.** Levi Strauss example from "More Effective Walking Around Management," by Tom Peters, *Boardroom Reports*, March 1, 1987.

Chapter Seven
116. Bob Waterman, quoted in "Rediscovering the Customer," special supplement, *Fortune*, January 18, 1988; **116.** *Fortune*, "Companies That Serve You Best," Bro Uttal, December 7, 1987, pp. 98-116; **117.** Strategic Planning Institute research from "The Strategic Management of Service Quality," PIMSletter, no. 33, pp. 7-8; **117.** "Rather than focusing . . ." PIMSPrinciples, p. 116; **117.** Tom Peters, quoted in SE, p. 29; **117.** Richard E. Heckert, quoted in "Getting customers to love you," Patricia Sellers, *Fortune*, March 13, 1989, p. 38; **118.** SQ, p. 39; **118.** James Brian Quinn, "Managing Innovation: Controlled Chaos," *Harvard Business Review*, May-June 1985, p. 80; **119.** Jack Welch, quoted in "The Strategic Management of Service Quality," PIMSletter, no. 33; **120.** SE, p. 31; **121.** *Thriving on Chaos*, Tom Peters, Knopf, New York, 1987, pp. 100-101; **122.** Buck Rodgers, *The IBM Way: Insights Into the World's Most Successful Marketing Organization*, Harper and Row, New York, 1986, pp. 60-61; **123.** Gordon Forward, interviewed by Alan M. Kantrow, "Wide-open Management At Chaparral Steel," *Harvard Business Review*, May-June 1986, pp. 100-101; **124.** Southern New England Bell, features in SEN, December 1988, p. 4; **124.** GE Answer Center, from a special supplement to SEN, and "Consumer Complaint Handling in America: An Update Study – Part II," Technical Assistance Research Programs for the United States Office of Consumer Affairs, March 31, 1986; **124.** Church's and Tony Lama examples from *Boardroom Reports*, September 15, 1985; **124.** IBM and Buck Rodgers, *Success* magazine, February 1986, p. 57; **125.** "Sidewalks between office buildings" from *A Kick in the Seat of the Pants*, Roger von Oech, Harper and Row, New York, 1986, p. 84; **125.** First Union Corporation cited in SE, p. 31; **125.** SE, p. 33; **125.** Piedmont Airlines example from SE, p. 33; **125.** Quad/Graphics and 3M examples from SE, p. 34; **126.** Cadillac example from "Getting Your Customers to Love You," Patricia Sellers, *Fortune*, March 13, 1989, p. 38; **126.** Techsonic Industries from "Getting Your Customers to Love You," Patricia Sellers, *Fortune*, March 13, 1989, p. 38-39; **126.** Land's End example from "Getting Your Customers to Love You," Patricia Sellers, *Fortune*, March 13, 1989, p. 45; **126.** Northwestern Mutual Life from "Getting Your Customers to Love You," Patricia Sellers, *Fortune*, March 13, 1989, p. 40; **129.** Christopher Hart, quoted in "Companies That Serve You Best," Bro Uttal, *Fortune*, December 7, 1987, p. 108; **130.** SE, p. 34.

Chapter Eight
131. *Total Customer Service*, p. 102; **132.** WP, p. 78.

Chapter Nine
138. SE, p. 59; **140.** Richard Pascale, "Fitting New Employees Into the Company Culture," *Fortune*, May 28, 1984, p. 28; **141.** TC, p. 315; **142.** Wexley and Latham's study cited in SEN, April 1989, pp. 6-7; **143.** *Corporate Cultures: The Rites and Rituals of Corporate Life*, Terrence Deal and Allan Kennedy, Addison Wesley, Reading Mass., 1982, pp. 49 and 144; **143.** Peter Drucker, *The Changing World of the Executive*, Times Books, New York, 1982, p. 12; **144.** "Pan Pacific hotel"

example from "Standards Bearer," by Patricia Davies, *Canadian Business*, March 1988, p. 123; **145.** Sporting Life example cited in "Disappearance of 'service' with a smile leaves consumers nostalgic and angry," by Patricia Owen, *Toronto Star*, May 14, 1988, p. A8; **147.** Merck example from "Companies That Serve You Best," Bro Uttal, *Fortune*, December 7, 1987, pp. 98-116.

Chapter Ten
149. TC, p. 324; **150.** Richard Schonberger, *World Class Manufacturing: The Lessons of Simplicity Applied*, The Free Press, New York, 1986, p. 215; **150.** Masaaki Imai, quoted in TC, pp. 75-76; **152.** Zenger-Miller research was published in "Company-Wide Quality Programs: How to Avoid Common Pitfalls and Create Competitive Challenge," Roland Dumas, *Quality Progress*, May 1989; **152.** Roland Dumas, "Join Forces for Total Quality Control," *Quality*, May 1989; **155.** "Two training experts" John Gunkler and Ron Zemke, "28 Techniques for Transforming Training into Performance," *Training*, April 1985, p. 54; **156.** William Cone, MBQ, p. 489; **156.** Theodore Caplan, MBQ, p. 488.

Chapter Eleven
158. "Pul-eeze! Will Somebody Help Me?" *Time*, February 2, 1987, pp. 47-53; **159.** John Opel, quoted in "On a Silver Platter," p. 21, American Society for Quality Control, Milwaukee, Wis.; **160.** ASQC quote from "On a Silver Platter," p. 21, American Society for Quality Control, Milwaukee, Wis.; **161.** *The New Achievers*, Perry Pascarella, Free Press, New York, 1984, p. 123; **162.** John Kotter, *Power and Influence: Beyond Formal Authority*, Free Press, New York, 1985, p. 68; **164.** "University of Manitoba" example from "Lets Make Good Service Part of the Job," *Toronto Star*, April 28, 1988, p. D5.

Chapter Twelve
167. George Odiorne, *How Managers Make Things Happen*, Prentice-Hall, Englewood Cliffs, N.J., 1982; **168.** Harvey Miller, quoted in *Nation's Business*, March 1988; **168.** Gene Dalton and Paul Thompson, *Novations: Strategies for Career Management*, Scott, Foresman and Company, Glenview, ILL., 1986; **169.** Richard Walton, "From Control to Commitment in the Workplace," *Harvard Business Review*, March-April 1985; **169.** Ernesto Poza, "Twelve Actions to Build Strong U.S. Factories," *Sloan Management Review*, Fall 1983; **170.** Henry Mintzberg, *The Nature of Managerial Work*, Harper and Row, New York, 1973; **171.** Joseph Leonard, "Why MBO Fails So Often," *Training and Development Journal*, June 1986, p. 38; **171.** Gary Jonas, MBQ, p. 458; **171.** *The New Achievers*, Perry Pascarella, Free Press, New York, 1984, p. 23; **172-3.** Bum Phillips and Tom Peters/ Nancy Austin quotes are compiled from *A Passion for Excellence: The Leadership Difference*, Random House, New York, 1985, pp. 325-330; **173.** Patricia Carrigan, quoted in *MTS Digest*, April/June 1987; **173.** Ralph Nader, quoted in *Time*, November 8, 1976; **176.** MBQ, p. 461; **178.** "not following through with on-the-job coaching," see "The Coaching Controversy," Neil Rackham, *Training and Development Journal*, November 1979.

Chapter Thirteen
180. Robert Daniell, quoted in the *Harvard Business Review*, September/October 1987; **180.** For studies on effectiveness of teams, see VIP, Chapter 9; **181.** Norman Maier, *Problem Solving Discussions and Conferences*, McGraw-Hill, New York, 1963; **181.** Janice Klein/Pamela Posey quotation from *Harvard Business Review*, November/December 1986; **181.** Koichi Tsukamoto, MBQ, p. 475; **182.** David Bradford and Allan Cohen, *Managing for Excellence: The Guide for Developing High Performance Contemporary Organizations*, Wiley, New York, 1984; **183.** Charles Garfield, *Peak Performers: The New Heroes of American Business*, William Morrow and Company, New York, 1986, p. 182; **184.** Winston Churchill comment from a speech he gave in Parliament on September 27, 1926; **185.** Chris Argyis, *Harvard Business Review*, September/October 1986/ **186.** George Polya, MBQ, p. 356; **187.** *The Plateauing Trap*, Judith M. Bardwick, AMACOM, New York, 1986; **187.** George Odiorne, *How Managers Make Things Happen*, Prentice-Hall, Englewood Cliffs, N.J., 1982; **187.** John Kotter, *Power and Influence: Beyond Formal Authority*, Free Press, New York, 1985, pp. 32-33; **188.** Dagobert Runes, MBQ, p. 80; **188.** Andy Grove, "How (and why) to Run a Meeting," *Fortune*, July 11, 1983, p. 132; **189.** Robert Half, quoted in "Meeting of the Minds," *Success*, December 1986; **192.** Ernesto Poza, "Twelve Actions to Build Strong U.S. Factories," *Sloan Management Review*, Fall 1983.

Chapter Fourteen
193. Ted Levitt, from "Rediscoverying the Customer," special supplement, *Fortune*, January 18, 1988; **195.** W. Edwards Deming, from an unpublished abstract of his book, *Quality, Productivity and Competitive Position*; **195.** Peter Drucker, *The Changing World of the Executive*, Times Books, New York, 1982, pp. 114-115; **196.** Karl Albrecht, from a summary of his book *At America's Service*, July 1988, Soundview Executive Book Summaries, Bristol, Vt.; **196.** Donald Porter, quoted in *Service America: Doing Business in the New Economy*, Karl Albrecht and Ron Zemke, Dow Jones Irwin, Homewood, Ill., 1985, p. 34; **197.** "American Society for Quality Control" from their booklet "On a Silver Platter," p. 27; **197.** "Strategic Planning Institute conclusions" from "Formulating a Quality Improvement Strategy," PIMSletter, no. 31, p. 13; **199.** Four Seasons example from "Getting Your Customer to Love You," Patricia Sellers, *Fortune*, Mar. 13, 1989; **200.** GE Answer Center and Georgia examples outlined in "Consumer Complaint Handling in America: An Update Study – Part II," Technical Assistance Research Programs for the United States Office of Consumer Affairs, March 31, 1986, p. 5; **201.** Xerox Canada cited in "Standards Bearer," Patricia Davies, *Canadian Business*, March 1988, p. 126; **201.** George Butts, quoted in "The Renaissance of American Quality," *Fortune* supplement, October 14, 1985; **201.** Fred Smith, from a letter he wrote to *Harvard Business Review*, September-October 1988. p. 174.

Chapter Fifteen
204. National Science Foundation study cited in IP, p. 191; **205.** Robert Desatnick, "Service: A CEO's Perspective," *Management Review*, October 1987; **205.** Alvin

Burger, quoted in *Inc.*, June 1984; **206.** National Science Foundation study cited in SE, pp. 71-72; **206.** Public Agenda Foundation study cited in IP, p. 191; **206.** Akio Morita, MBQ, p. 401; **207.** SE, p. 71; **207.** Robert Kelley, "Poorly Served Employees Serve Customers just as Poorly," *Wall Street Journal*, October 13, 1987, p. 15; **207.** Thomas J. Peters and Robert H. Waterman, *In Search of Excellence: Lessons from America's Best-Run Companies*, Harper and Row, New York, 1982, p. 269; **208.** George Blomgren, quoted in IP, p. 191; **208.** Paul "Bear" Bryant, quoted in *GMP: The Greatest Management Principle in the World*, Michael LeBoeuf, Berkley Books, New York, 1985, p. 88; **208.** TC, p. 307; **208.** *Total Customer Service*, p. 129; **210.** Cathy Deforest, quoted in SEN, October 1988, p. 3; **210.** TC, p. 311; **212.** H. Ross Perot, quoted in *Life*, February 1988; **212.** Domino's Pizza example from TC, pp. 309-310; **213.** Security Pacific National Bank example from SQ, p. 94; **213.** American Express example from "Companies That Serve You Best," Bro Uttal, *Fortune*, December 7, 1987, pp. 98-116; **215.** Northwest Airlines example from SEN, April 1989, p. 5; **215.** Holiday Inns and Transco Energy examples from "Accentuate the Positive," Ken Blanchard, *Success*, November 1986, p. 8; **216.** Ken Blanchard, "Jelly Bean Motivation," *Success*, February 1986, p. 8; **216.** Tom Peters, "Is a Paycheck Enough?" *Success*, November 1985, p. 14.

Chapter Sixteen
218. Takashi Ishihara, MBQ, p. 469; **218.** Bob Waterman, RF, p. 74; **218.** Allan "Mogie" Morgenson, quoted in *Working Smarter*, Editors of *Fortune*, Viking Press, New York, 1982, pp. vii-ix; **218.** Philip Caldwell, quoted in "Cultivating Human Potential at Ford" *The Journal of Business Strategy*, Spring 1984, p. 75; **219.** Jack MacAllister, quoted in RF, p. 98; **219.** Walter Fallon, quoted in IP, p. 88; **219.** Bob Waterman, RF, p. 90; **220.** James Harrington, IP, p. 86; **220.** A.T. Kearny study cited in TC, p. 282; **221.** James Harrington, IP, pp. 95-96; **223.** Tom Peters, TC, p. 286; **223.** James Harrington, IP, p. 87; **224.** Fred Allan, MBQ, p. 164; **224.** Bob Waterman, RF, p. 97; **224.** John Young, quoted in IP, p. 86; **227.** Bob Waterman, RF, p. 55; **227.** James Harrington, IP, p. 105; **227.** George Weyerhaeser, from "Quality: The Competitive Advantage," special supplement, *Fortune*, September 28, 1987; **228.** Bev Moser, quoted in IP, p. 86; **228.** Toyota, cited in IP, p. 88; **228.** Motorola and Hewlett-Packard examples from IP, p. 96; **228.** IBM examples compiled from IP, p. 96, 102, and 113; **229.** Ford Taurus example from RF, pp. 81-83; **229.** Dow Jones example from RF, pp. 72-73; **229.** NUMMI example from TC, p. 290; **229.** "The Task Facing General Motors," *Fortune*, March 13, 1989, p. 53.

Chapter Seventeen
232. James Harrington, IP, p. 140; **232.** Ron Zemke, SE, p. 47; **233.** *Relevance Lost: The Rise and Fall of Management Accounting*, Thomas Johnson and Robert Kaplan, Harvard University Press, Boston, 1987; **233.** Tom Peters, TC, p. 488; **234.** J.W. "Bill" Marriott, Jr., quoted in SE, p. 48; **235.** "ServQual" outlined in SE, p. 53; **235.** John Naisbett, *Megatrends: Ten New Directions Transforming Our Lives*, Warner, New York, 1982; **236.** *Fortune*, "Getting customers to love you," Patricia Sellers, March 13, 1989, p. 39; **236.** James Harrington, IP, p. 140; **238.** Ford's rating

system outlined in "Would You Buy a Car from This Man?" Thomas Moore, *Fortune*, April 11, 1988, pp. 72-74; **238.** American Airlines example and quote from "Rediscovering the Customer," special supplement, *Fortune*, January 18, 1988; **238.** Travel Related Services example from "Companies That Serve You Best," Bro Uttal, *Fortune*, December 7, 1987, pp. 98-116; **239.** Diners Club example outlined in a letter from James R. Emshoff, President and CEO, published in *Harvard Business Review*, September-October 1988, p. 172; **239.** Sewell Village Cadillac cited in SQ, p. 178; **240.** Domino's Pizza example from "Getting customers to love you," Patricia Sellers, March 13, 1989, p. 43; **240.** Deluxe Check example from TC, p. 485; **241.** Richard Schonberger, *World Class Manufacturing: The Lessons of Simplicity Applied*, The Free Press, New York, 1986, p. 13; **241.** SE, p. 57.

Chapter Eighteen
243. Jim Mitchell, quoted in SQ, p. 38; **244.** Steve Estridge, quoted in *Inc.*, February 1988; **245.** Peter Drucker, *People and Performance*, Harper and Row, New York, 1977.

Chapter Nineteen
249. John Fisher, quoted in SQ, p. 38; **263.** Karl Albrecht, from a summary of his *At America's Service*, July 1988, Soundview Executive Book Summaries, Bristol, Vt.; **266.** William Weisz, quoted in IP, p. 84.

Chapter Twenty
270. Karl Albrecht, quoted in a summary of his book *At America's Service*, July 1988, Soundview Executive Book Summaries, Bristol, Vt.; **274.** Charles Garfield, PP, p. 132; **274.** James Hickman, quoted in "The Power of Your Mind's Eye," Alan James Mayer, *Enroute*; **274.** Lee Pulos, quoted in PP, p. 131; **274.** Bruce Jenner, quoted in PP, p. 9; **274.** Jack Nicklaus, quoted in PP, p. 145; **275.** Warren Bennis and Burt Nanus, *Leaders: The Strategies for Taking Charge*, Harper and Row, New York, 1985, p. 70; **276.** Charles Garfield, *Peak Performers: The New Heroes of American Business*, William Morrow and Company, New York, 1986, p. 146.

INDEX

Corning Glass Works, 106, 108, 112
Corporate Plan, 263-65
Corporate Steering Committee, 258-59
"cost of doing business", 92-93
Cost of Quality (COQ), 2, 20, 152, 188, 228
Crouse-Hinds, 228
cultural change:
    and "mundane action plans", 111
    in organizations, 95-97
    and training, 99
cultural factors and service/quality teams, 223
culture (corporate):
    and motivation, 204
    public and private sectors, 39-41
    service/quality, 101-102
customer complaints, 21-28
customer expectations, 78-79
customer listening, 118-32
    examples of, 123-28
    pitfalls and traps, 128-30
customers, public sector, 42-43

D

deadly assumptions, 72-94
Delta Airlines, 112
Deluxe Check, 240
demotion, 143-44
Diners Club, 239
dismissal, 143-44
Disney Resorts, 135, 245
Domino's Pizza, 212, 240
Dow Chemical, 189-90
Dow Jones, 229
downsizing in organizations, 16, 47-49

E

Eastman Kodak, 90, 219
Electronic Data Systems, 212
employee:
    participation, 2
    relations, 16
    training, 84-87
employees:
    and commitment to service, 79
    and decision-making, 218

and human-resource policies, 101
and improvement efforts, 133
and participation, 167-68, 218
satisfaction and commitment, 140
treatment of, 100, 122
environment, organizational, 158
excellence, 3
executive retreat agenda, 252-53

F

Federal Express, 101, 201
financial rewards, 205-207
Flintstones Bedrock City, 64, 144
flow charts, 226
Ford Motor Company, 8, 92, 218, 229, 238
Four Seasons Hotels, 62, 112, 199, 245
Free Trade Agreement, 31

G

General Electric, 26, 66, 119, 124, 200, 218, 241
General Motors, 8, 126, 190, 229
Georgia, Office of Consumer Affairs, 200
Green Bay Packers, 178
groupAction, 3

H

Hartford Insurance Group, 91
health-care field, 43
Hewlett-Packard, 91, 92, 118, 224, 228, 236, 241
Hilltop Auto Service, 63
hiring:
    and orienting, 138-40
    pitfalls and traps, 147-48
    selection process, 139-41
Hockey Hall of Fame, 64
Holiday Inns, 215
Holland America, 146-47
Honeywell Bull, 239
Hyatt Hotels, 59

I

IBM, 18, 60-61, 93, 105, 122, 124-25, 159, 207, 220, 228, 236, 245

ABOUT THE AUTHORS

Jim Clemmer is a co-founder and operating executive of The Achieve Group. He is co-author of the Canadian best-seller, *The VIP Strategy: Leadership Skills for Exceptional Performance* and its companion workbook, *The VIP Leadership Action Planner.* Jim appears regularly on television and radio and is a popular keynote speaker and executive workshop leader.

Barry Sheehy is an operating executive of The Achieve Group and leader of Achieve's Service/Quality Academy. He holds undergraduate and graduate degrees from Loyola and McGill Universities. Barry developed an award-winning productivity and service improvement process while with a major Canadian public sector organization and later directed quality improvement efforts for a large international high technology company. He has been widely published in quality and management journals across Canada and the U.S.